SELECTING
THE
POPE

ALSO BY GREG TOBIN:

Nonfiction

The Wisdom of St. Patrick:
Inspirations from the Patron Saint of Ireland (1999)

Saints and Sinners:
The American Catholic Experience
Through Stories, Memoirs, Essays, and Commentary (1999)

Fiction

Conclave (2001)

Council (2002)

SELECTING
THE
POPE

Uncovering the Mysteries
of Papal Elections

Greg Tobin

With a Foreword by Monsignor Robert J. Wister

BARNES
&NOBLE
BOOKS
NEW YORK

This book is dedicated to my friend Joseph Michael Sopcich.

A Barnes & Noble Publishing Book

Library of Congress Cataloging-in-Publication Data

Tobin, Greg.
Selecting the Pope : uncovering the mysteries of papal elections.
/ Greg Tobin.— 1st ed.
p. cm.
Includes bibliographical references and index.

ISBN 0-7607-4032-1

1. Popes—Election. I. Title.

BX1805 .T63 2003
262'.13—dc21   2003000659

Printed and bound in the United States of America

1 3 5 7 9 10 8 6 4 2

First Edition

CONTENTS

FOREWORD

"You are Peter . . . on this rock . . . I will give you the keys of the
kingdom of Heaven. . . . Feed my lambs . . . feed my sheep."[1]

SINCE THESE WORDS WERE UTTERED, some thirteen score
(perhaps 261–264 men, the exact number is disputed) have exercised the ministry first entrusted to St. Peter the Apostle. It is a
ministry of faith, of unity, of love. Linus, Cletus, Clement,
Cornelius . . . Pius, John, Paul, John Paul I and II . . . and almost
two hundred fifty names in between. Not a dynasty, not a royal
family, but a series of bishops, and we cannot even say an unbroken series, although it is difficult to imagine the multi-year gaps
during the Middle Ages while the succession was disputed. Who
were they? How did they achieve the pinnacle of authority in the
Catholic Church? How were they chosen? And how will the next
leader of the Catholic Church be elected?

The past two thousand years have witnessed a succession of
holy men and scoundrels, of geniuses and mediocrities, no one
exactly like the other. Alexander VI's eleven-year reign
(1492–1503) was marked by corruption and licentiousness, as he
notoriously fathered several children, including Cesare and
Lucretia Borgia, and his papal policies were aimed to destroy rival
families and subdue nations to his will. Contrast his papacy to that
of Gregory I, one of the true saints to occupy the Throne of St.
Peter. A patrician Roman of the late sixth century, he renounced
civil office and became a monk, then (in his late thirties) was called
to serve the pope as a diplomat. When he was elected in A.D. 590,
he put his family's wealth to the service of the church and the city
of Rome, and during his fourteen-year pontificate he fully embodied the papal title that he coined, "Servant of the Servants of God."

Saint, sinner, warrior, judge, leader, viceroy, rock—for every age
a different face. And yet, the mystery and the man endure. For or

against him—and for or against his cause—nations have schemed, diplomats have plotted, priests have prayed, armies have clashed, Swiss Guards have died.

We stand today at a crossroads, a crossroads at which the Catholic Church has stood hundreds of times across the millennia. We are in the waning days of a pontificate, but not just any pontificate. It is the pontificate of a man whom many are already calling "John Paul the Great," a title universally attributed to only two of his predecessors (Leo I and Gregory I). Only three popes (as of this writing) served longer than Pope John Paul II. A paltry few of them have left a mark upon the church equal to his. While it is too early to evaluate the long-term influence of John Paul II's pontificate, we can safely say that his impact on the world has been enormous. Thanks to the proliferation of modern media, he has been more visible than any pope before him. Thanks to the population explosion, and the length of his pontificate, for two-thirds of the people of the world, he is the only pope they have known. The volume, breadth, and intellectual depth of his writings—books, encyclicals, meditations, and speeches—fill not several volumes, but many shelves. Generations will pass before their value can be appraised properly.

For more than a decade the foreign ministries and state departments of the world have pressed their "intelligence communities" for reports on the health of the pope. To their frustration, all they have been able to obtain are snippets of gossip from "informed sources" and an occasional tidbit, perhaps of misinformation, from the Vatican Press Office. The media, press, and worldwide networks have produced, edited, and re-edited the papal obituary. Publishers have printed books of the various "*papabili*" (papal candidates) only to have some of the "front runners" pass away while the pope lived on. Clerical gossips have chattered about the qualities and characteristics of individual cardinals. Scarlet-robed members of the Sacred College have inquired more discreetly of the views of their confreres on issues of ecclesiastical and political import.

Analysts, historians, politicians, and ecclesiologists continue to try to "handicap" the next papal election. What are the "voting blocs" in the next conclave? Who are the "liberals"? Who are the "conservatives"? Will the conclave pit the "centrists" against the more "collegially minded"? What are the possible coalitions? Which are the various ethnic groupings? How might these various groups coalesce to form a compromise? Since John Paul II named almost all of the voting cardinals, won't the next pope be in his mold? What "deals" (even though forbidden) are being made?

In this book, *Selecting the Pope: Uncovering the Mysteries of Papal Elections*, Greg Tobin gives us the tools to watch the next conclave, which will be a "world historical event." In a charming, popular style that never sacrifices accuracy for clarity, Tobin gives us a tour of the papal elections—past and future—and what a tour it is! He lets us see the spiritual and secular forces that have made and, in some cases, unmade popes. He sets before us the politics and intrigue of past conclaves, and with an eye for the telling, minute detail, he shows the mechanics of the next conclave, a conclave that will be unlike any other. For the first time in almost a millennium, it will be possible (though not probable) for a pope to be elected by a simple majority rather than the normal two-thirds. For the first time, cardinals will not be "locked up" all day in a conclave. Instead, they will stay in comfortable modern accommodations (more like a Holiday Inn than a Ritz-Carlton); they will commute in a comfortable bus to the Sistine Chapel where they will be truly locked up for the day but return to their lodgings for meals and repose. If necessary, they will rise the next day and start all over.

When the governor of Arkansas or of Texas becomes president, he is still Bill or George. Political pundits plumb his previous record to discern his future policies as president. This works to a degree. However, he now faces new issues. He is the chief magistrate of the entire nation, not only of a state. The new pope is the spiritual leader, not of a local or regional faith, but of a worldwide church. In the face of this mission, he cannot, of

course, change the faith, but he may change his views or his policies. Unexpected changes in the world at large may also alter the
cardinals' vision of the papacy, and therefore, of the man they
elect. In the final analysis, a conclave is both a roll of the dice and
a prayer to the Holy Spirit.

Recent conclaves (by recent, I mean within the last two centuries) have produced several surprises. Obviously, to some degree,
the cardinals know the man they elect, but something often makes
their own hopes and predictions for him as pope go awry. Sometimes,
he is not exactly the personality they imagined. Sometimes, events
move quickly and he changes his own direction. Sometimes, he
changes radically.

We should not be surprised. In 1846, after the gloomy pontificate of Gregory XVI, the cardinals elected the young (age fifty-
four), gregarious Giovanni Maria Mastai-Ferretti, Pope Pius IX.
While he at first appeared open to the contemporary world (as
opposed to his predecessor, who had condemned railroads), after
revolutionaries drove him into exile and assassinated his prime
minister, Pius came to see most of the world as the church's enemy.
Events beyond his control changed him into a very different person
from the one the cardinals thought they elected.

The 1903 conclave elected Giuseppe Sarto, perceived to be a
gentle pastor. The gentle pastor, Pius X, encouraged frequent
reception of the Eucharist and allowed children as young as seven
years of age to receive Communion. But, dismayed by theological
currents of the time, he allowed his subordinates to engineer a persecution of theologians, thus weakening the development of
Catholic theology for a half-century. The gentle man turned out to
be a strong and powerful man.

Fast forward to the 1970s: the pontificate of Paul VI seemed to
be wearing out, as the aging pontiff, beset with turmoil in the
church, became increasingly melancholy. When the cardinals met
in August 1978 to choose his successor, they wanted a pope who
would radiate joy. Albino Luciani was their choice. His first surprise was the choice of a double name, John Paul. The so-called

"Smiling Pope" then rejected the centuries-old triple tiara and the triumphal coronation prayer, "Receive this tiara, adorned with three crowns, and know that you are the father of kings and princes, ruler of the world and Vicar of Jesus Christ on earth." They were in for yet another surprise. Four weeks later, John Paul I was dead and they were back in Rome again.

There is not enough space here to recount the surprises of John Paul II. But when the cardinals meet to choose his successor, they should not assume that they know the route the man they choose will take. There is an old Scottish proverb, "The best laid plans of mice and men gang aft agley (often go awry)." The next pope will have a few—perhaps more than a few—surprises for us, and for his electors.

The author of this book appreciates the element of the unexpected and is aware of the quicksand of papal predictions—yet he clearly presents the new rules of the conclave (written by John Paul II himself in 1996) and is not reluctant to analyze the whys and what-ifs that flow from the contemporary situation of crisis, scandal, and uncertainty.

Many of the readers of this book, if they happen to be Catholic, may more than likely be what I consider "minority" Catholics. They are probably well educated and relatively comfortable; they are probably white. As such, they probably do not realize that they are a minority in the Roman Catholic Church. Yet the image of the Catholic Church in the minds of many is one of soaring Gothic cathedrals, bustling suburban parishes, the Knights of Columbus, and the Notre Dame football team. The average or "majority" Catholic today is a poor woman of color living in a village on about two dollars a day. The Catholic Church is literally a "church of the poor." While a century ago eight of ten Catholics lived in Europe or North America, and the remainder in Latin America, Africa, and Asia, today the numbers are reversed. Today, eight of ten Catholics are Latino, African, and Asian, and they are, indeed, poor.

Therefore, the next pope may come from the major part of the Catholic world, the world of the poor. Whoever he is, the great majority of his flock live in what are euphemistically called "developing" (that is, very poor) nations. This shift will grow greater as the twenty-first century progresses. In 1978, the cardinals ended the 455-year Italian monopoly of the papacy. Will the cardinals of the next conclave end the millennium and a half European monopoly? Only time will tell. Two things we do know. The next pope will be a man as different from John Paul II as John Paul was different from all of his predecessors, dating to Peter the Apostle. The next pope will, even in his uniqueness, claim the same apostolic authority as those thirteen score others, with all their sublime charismata and moral warts.

Greg Tobin writes fluently and authoritatively about a subject that has fascinated the world for two millennia. In *Selecting the Pope*, he has given us a handbook as well as a history, which will enable anyone to appreciate the "hows" and "whys" of the next papal conclave. The election of the pope is a process unlike any other in the world. The papacy is not a dynasty, as we commonly understand the term. We cannot say, "The pope is dead, long live the pope." When the pope dies, we have to wait for a prescribed period of mourning, then the conclave. As the Romans themselves say, "The pope dies, we make another one." This is the story of the making of popes.

Rev. Msgr. Robert J. Wister, Hist. Eccl. D.
Seton Hall University
South Orange, New Jersey
February 2003

PREFACE

Monday, October 16, 1978

In the wake of John Paul I's sudden death on September 28, 1978, only thirty-three days after his election, the college of cardinals was faced with painful, difficult choices. The near-universal euphoria over the Smiling Pope—who later came to be known as the September Pope—had been shattered. There was an element of panic over who was the right man for the seemingly impossible job of pope in a post-Vatican II world, divided by cold war and spiritual ferment within the church itself. (The effect of the Second Vatican Council, known as Vatican II—a meeting of all the world's Catholic bishops in the early 1960s—cannot be overemphasized here or throughout the discussion of the next papal election.)

The world awaited news from the papal conclave, now in its second day. The odds-on favorite to succeed Pope John Paul I was Cardinal Giovanni Benelli, relatively young and hard-charging at age fifty-seven, the archbishop of Florence and one-time confidant of Pope Paul VI. But Cardinal Giuseppi Siri, the seventy-two-year-old archbishop of Genoa, a conservative lion, had more or less solidified the right wing votes before entering the conclave and promised to be the conservatives' stalking horse. Both were Italians, as was the Patriarch of Venice, Albino Luciani, who had been elected as John Paul I in a one-day conclave on August 26 of that year. And as had been the previous forty-four popes in the past four hundred fifty-five years.* Benelli was said to have been Paul VI's favorite. Siri had been a "bridesmaid" at three previous conclaves: in 1958, 1963, and August 1978.

There were one hundred eleven cardinal-electors, the same number as in the previous conclave but slightly different in com-

---

*Hadrian VI, a Dutch cardinal, was elected in 1522 and reigned for one and one-half years.

position (the American cardinal John Wright had missed the August gathering due to severe illness, but was able to attend the October meeting—and, of course, Luciani was deceased). The world could not know what was going on inside the Sistine Chapel, as the sacred college of cardinals gathered to perform their most important and awesome responsibility, the election of the Successor of St. Peter and Supreme Pontiff of the Universal Church. The people of Rome and Catholics around the world could not know that the cardinals were deeply, bitterly divided and had come to a near deadlock after four ballots on Sunday, the first day of voting.

Siri's support had scattered to the winds—in part as the result of a disastrous public relations mistake the cardinal himself had made and, it was whispered, a sharp political maneuver by the pro-Benelli forces. And, although Benelli had gained in strength and remained the top vote-getter from the second through the sixth ballots, the cardinals knew a compromise was needed. Benelli's highest vote total was seventy, well short of the eighty-four (two-thirds plus one) required for election.

A luncheon held in the Borgia apartments of the Apostolic Palace was extended to give the cardinals time to regroup and discuss alternatives. On the sixth ballot, just before the break, a new name had rocketed to close second place behind Benelli: Cardinal Karol Wojtyla, the archbishop of Krakow, Poland. Wojtyla was not an unknown quantity among the sacred college, but a well-liked and respected junior cardinal at age fifty-eight. His reputation as an effective pastor under a communist regime, as an author and theologian, as an athletic and congenial, if deeply spiritual prelate, was indisputable. And he was conservative enough theologically to be acceptable to Cardinal Siri's supporters who were now disunited, looking for another leader. At the same time, Wojtyla was more than acceptable to the progressive or liberal group of cardinals who sought a vibrant new face for the church in the world—which is what had appealed to them with Luciani, John Paul I.

So, the classic Siri-Benelli confrontation in October 1978 was representative of the opposing forces within the powerful Roman Curia that threatened disunity and discontent in the church itself. The curia, which is the complex system of congregations and commissions known as "dicasteries," operates like any long-established bureaucracy. Self-conservation is a high priority in any such organization, and generally conservative policies serve the congregations and their leaders, prefects and presidents (who themselves are always cardinals or archbishops). Paul VI had attempted to "liberalize" these agencies, and Benelli had been the chief architect of Paul's internal reorganizations. This is not to say that Benelli himself was "liberal," per se. But as compared to Siri, who may fairly be described as "reactionary," he was seen as a potential heir to the more open and pluralistic impulses of the council of the previous decade. (Paul VI had presided over the last three sessions of Pope John's council, 1963–65.)

The cardinals of the October conclave were of a mind to seek pastoral stability and long-term viability for the papacy, not to "turn back the clock" as Siri promised to do in the interview that was leaked just as the doors to the conclave closed on the electors. The archbishop of Genoa had shot himself in the foot, and only the diehards would be willing to go all the way with him. Benelli, on the other hand, was a supremely pragmatic operator who, once he saw the emerging will of the conclave, gave way gracefully to the eventual winner. By the sixth ballot, "Wojtyla had taken eleven votes from Benelli in the most surprising shift in the history of modern conclaves."[1]

The author of an authoritative work on the conclaves of the past century, Francis Burkle-Young maintains that the seismic shift that played out in 1978 could actually be traced to February 18, 1946, when Pius XII announced the elevation of thirty-two new cardinals—the largest number of new cardinals in a single day since Leo X in 1517. In that first postwar consistory, later called the Grand Consistory, Pope Pius XII had internationalized (and "de-Italianized") the college of cardinals to a greater degree than anyone before. Paul VI continued the trend in the six consistories of his reign, and at his death had chosen 100 of the 111 eligible electors, of whom only thirty were Italians. Americans were the second-largest contingent of electors from a single nation, with nine eligible electors. Non-Europeans held fifty-six votes, a simple majority, for the first time in history.

And so, in that historic conclave of 1978, not only did the electoral college embrace the notion of a non-Italian pope, but they focused on an East European, a Slav, a man from behind the Iron Curtain! Outside, beneath the balcony upon which the new man would appear before them, the large, restless crowd awaited the dramatic moment, and John Paul II, the former Karol Wojtyla, would not disappoint them. . . .

Wednesday, October 16, 2002

Twenty-four years later: Pope John Paul II is still the Supreme Pontiff of the Roman Catholic Church. As of April 17, 2003, his will be the third longest pontificate in history, following Popes Pius IX (thirty-one years eight months), Leo XIII (twenty-five years seven months), and Pius VI (twenty-four years six months)—all within the past two hundred years. His obituary has been written many times over, but he continues to survive and to surprise. His physical health has been deteriorating for more than a decade, though his mental acumen has never been questioned, and his spiritual power remains undiminished, even stronger than ever. He has always been known as a man of prayer, a devoted Marian, a writer and linguist of great power. His pontificate has dazzled people throughout the world, disappointed some, and brought the office itself into new focus and scrutiny. In fact, he even called for a discussion among Catholics and other Christians of the "primacy," that is, the Catholic doctrine identifying the pope as the head of the college of bishops and the supreme pastor of Christianity, in his encyclical *Ut unum sint* (that all may be one). He has devoted himself to ecumenical outreach, especially to the Eastern

Orthodox churches, where he has often been rebuffed. Further, he has sought to reconcile Jews and Catholics in numerous statements and gestures throughout his pontificate.

The Catholic Church itself has endured a long, debilitating season of scandal with revelations in the United States and elsewhere of sexual misdeeds by some clergy and bishops, severely eroding the credibility of those members of the hierarchy who have denied or actively covered up the abuse of children. Tensions between the Vatican and the Russian Orthodox Church—a festering sore resulting from the thousand-year schism between East and West—continue to cause disappointment and anxiety for the pope and others who hope for reunion among all the churches.

And on Wednesday, October 16, to commemorate the anniversary of his election and to inaugurate his twenty-fifth year, the Holy Father announced a major change in the prayers of the rosary. In an apostolic letter, *Rosarium Virginis Mariae* (the Rosary of the Virgin Mary), John Paul declared a Year of the Rosary and reiterated his dedication to this "prayer loved by countless saints and encouraged by the magisterium. Simple yet profound, it still remains, at the dawn of this third millennium, a prayer of great significance, destined to bring forth a harvest of holiness." Additionally, he proclaimed a new set of mysteries, the so-called mysteries of light or luminous mysteries, to be recited and reflected upon with the rosary. Along with the joyful, sorrowful, and glorious mysteries, these new meditations on significant moments in Christ's public ministry are meant to give "a fresh life and to enkindle renewed interest in the rosary's place within Christian spirituality as a true doorway to the depths of the Heart of Christ, ocean of joy and of light, of suffering and of glory."[2] The papal letter was worldwide news.

There is a sadness in the air of this autumn day, the twenty-fourth anniversary of the last conclave, and an unease. Many Catholics speak in hushed tones of "that day," the inevitable and all-too-foreseeable day when the famously tight-lipped Vatican will announce the passing of the pope. In a recent *Wall Street Journal* column, author and commentator Peggy Noonan called the reigning pontiff "John Paul the Great."[3] More and more people are reaching the same conclusion; that he will not only be sainted, but that he will go down in the historical record as one of the most important figures in the history of the church.

Almost forgotten, after the passage of a generation, is the circumstance and method of his election. With such a long pontificate still in progress, so many Catholics, especially the youth, take for granted that John Paul is and "always" has been the pope. Yet he is the 262nd man to be so designated, and the history of the past two millennia proves that his election was no accident—just as the next man, whoever he may be, whether an "obvious" choice or a compromise among the cardinal electors, will take the chair of St. Peter for a purpose that we cannot yet know. A billion people and more, and especially the people of Rome, await the promptings of the Holy Spirit to reveal who he will be. Only time and history can reveal why he is the choice of the elite college of electors who, in turn, pray that they may discern the will of God as they deposit their secret ballots in the chalice on the altar of the Sistine Chapel.

Selecting the Pope

This book was written for anyone and everyone—Catholic and non-Catholic alike—who is interested in the process by which the pope is elected to be the head of the Roman Catholic Church. In these pages, presented as a handbook of sorts, you will learn about the historical and religious significance of the papal election, as well as the actual rules and regulations of the next conclave (the meeting of the cardinals to cast their secret ballots), which will be held shortly after the death and burial of the pope.

It is a rather tall order to condense nearly two thousand years of historical experience and hundreds of pages of ecclesiastical documents into this (I sincerely hope) easily accessible and readable format—but the process of research and writing for this book has proven to be a wonderful, worthwhile educational and spiritual experience. Amid the controversies and uncertainties of our age, at the dawn of the third year of the third millennium, I find it to be a source of some solace and hope to reflect on the meaning of the apostolic succession that traces its origin to St. Peter, the acknowledged head of the apostles. As the eminent British historian Lord Macaulay wrote in 1840: "The proudest royal houses are but of yesterday when compared with the line of Supreme Pontiffs. . . . The papacy remains, not in decay, not a mere antique, but full of life and youthful vigor."[4] Remarkably, Macaulay's analysis is as true today as it was 160 years ago; the papacy has never been more visible, more vital than it is today. The current pope has elevated the office and renewed its relevance in the contemporary world. So, let's take a look at how one is chosen to fill this historic office.

The organization of the book is designed to provide a framework for the examination of the papal legislation that governs the election process. That law is contained in the Apostolic Constitution, *Universi Dominici Gregis*, promulgated by Pope John Paul II on February 22, 1996 (reproduced in full as Appendix D). In the introduction to the document, Pope John Paul II states:

> The Shepherd of the Lord's whole flock is the Bishop of the Church of Rome, where the Blessed Apostle Peter, by sovereign disposition of divine Providence, offered to Christ the supreme witness of martyrdom by the shedding of his blood. It is therefore understandable that the lawful apostolic succession in this See, with which 'because of its great pre-eminence every Church must agree,' has always been the object of particular attention.[5]

The peculiar ecclesiastical language that characterizes such documents is apparent in this passage, which sums up the reasons that hundreds of millions of people around the world will watch and wait with intense, sincere interest as the cardinals gather to elect the successor of John Paul, the Successor of St. Peter.

In previous books and articles on the subject of the Roman Pontiff, I have treated the papacy in some depth, and I still find it endlessly fascinating; always there is new information or perspective to discover about the history and future of the papacy and the papal elections. Many people have asked me, "Where did you find this information?" The simple answer is, it is available to anyone who is willing to research the subject matter. It is available in books, magazine and newspaper reports, official documents, and, of course, on the World Wide Web at sites of varying quality and credibility. There are also "inside" sources, such as cardinals who have participated or will participate in a conclave, and other clergymen who are experts in canon law and church history. It is up to the researcher, then, to sift, choose, and apply the available information to the subject at hand. That is what I have tried to do in this book. In the process of the research and writing, I have learned even more than I expected about the intricacies and somewhat arcane details of this slice of history.

Behind the frequent question about sources, quoted above, lies a nearly universal fascination with the inner workings of the Vatican. The institution of the papacy, now nearly two thousand years old, has always been a lightning rod for criticism, both internal and external, of the Roman Catholic Church. The pope is a figure unique in all the world, the issue of his succession "has always been the object of particular attention,"[6] and the super-charged pontificate of Pope John Paul II has raised to new and dizzying heights the profile of the papacy. The burning question in the twilight of his pontificate has been, "Who will be the next pope?" And to point us toward an answer, I propose to examine the document that governs the next papal conclave and to place it in historical context with the previous elections, some of which we know about in intimate detail (despite the explicit official policy of secrecy regarding conclaves).

In this book we will first examine the office of the papacy and its claim to have succeeded directly from "the Blessed Apostle Peter" and to embody the primacy as "the Shepherd of the Lord's whole flock." These are hugely important historical and theological claims, supported by scripture, tradition, and faith—and vehemently criticized by some Christians outside the Roman Catholic communion. The credibility and position of the pope as leader of the Catholic Church reside within this scriptural and traditional context.

Second, we will look at the sources and meanings of the current election process. The conclave has a history of its own, which parallels and supports that of the papacy. The rules of the election outlined in *Universi Dominici Gregis* reflect a continuity with the experience of the church from its very first days of existence. In itself, this document is a fascinating combination of faith, history, tradition, theology, politics, and common sense. The author, the reigning pontiff, has personally experienced two such elections as a cardinal himself.

From those experiences, as well as the Code of Canon Law (revised under John Paul's supervision in 1983) and previous papal pronouncements, he has fashioned the new rule book—which differs somewhat but not substantially from the procedure first outlined 730 years ago, on July 7, 1274, by Pope Gregory X. In that medieval document, titled *Ubi majus periculum*, the concept of a secret, closed-off meeting of the cardinals, the conclave, was officially legislated for the first time. So, the next time the one hundred-plus cardinal electors meet, they will, in effect, follow the same procedure that has been in effect for eight centuries, with a traditional and scriptural foundation that dates even further back, to the earliest days of the church as described in the Acts of the Apostles.

But the political and ecclesiastical developments of subsequent centuries are just as clearly reflected. The election of the pope incorporates the highest spiritual aspirations (i.e., the guidance of the Holy Spirit and the will of God) with the simplest and basest of human realities, such as money, politics, and conflicting personalities. It is the church in microcosm. I recommend that the reader glance at the document and become familiar with its provisions, with the understanding that the language is sometimes difficult, seemingly obscure, even exasperating. I will try to make it clear—even interesting and alive—for the lay reader in the course of this book.

Also in this section, we will discuss the role of the sacred college of cardinals. Most Catholics and other interested observers do not know very much about the so-called sacred college and the key role that the cardinals play in the governance of the church, both in local dioceses and in the Roman Curia, the administrative departments of the Holy See. These men—numbering approximately 170, of whom about 110 are eligible to elect the next pope (being under the age of eighty), and from whose number will come that future leader—are the key players in the pageant, and they have been for well over a thousand years. Who are they? Where do they come from? How do they relate to one another—theologically, politically, fraternally? Like CEOs of major corporations (which, in fact, many of them are) or sovereigns unaccountable to any parliament (which, as "princes of the church," they are, in fact), they can be coy or frustratingly inscrutable. It is important to remember that they wouldn't hold the positions they do if they were not the inheritors and protectors of orthodoxy. Yet among them are unique traits and biases, endearing or off-putting personalities, formidable skills, and personal holiness. The college of cardinals is the most exclusive club in the world, and one with the weight of the entire church on its shoulders during the vacancy and the papal election.

Finally, this topic provides a point of view from which to observe today's Catholic Church and the church of the near future. The anticipated passing of a pope (any pope, but perhaps John Paul II in a special way because he is so intelligent, so dynamic, so beloved—and at once so highly revered and so acutely controversial) must be discussed with sensitivity and historical awareness. John Paul I, Albino Luciani, reigned for only a month, the shortest pontificate in five hundred years. John Paul II, Karol Wojtyla, has reigned for nearly twenty-five years. The latter's obituary has been written and rewritten many times over during the past twenty years, ever since the assassination attempt in St. Peter's Square in May 1981. The death of the former, who was hailed as a new kind of pope because he smiled and eschewed the cumbersome medieval coronation in favor of a simple installation mass, is still considered suspicious by some, the subject of lurid speculation in books and films. And so today's church—and today's pope—will one day pass from the scene, forcing the church to change and develop and form itself anew as the body of Christ and the community of the saints.

Today's Catholic Church in the United States is changing despite the apparent resistance of some in the church's hierarchy (as embodied by the national bishops' conference) to embrace the need for changes expressed by a newly energized (and in some cases, angry) laity. The Roman Catholic Church around the world, especially in Africa and Asia, is changing, growing, experiencing an evangelistic renewal and expansion in hitherto "pagan" (i.e., non-Christian or local religions) territories. In Europe, the church seems tired, though the youth may spearhead a restoration of its spiritual preeminence in many nominally Catholic countries; the episcopal hierarchies of Europe are as scandal-fatigued as the American church, if not more so. The universal church, which is one meaning of "catholic," may or may not be able to manage these conflicting trends and maintain the theological discipline necessary to preserve its very identity. Even the post-conciliar church, i.e., the church after the Second Vatican Ecumenical Council (1962–65), which updated many church practices for the contemporary world, is decidedly pre-modern, even medieval in so many of its ways. It is also ancient and apostolic in its preservation of the precious "deposit of faith" that it believes has been passed down directly from the apostolic age to our own, protected by popes and councils, and by direct divine involvement through the Holy Spirit in the very life of its people.

Yet change is nothing new. Change is a constant in the history of the one holy Catholic and apostolic church professed at Sunday mass in the familiar *credo* (creed, or symbol of faith) that itself evolved during the first crucial centuries of doctrinal conflict and development. The church has nearly always confronted such changes and challenges with a wince—or sometimes a sterner response. Pluralism of thought and expression is another necessary aspect of the responses within the church, among theologians and the rank-and-file faithful (an important aspect of the American Catholic Church since its foundation).

What will happen in the next conclave? How will the cardinal electors respond to pressures from angry and frustrated American Catholics, and cries for pluralism and justice among the burgeoning Catholic communities in poor countries? Will the next conclave experience the same factional divisions as that of the 1978 conclave, which elected John Paul II—the same conflict between wanting to "turn back the clock" and needing to find a way to acknowledge the contemporary laity who increasingly demand internal reforms? As the Catholic Church confronts some of the most extreme and public pressures of its existence, the upcoming conclave holds profound significance, as electors—and ultimately the next pope—must find a way to give direction and unity to a bitterly divided and besieged church.

How, then, will the church as the people of God respond, in the person of the pope, to the as yet unknown twists and turns that lie ahead on the road to the future? Will the next Supreme Pontiff bend, as many have before him, or assume a sterner defensive posture, as have so many others throughout history?

PART I

History and Development of Papal Elections

- ◆ The Petrine Ministry

- ◆ Primacy and Succession

- ◆ Scriptural Sources: The Gospels and the Acts of the Apostles

- ◆ The Early Church of Rome: A.D. 64–476

- ◆ Eight Turbulent Centuries: 476–1274

- ◆ The Origin of the Conclave: 1274–1303

- ◆ Exile and Schism, Reformation and Revolution: 1303–1800

- ◆ The Holy Father: 1800–1903

- ◆ Modern Popes and the Papacy: 1903–2003

History and Development
of Papal Elections

IN HIS MAY 25, 1995, ENCYCLICAL LETTER, *Ut unum sint* (that all may be one), Pope John Paul II acknowledged that the papacy remains an obstacle to Christian unity among the Orthodox, Protestant, and Catholic churches. The Roman Pontiff called for an ecumenical dialogue on the nature and value of the papacy, an invitation to reflect, pray, and comment upon the primacy, with an end goal of possible reform of the office and its relationship to the church and the world.

In order to understand the varying, powerful reactions provoked by this supreme religious office, it is first necessary to understand the basic concept of the papacy and how the head of the church is chosen. Who is the pope, then, and how did his role develop over time into what it is today? Why should we care about this antique office that often seems swaddled in medieval trappings? Who can fill the shoes of the Fisherman? Who would want to? Like the church itself, the papacy has survived against all odds—against all the assaults and tides of history. The papacy has persevered, upheld by the fundamental belief that the Holy Spirit sustains the church and the pope in his authority and teaching office—that there is reason and purpose beyond mere human understanding of his role in keeping the church one, holy, catholic, and apostolic.

The Petrine Ministry

The papacy, also called the Petrine ministry, or office held by the pope, is a concept that has developed from the tradition surrounding the apostle Peter's life, ministry, and martyrdom in Rome into its contemporary form through twenty tumultuous centuries. We count 261 men as legitimately elected successors of St. Peter as bishop of Rome.* The titles of the pope are numerous, historically and theologically significant, and somewhat mind-boggling to the contemporary observer (especially a non-Catholic). Here is a brief description of his official titles:

1) **Bishop of Rome**: First and always, the pope is bishop of Rome, the overseer and chief shepherd or pastor of what is called the "Holy See" or the "Apostolic See," a diocese comprised of parish churches, parish priests, local church members, and all of the administrative apparatus required for diocesan administration. Of course, he requires much assistance in carrying out this important responsibility. The vicar general of the diocese is usually a cardinal—currently Camillo Ruini, since 1991, who also serves as president of the episcopal conference (the bishops' national organization) of Italy. The pope's local cathedral is the basilica of St. John Lateran, which is a legacy from the emperor Constantine; it had been a palace of the Laterani, a noble Roman family.

2) **Vicar of Jesus Christ**: The title Vicar of Jesus Christ supplanted the more common, earlier term "Vicar of Peter," which was adopted by Pope Leo the Great in the fifth century. Vicar of Christ

---

*For purposes of our discussion here, I will not enter into the debate over the exact number, but adopt the dating and numbering of legitimate popes from two modern sources: McBrien's *Lives of the Popes* and Kelly's *Oxford Dictionary of the Popes*.

is, arguably, applicable to any bishop, not just to the pope. Its adoption as an official title coincided with the monarchical development of the papacy. In his coronation address, Pope Innocent III (1198–1216), who raised the papacy to the pinnacle of its temporal power and prestige, stated that he was: "Verily, the *Vicarius Christi* (vicar of Christ), the successor of Peter, the anointed of the Lord, the god of pharaoh set midway between God and man, below God but above man, less than God but more than man, judging all other men, but himself judged by none."[1]

3) **Successor of the Chief of the Apostles**: This title, also commonly known as the "Successor of Peter," which even Innocent did not dispute (though he downplayed), defines the papal succession in a way unique to any office in the church. There are other bishops and archbishops, vicars and patriarchs, but only one successor of St. Peter: "You are Peter. . . . I will give you the keys of the kingdom of Heaven," Jesus said in Matthew, Chapter 16. And the text of this Gospel passage is engraved in the dome of St. Peter's Basilica in letters six feet high—above the main altar where the pope says mass, and above the statue of Peter, attributed to the thirteenth-century sculptor Arnolfo di Cambio, with the foot worn away by the touch of countless pilgrims.

4) **Supreme Pontiff of the Universal Church**: As Supreme Pontiff of the Universal Church, a title and theological statement that has caused centuries of dispute and division among Christians, the pope claims jurisdiction over all other priests and pastors in the world. The title is adapted from the Roman *Pontifex Maximus* (Supreme or High Priest), a responsibility held by the head of the college of pontiffs, a sacred society of ancient Rome. *Pontifex* itself is Latin for "bridge builder," signifying the high priest's role in bridging the divine and material worlds. It illustrates, as do so many aspects of the papacy, the influence of the imperial style and organization on the Catholic Church. The issue of papal primacy, which has been the source of schisms and lingering resentments among Christian denominations worldwide, is encompassed by the scope of this title. The pope is also sometimes called the "Roman Pontiff."

5) **Patriarch of the West**: The pope is one of several patriarchs, the "fathers" of sees that trace their origin directly to the apostles and to centers of imperial government. Other sees include Constantinople, Jerusalem, Antioch, Alexandria, Venice, and Lisbon. The latter two are add-ons from later centuries. (Note: The Patriarch of Venice was thrice elected pope in the twentieth century, in 1903, 1958, and 1978.)

6) **The primate of Italy**: The primate of Italy is, simply, the titular chief national bishop of Italy. By tradition, a number of European and Latin American nations (e.g., Hungary, Poland, and Mexico) have employed such a designated honorary title. The primate also ranks as a metropolitan (see below).

7) **Archbishop and metropolitan of the Roman Province**: This title reflects a number of things, including further vestiges of imperial prestige that began to accrue to the bishop of Rome during the early medieval period. "Archbishop" and "metropolitan" are roughly equivalent terms, signifying the jurisdiction over other local bishops in the province, a territory that extends beyond more than one diocese; the bishops within the province are answerable in some ecclesiastical matters to the archbishop. (The terms "diocese" and "province" also reflect the administrative organization of the Roman Empire.) As a metropolitan, the bishop wears the pallium within his jurisdiction whenever vested in sacred vestments, as for the mass. The pope wears his pallium at all times and places when properly vested, as a sign that his jurisdiction alone is universal.

8) **Sovereign of the Vatican City State**: The pope, as Sovereign of the Vatican City State, is the political ruler of a diplomatically recognized state. Today, there are about 175 ambassadors to the Holy See, including the mission from the United States (since 1983). The pope holds secular legal authority in all state matters and royal status among other sovereigns of the world. The title itself was formalized in the Lateran Treaty of February 11, 1929, between Pope Pius XI and Mussolini, the prime minister of Italy. This temporal papal function is the remnant of the "Papal States" that existed from 754 (the so-called Donation of Pepin) to 1870 (the loss of territories to the Italian government during the Franco-Prussian War).

9) **Servant of the Servants of God**: Servant of the Servants of God (Servus Servorum Dei) was proclaimed in A.D. 602 by Pope Gregory the Great (590–604), the scion of a noble Roman family and a skilled government administrator who resigned his temporal office to become a monk at about thirty-five. He strongly affirmed that the primacy of the Roman pontiff was rooted in humility and service; that a bishop is one who seeks "to subdue himself rather than his brethren" and to be "a minister, not a master."[2] Popes employ this title especially when they address fellow bishops, as does Pope John Paul II in *Universi Dominici Gregis*, the constitution governing the papal conclave.

Primacy and Succession

The concept of "the apostolic succession" is key to understanding the papacy and how and why the pope is elected in the particular way that has developed over the centuries. Today's bishops are seen as direct successors to the apostles of the first century; the apostles themselves were first chosen by Christ (the Anointed One of God) and were witnesses to his resurrection. Jesus himself commissioned them as apostles or "messengers." Then the earliest churches (in Jerusalem, Antioch, Corinth, Rome, etc.) elected elders to be their authorized representatives to other churches and among other Christian leaders. These were the two categories or classes of "apostle" as described by the ancient writers.

Catholic doctrine, the so-called sacred "deposit of faith" based on the twin sources of scripture and tradition, holds that these apostles, especially the Twelve selected personally by Jesus of Nazareth, directly and fully transmitted the words of the Master that revealed the nature of God and the foundation of the divine assembly of God's people, which came to be known as the church. Into the hands of the apostles, then, Jesus placed the duty to build his church and the authority to govern that church. Against the heresies that grew up quickly in the Christian communities, the apostles of both kinds and those selected to preach after them presented the entirety of their Lord's teaching to the faithful in the churches and to those seeking to join the church.

So, the apostolic succession encompasses two factors: 1) *authority*—the unbroken lineal and historical passing on, through laying on of hands, of the commission and the authority of Christ; 2) *teaching*—the strict maintenance and passing on of the purity and authenticity of that first preaching. There has been, according to the understanding of the Catholic Church, no dilution or innovation of the original message of Jesus within the church, but a true, faithful, and infallible transmission of the Word. The church of Rome, from the first century onward, gained a reputation as the seat of orthodoxy and authority, with a nod to the political preeminence of the city itself, but mostly because Peter and Paul were understood to have led the church there before their martyrdom. There was little challenge among Christians throughout the Roman world that some measure of authority resided in the capital city within the church leadership there.

Today, in Catholic churches throughout the world, the list of episcopal succession is advertised explicitly, sometimes enshrined prominently in the cathedral. In some Protestant churches, the claim of succession from the apostles is also upheld. As regarding the papal succession, as the title of this book indicates, the line traces back to St. Peter himself, sometimes called the chief of the apostles.

In the creeds (Nicene Creed and Apostles' Creed), "apostolic" is one of the marks or fundamental characteristics of the church. It is understood, in the Catholic context, that the successors of the apostles are the bishops: the chief pastors, teachers, administrators of the local churches, wherever they may be throughout the world. The bishops together form a community of authority known as the "college of bishops." From this overall concept comes the further, more specific concept of collegiality; that is, the sharing of the apostolic authority among all the bishops (now numbering about four thousand) who are more or less equals and hold the entire and exclusive authority within their own dioceses, though some hold certain jurisdictional authority over others. An archbishop, as a "metropolitan," has limited oversight of the bishops of his province. The pope holds a position of preeminence over the entire college of bishops; this preeminence is known as "the primacy."

There are historical and theological arguments for and against the primacy of the bishop of Rome over all other bishops, over councils, and over all the members of the church. Arguably, the schism of the Eastern Orthodox churches (from 1054 to the present day), the so-called Great Western Schism of 1378 to 1417, and the Protestant Reformation all resulted in some measure from the exercise of primatial authority by the pope and the church of Rome. Even some Catholic bishops, and especially some national or regional conferences of bishops, question the absolutist and monarchical implications of the papal primacy. It is offensive to some Christians, and perhaps to a handful of Roman Catholics, for the pope to claim to be the Supreme Pastor of the Universal Church, or even the head of the college of bishops. After the Council of Constance (1414–1418), a movement grew up which posited the authority of a worldwide or ecumenical council of the church over the pope, but this "conciliar theory" never took root within the structure of the church. Protestantism, then and now, is to a greater or lesser degree a rejection of papal authority.

Scriptural Sources:
The Gospels and the Acts of the Apostles

Where did the papal office come from and who was the first pope? We can look to scriptural sources for some answers. Here we will find out why, as in the listing of papal titles, that the pope is called the Successor of Peter, why his office is called apostolic and his diocese the Apostolic See. The word "pope" comes from the Greek *papa*, a term of reverence and affection that was used for centuries for bishops throughout the Christian world. Over time, it became more associated with the bishop of Rome than with any other bishop, and in the late eleventh century, Pope Gregory VII (of whom more to follow later) reserved the appellation exclusively for the pope of Rome, the patriarch of the western church. In the east (even today), the title is sometimes used for high-ranking church-men, such as the leader of the Coptic Church in Egypt.

But let's turn now to the New Testament. . . .

From the earliest days of the Christian church, staring at Pentecost—the visitation of the Holy Spirit, as "violent wind" and "tongues of fire," upon the apostles in Jerusalem some seven weeks after the death, resurrection, and ascension of Jesus—its mission required some organizational framework. On that day, as recorded in the Acts of the Apostles, the church was first proclaimed in pub-lic by those who had trod the countryside of Roman-occupied Judea and the Galilee with their Lord. To the "devout men living in Jerusalem from every nation under heaven," the apostles were inspired to preach in many languages about "the marvels of God." Acts describes the activities of that day and the primitive organiza-tion of the church in Jerusalem while chronicling the growth of Christianity throughout the eastern Roman Empire in Judea, Syria, Asia Minor, Phoenicia, Cyprus, and Greece.[3]

Even before that, the Gospel of Matthew relates, the teacher from Nazareth foretold the need for a structure to support the anticipated missionary activities of the apostles. Significantly, in this passage, Jesus changed the name of the apostle Simon bar Jonah to Cephas (Aramaic), or Petros (Greek)—Peter, in English—meaning "rock":

> When Jesus came to the region of Caesarea Philippi he put this question to his disciples, "Who do people say the Son of man is?" And they said, "Some say John the Baptist, some Elijah, and oth-ers Jeremiah or one of the prophets." "But you," he said, "who do you say I am?" Then Simon Peter spoke up and said, "You are the Christ [the Anointed], the Son of the living God." Jesus replied, "Simon son of Jonah, you are a blessed man! Because it was no human agency that revealed this to you but my Father in heaven. So I now say to you: You are Peter and on this rock I will build my *ekklesia*.* And the gates of the underworld can never overpower it.

---

*The Greek word *ekklesia* means "assembly," and is most often translated as "church."

I will give you the keys of the kingdom of Heaven: whatever you bind on earth will be bound in heaven; whatever you loose on earth will be loosed in heaven." Then he gave the disciples strict orders not to say to anyone that he was the Christ.[4]

In the quest to understand Peter's leadership role among the first disciples and in the young church, it is important to note that in the first two chapters of Acts he is the first-mentioned of the apostles who were "joined constantly in prayer." Before a congregation of believers he urged the election by lot of a new apostle to replace the deceased Judas. And he was the primary spokesman for the other apostles on the day of Pentecost:

Hearing this [Peter's exhortation], they were cut to the heart and said to Peter and the other apostles, "What are we to do, brothers?" "You must repent," Peter answered, "and every one of you must be baptized in the name of Jesus Christ for the forgiveness of your sins, and you will receive the gift of the Holy Spirit. The promise that was made is for you and your children, and for all *those who are far away, for all those whom the Lord* our God *is calling to himself*." He spoke to them for a long time using many other arguments, and he urged them, "Save yourselves from this perverse generation." They accepted what he said and were baptised. That very day about three thousand were added to their number.[5]

Throughout the first fifteen chapters of the Acts of the Apostles, Peter is the most visible representative of the church, though certainly not the only voice: also prominently mentioned are John (the beloved disciple), Stephen (the first Christian martyr), Saul (later Paul) of Tarsus, and James (the "brother of the Lord"), along with a score of other important men and women in the growing Christian community. Peter preaches, argues, performs miracles, converts a Roman centurion, is arrested and delivered from Herod's jail by an angel, is a leading figure at the Council of Jerusalem (circa A.D. 49)—then disappears from the record as the mission of Paul the apostle becomes the sole subject of Acts. By his own actions and by the commission from Jesus, Peter became the first among the apostles, the president of the "college of apostles," if you will, eventually taking that mission to Rome, the capital of the empire. These visible activities, along with the weight of tradition from oral sources and non-canonical writings, arguably place Peter in the position of the first pope.

Also of significance is the organizational activity described in the Acts of the Apostles, such as the creation of the order of deacon:

> About this time, when the number of disciples was increasing, the Hellenists [Jews from outside Palestine, or Greek-speakers] made a complaint against the Hebrews: in the daily distribution their own widows were being overlooked. So the Twelve called a full meeting of the disciples and addressed them, "It would not be right for us to neglect the word of God so as to give out food; you, brothers, must select from among yourselves seven men of good reputation, filled with the Spirit and with wisdom, to whom we can hand over this duty. We ourselves will continue to devote our-selves to prayer and to the service of the word." The whole assem-bly approved of this proposal and elected Stephen, a man full of faith and of the Holy Spirit, together with Philip, Prochorus, Nicanor, Timon, Parmenas, and Nicolous of Antioch, a convert to Judaism. They presented these to the apostles, and after prayer they laid their hands on them.[6]

These *diakonoi* (servants) were created to help the apostles handle the increasing amount of administrative work that threat-ened to overwhelm "the word of God" in the practicalities of life, providing for those in need. The order of deacon would be carried over into the other churches throughout the Christian world, including the church of Rome. Eventually, other holy orders— including those of priest and bishop—would emerge and develop into formal and necessary offices within the church as well.

The Early Church of Rome: A.D. 64–476

Tradition places both St. Peter and St. Paul in Rome (at different times) during the reigns of the emperors Claudius and Nero, that is, from about A.D. 40 on. It is held that Peter's "episcopate" lasted about twenty-five years, though we are not sure how long he lived and preached in Rome. It was believed for nearly two millennia that no pope would ever reign for as long as Peter, until Pius IX (elected in 1846) shattered the supposed sacred ceiling during his nearly thirty-two-year pontificate.

Paul, the first chronicler of the new religion and its most indefatigable apostle, journeyed extensively throughout the Mediterranean region beginning about A.D. 35. Following his conversion experience in Damascus, he preached the risen Christ in Asia Minor, Syria, and Greece. Paul was arrested in Jerusalem and appealed to the emperor, as a Roman citizen. He was put under house arrest in the capital city in about A.D. 62, and executed some time later. The church historian Eusebius of Caesarea relates the story of Peter's trial and execution at about the same time, perhaps a couple of years later, which would put his martyrdom at about A.D. 64. Legend puts St. Peter on a cross upside down, in deference to his Savior's death.

There is little to no direct evidence of either Peter or Paul in Rome, let alone their activities there. But for two and a half centuries the belief among Christians—the unshakable belief—held that both apostles were buried in Rome; Peter on the Vatican Hill near the site of Nero's circus, in a pagan necropolis. In the early fourth century, Constantine decreed that a huge basilica be built over the presumed gravesite of St. Peter.

By the late fourth century a tradition had developed that Peter resided in Rome for twenty-five years, but there is no historical verification of this assertion. Today's Vatican Press Office supports the quarter-century span in its official recounting of the historical lengths of various pontificates. According to Eusebius, who wrote in the early fourth century, "Peter is reported to have preached to the Jews throughout Pontus, Galatia, Bithynia, Cappadocia and, about the end of his days, tarrying at Rome, was crucified."[7] Paul, whose remains are also claimed by the church in Rome, is considered a co-founder of sorts of the Christian community in the imperial capital. His Letter to the Romans is the first epistle in the New Testament, and Protestant Christians put him in a position of spiritual and theological preeminence over even Peter, contrary to the Catholic tradition.

Starting at an undetermined point after Peter's death, the bishops of Rome were elected by the clergy and people, as were bishops throughout the Christian world. History has not recorded the precise method of such elections in the first few centuries after Christ, nor do the accepted listings of the earliest popes stand up to the most rigorous historical standards. St. Irenaeus, a Syrian theologian and bishop of Lyons (died circa 200), wrote, in his *Adversus Heraesus* (Treatise Against the Heresies) in A.D. 180, that there had been twelve successors of St. Peter through the reign of his friend Eleutherius (174–189). He named Linus first, then Cletus (or Anacletus), Clement (author of an important letter from the church of Rome to the church of Corinth, c. 96), Evaristus, Alexander, Sixtus (the sixth), Telesphoros, Hyginus, Pius, Anicetus, and Soter. This listing was adopted by Eusebius and recorded in the *Liber Pontificalis* (Book of the Popes), the collection of papal biographies from St. Peter to Pius II (died 1464), considered the "official" listing by the Holy See itself (from its first compilation in the sixth century through later redactions).

Before the emergence of a single overseer or bishop (or the papacy as we now know it), it is probable that a council or "college" of elders governed the Christian community of Rome until the mid-second century. Someone such as St. Clement I (c. 90–100) may have been the presider or spokesman for such a pastoral group or council. But it did not take very long before a "monoepiscopal" (or single-bishop) stamp was imprinted on the church of Rome—with St. Pius I (c. 140–155), who was followed by Anicetus (c. 155–166), the champion of the western (Roman) dating system of Easter in the long-simmering controversy with the eastern churches. Anicetus cited Peter to justify the custom of celebrating the

Resurrection on the Sunday following the fourteenth day of Nissan (the equivalent in the Jewish calendar of the lunar month of March), rather than on the date itself. Most of the fragmentary knowledge we have of this period—the first two centuries of the church in Rome—comes from oral tradition and later-written annals. But it is "safe" to date the establishment of the bishop of Rome as a single, authoritative leader with some influence throughout the Christian world at about A.D. 150.

From this period, a monarchical aspect of the papacy also seems to have flowered. The see of Rome had very early become a repository and protector of orthodoxy, unity, and "apostolicity"; bishops and Christian churches throughout the Mediterranean basin appealed to Rome in matters of heresy (i.e., theological disputes) and as a model of ecclesiastical governance. The churchmen of Rome were more than pleased to provide guidance and clarification on these issues for the brethren throughout the known world. It only helped the cause of "primacy" that Rome was the ancient political capital of the empire.

Thus, we see an ever stronger claim for Rome's local church to assume a primatial, apostolic status among the other churches, including those with legitimate, if competitive, patriarchal and apostolic foundations, such as Jerusalem, Antioch, Alexandria— and from the late fourth century, Constantinople, which assumed second-place ranking to Rome. The temporal power and prestige of the Roman church increased as the imperial power and glories of the western Roman Empire faded and, finally, disappeared. By the time of St. Gregory I, in the late sixth century, as barbarian invasions and internal corruption exacted their toll on the city, the local populace would look to the bishop of Rome for governmental stability and for spiritual and material sustenance.

The church was an urban institution, particularly in its evangelization and governance. It grew rapidly, first among far-flung Jewish communities in cities throughout the Roman Empire. Hundreds of years passed before the Gospel was carried in a systematic fashion by missionaries among the barbarians (foreigners, non-Romans) and the pagans (people of the countryside). Rome itself was a city *sui generis*, and its church took on some of the characteristics of the place in which it was situated.

Twenty-six religious community centers, which became the *tituli* (parish churches) were evidently well-established in Rome by the time of the emperor Constantine (312). The Roman *diakonoi* (deacons or servants) served as pastors or leaders of these confederated communities and supervised secular services for the needy, providing food and shelter in the churches. Within a few generations the *presbyteroi* (priests or elders) had emerged as the primary spiritual fathers and ministers to the Christian population, preaching "the word of God" and presiding at the eucharistic commemoration of the Last Supper. The *episkopoi* (bishops or overseers) emerged in the second century as the principal teachers of doctrine and final appeal in disputes among the larger city-based communities.

The role of bishop and the notion of apostolic succession developed in the writings of important churchmen over two centuries since the time of St. Peter. St. Clement I of Rome wrote his corrective letter to his fellow Christians in Corinth that stressed the succession of authority from God to Jesus Christ to the apostles, thence to the bishops and the deacons and to their successors. St. Ignatius of Antioch (died c. 107) wrote, also in letters, that the local church ought to be subject to its bishop: that where the bishop is, there the Eucharist is; without a bishop there is no Eucharist. Then St. Irenaeus of Lyons (died c. 200), the author of the first list of popes, allowed that the bishops, as successors of the apostles, are the repositories of the apostolic faith, "from the mouths of the apostles themselves."[8] Cyprian of Carthage (died c. 258), the African bishop who was deeply involved in some of the theological controversies of his day—and who clashed with Pope Stephen I—maintained that, though the Roman see was the "primordial" (or "principal") church in the Christian world, each bishop shared in the apostolic authority: "The bishop is in the church, and the church in the bishop."[9]

To fill a vacancy in the episcopal leadership of the diocese of Rome quickly became a very important function of the local church.

Remember too, that the Christians of Rome (and many throughout the empire) faced fierce, if sporadic, imperial persecutions for nearly three hundred years, putting increasing pressure on the people and their leaders.

Among the first dozen or so popes were Jews, Italians, Greeks, a Syrian, and an African. This factor gave the Roman church its cosmopolitan and catholic (universal) character. At least one pope, Callistus I, was once a slave, and many (we do not know the exact number) were martyrs in witness to their faith. All, presumably, served in visible positions of responsibility in the local church before being elevated to the *cathedra* (chair) of the see of Rome. In this early period (throughout the first few centuries of Christianity), the deacons and presbyters in Rome gained power and influence under the aegis of the bishop—which gave rise to the office of cardinal that would become solidified in the ninth and tenth centuries.

The popes during this time were elected not by a formal ballot but by a consensus among the local clergy, with the involvement of "the people," as represented by the patrician class (who were soon to populate the ranks of the clergy, as well). They were conscious, from at least the mid-second century (thanks to Irenaeus), of the importance of their direct succession from St. Peter, the traditional co-founder of the Roman see and first among the original Twelve Apostles. The evidence and theological justifications of the direct apostolic succession were not taken lightly by these men and their fellow Christians.

The story of the first supposed "antipope" illustrates the theological clashes and the state persecutions of the period, in which the pope was a central player and sometimes victim. Hippolytus (died c. 235) was a vocal intellectual, prolific author, and respected presbyter of the Roman church well schooled in the Greek philosophers and theologians of the time. Along with the North African Tertullian (died c. 222), considered one of the great Latin fathers of the church, Hippolytus fell into the heresy of Montanism, a severely ascetic doctrine that preached the imminent apocalypse. He was a harsh critic of Pope Zephyrinus (199–217) and an opponent of Callistus, Zephyrinus's most trusted deacon and successor (217–222). In 217, a schismatic Roman faction named Hippolytus bishop. For the next eighteen years, Hippolytus continued to press his rival claim to the papacy through the reign of Urban I (222–230) and Pontian (230–235), who was arrested in the persecution of Christian leaders by the Emperor Maximinus Thrax—as was Hippolytus!—and exiled to Sardinia. Pontian abdicated (the first, but not last, pope to resign), he and his papal alter ego reconciled, and both men died martyrs and were sainted. The reunified Roman church elected a single successor. Thereafter, there would be more than three score antipopes scattered throughout the history of the church, but with rare exception none materially threatened the existence of the papacy, the canonical election process, nor the church itself.

Pontian's abdication in the face of persecution took place on September 28, 235—the first exact date in recorded papal history. Anterus, who reigned less than two months, was elected on November 21, the next reliable date of record that survives this early period. We have thus entered the realm of history versus informed (or inspired) speculation.

According to Eusebius, when the Roman clergy met in 236 to choose a successor to the short-lived Pope Anterus, a miracle occurred in the form of direct intervention by the Holy Spirit:

It is said that after Anterus's death Fabian [a presbyter] came with a party from the country and paid a visit to Rome, where by a miracle of divine and heavenly grace he was chosen to fill the place. When the brethren had all assembled with the intention of electing a successor to the bishopric, and a large number of eminent and distinguished men were in the thoughts of most, Fabian, who was present came into no one's mind. But suddenly out of the blue a dove fluttered down and perched on his head (the story goes on), plainly following the example of the descent upon the Savior of the Holy Spirit in the form of a dove. At this, as if moved by one divine inspiration, with the utmost enthusiasm and unanimity the whole meeting shouted that he was the man, and then and there seized him and set him on the bishop's throne.[10]

Fabian became a widely admired pope and was martyred in 250 during the Decian persecution. During his reign the *Liber Pontificalis* (Book of the Popes) was instituted, which incorporated dates and details of papal elections. In these years there were lengthy vacancies in papacy due to continued persecutions. Sixtus II was dragged from the episcopal chair by the emperor Valerian's troops on August 6, 258, and beheaded; all seven Roman deacons were summarily executed, which chilled the remainder of the clergy and caused a delay of nearly two years before the next election (Dionysius on July 22, 260). The longest vacancy on record, nearly four years, occurred after the abdication of Marcellinus (296–304), who was accused of apostasy (a self-separation from the church) during the persecutions of Emperor Diocletian and was deposed. He died shortly thereafter.

Another important instance of an antipope occurred upon the death of Pope Liberius (September 24, 366). Amid continued squabbles over the Arian heresy, both theological and street fighting broke out. The deacon Ursinus was elected and installed in the Julian Basilica by one faction, the presbyter Damasus elected by another; this was followed by a massacre of the followers of Ursinus and the consecration of Damasus at the Lateran Basilica. Bloody riots continued even after his installation, so Damasus sought the help of the prefect of the city and other civil authorities to secure his power— the first time a pope had enlisted the support of the civil powers. It would not be the last time, as we shall see. Unfortunately, bloodshed continued until the prefect successfully exiled the antipope Ursinus and his remaining supporters who were not dead in the streets.

Seventeen years later, Siricius was elected peacefully, unanimously, and with the emperor's approval. A disputed election in 418 (between Boniface and Eulalius—Boniface won) was followed by a unanimous, uncontested election on September 10, 422, of the Roman archdeacon Celestine. Another important deacon, Leo, was absent from Rome on a diplomatic mission when he elected in 440; he went on to become one of the greatest of all popes as Leo I, known also as Leo the Great, reigning until November 10, 461. Famously, Pope Leo held off the invading king of the Huns, Attila, in 452.

The last of the western Roman emperors, Romulus Augustulus, was deposed in September 476, and the barbarian kingdoms were soon established in the west, changing the political map of Italy and impinging on the security of Rome itself. Thus, for the first time ever, the newly elected Pope Felix III sent an ambassador to Constantinople to announce his election to Zeno, emperor of the east, and seek imperial support.

Eight Turbulent Centuries: 476–1274

Roughly the first thousand years of the papacy—up until 1059— saw the papal election laws and practices swing widely from simple acclamation by the clergy and people of Rome amid persecutions that persisted until Emperor Constantine's tolerance, then embrace of Christianity, to the intervention of emperors, corrupt politicians, and noble families. In the ensuing centuries, the papacy experienced some of its very worst moments, as well as some of its most glorious. Two of the greatest popes ever, Leo I and Gregory I, were elected in times of incredible turbulence. Other reforming popes, such as Gregory VII and Gregory X, served during the middle ages when the papacy became both more monarchical and more secularized. And during this time, some of the most depraved persons to occupy the Throne of Peter, such as Pope John XII, were elected, deposed, even murdered: the first pope to be assassinated, John VIII, was poisoned, then clubbed to death in 882.

In papal elections of late antiquity and the early middle ages, not only was the emperor's approval (or lack thereof) an issue, but popes sought to nominate their own successors, causing a series of new questions to arise. Pope Symmachus was one of two men elected as pope on the same day by different factions of Roman clergy, a situation that was appealed to the Ostrogothic king of Italy (remarkably, like the majority of Christians of the time, a believer in the Arian heresy, despite its rejection by the orthodox fathers of the church), who ruled that the one consecrated first should be the bishop of Rome. The "winner" of the dispute, Symmachus issued legislation the next spring (March 1, 499) banning all discussion of a pope's successor during his lifetime, allowing him to nominate a successor if he so chose, giving the electors the right to choose another candidate, and banning the laity from participation as electors. The practice of a pope nominating his successor was later rejected by successive electoral colleges of Roman clergy and laity. Up to the present day, popes are proscribed from directly naming their preferences, formally or informally.

Dual elections (even rival consecrations), antipopes, long vacancies, election intrigues, and compromises continued intermittently through the sixth and seventh centuries. Legislation by the king of Italy and the senate of Rome in 533 stated that there should be no improper practices in the election of the pope, under pain of severe penalties. In addition, there would be very strict limits on the amount of money to be expended at elections, and disputed elections were to be "referred to the court, on procuring the necessary documents from royal officials."[11]

Politics and intrigue became the norm in papal elections. King Theodoric intervened in the papal election of July 12, 526, which tipped the vote to Felix IV. After the pontificate of Agapitus I (535–536), King Theodahad, the last Ostrogothic king of Italy, pressured the clergy of Rome into electing a subdeacon, Silverius (the son of a previous pope, Hormisdas). In 556 Pelagius I was installed after appointment by the emperor, rather than by election. Imperial ratification—which sometimes took months to confirm— was now a requirement.

The pontificate of Gregory I the Great (590–604) was the pivotal event of the early middle ages. A wealthy Roman who had rejected family name and properties for the monastic life, he was an accomplished diplomat and scholar; he reluctantly accepted election. He later wrote, "Under the pretence of being made a bishop, I have been brought back into the world . . . I have lost the deep joy of my peace and quiet, and while I seem outwardly to have risen, inwardly I am in a state of collapse."[12] He became perhaps the greatest of all popes, but political turbulence and ill health plagued his reign. Those who elected him knew they had chosen a strong leader, but Gregory redefined the papacy as a civil as well as spiritual power, filling the vacuum that existed in the government of Rome. He dispatched missionaries to England, and presided over a revolution in liturgy (including the music that famously bears his name, the Gregorian chants). He left the church of Rome in a position of great prosperity and prestige; the only stable and universally recognized institution in western Europe.

After Gregory, there were anti-Gregory (anti-monastic) back-lashes and political interference began to plague the papal elections again. From May 685 through December 687, just a two-year span, there were four canonical popes (Benedict II, John V, Conon, and Sergius I) and two antipopes (Theodore and Paschal). After Pope Conon's death there was an electoral split that resulted in a vacancy of three months. During this vacancy, disaffected factions influenced by military threats and bribery elected two antipopes. Finally, at a meeting of civic, army, and clerical leaders, Sergius was chosen then installed at the Lateran Basilica, which was promptly stormed by citizens and factional partisans. The imperial exarch, who had been bribed by one of the antipopes, switched his approval to the new man, and Sergius (687–701) was secure. Gregory III was elected unanimously in 731 on the same day as the funeral of his predecessor, and he became the last pope to seek the formal mandate of the emperor in Constantinople.

It must be said, though, that some pontiffs continued to work hand in hand with the political authorities, such as the Roman emperor (based in Constantinople) or his exarch based in Ravenna, or the barbarian kings of Italy (very often an iffy proposition when the monarch was a heretic) or, after 800, the Holy Roman emperor. Stephen III (752–757) moved to detach from the Byzantine empire and ally the papacy with a rising power in the west, the king of the Franks. From King Pepin, the father of Charlemagne, Stephen sought and received political and military protection, as well as a "donation" of lands that would serve as a buffer between Rome (the pope) and hostile powers. These lands became the basis of the "papal states," territories over a significant portion of north-central Italy that expanded and contracted but remained under direct control of the pope for a thousand years.

The pope often needed military support to maintain the security of these papal states, and the emperor often wanted to assert his authority (widely believed to be divinely instituted) in Rome and central Italy. Thus, in subsequent years, the pope-elect was required to report his election for ratification by the Frankish king (soon, the Holy Roman emperor) before he could be consecrated, and by some he was not considered to be pope until that approval had been obtained.

Secular authorities even dictated papal election laws. In 824, seeing the urgent need for reform in the face of public disturbances and factional infighting, the Holy Roman emperor Louis I (known for his religiosity as Louis the Pious) dispatched his heir, Lothair, to formally codify the relationship between empire and Apostolic See. The result was the so-called "Roman Constitution," decreed on November 11. The constitution restored the traditional electoral participation of the people of Rome, along with the clergy, which had been suspended fifty-five years earlier by Pope Stephen III. Also, the legislation required that, prior to being consecrated as bishop of Rome, the pope-elect seek the emperor's confirmation of his election and swear an oath of loyalty to the emperor before the imperial envoy. Further, the citizens of the Papal States were required to swear allegiance to the emperor.

However, despite imperial oversight of the elections, some of the worst popes on record were elected within the century. As previously mentioned, John VIII (872–882) was assassinated. John's successor, Marinus I (882–884), was the first pope to have been a bishop of another diocese (contrary to one of the most important church laws of the previous six centuries that prohibited the "translation" of a bishop from one see to another). And in one period of less than two years, from April 896 to January 898, there were six canonically elected popes (Formosus, Boniface VI, Stephen VII, Romanus, Theodore II, and John IX). The first of these, Formosus (891–896) was later "tried" posthumously for perjury, coveting the papacy, and violating the canon that prohibited bishops from switching sees. In the infamous Cadaver Synod convened by his successor Stephen (896–897), Formosus's body was disinterred nine months after his death, clothed in papal vestments, and seated upon a papal throne; he was found guilty and his body dumped into the Tiber. Yet, in the same century, two of the greatest and most respected popes were also chosen: Nicholas I (858–867) and the cardinal priest Hadrian II, who accepted the papacy as a compromise candidate in 867.

The tenth century witnessed the nadir of the papacy with the election of ambitious bishops and profligate Roman aristocrats, the domination of elections by empresses and papal mistresses—and even the murder of a pope by a successor. In August 903, after the death of Benedict IV (900–903), a man who was not a member of the Roman clergy was elected. It seems that the clergy and nobility could not agree on a local candidate, so they chose a parish priest from a town about twenty-five miles away. The "stranger," who became Leo V (903–904), was pushed from the papal throne by an antipope named Christopher and jailed. In the meantime, after being elected twice (the first time, in 897, he was forced to decline even after being installed), Pope Sergius III returned from exile and marched on Rome. He jailed and eventually murdered both Christopher and his legally elected predecessor, Leo V.

Alberic II, the prince and patrician of Rome, as all-powerful dictator of the city from 932 to 954 made and broke several popes. On his deathbed, Alberic secured—through threats and bribery—the election of his eighteen-year-old son Octavian as pope. The youth was in fact elected, in violation of the ancient law of Pope Symmachus (499) against such nepotism and civil influence. Octavian changed his name to John XII (only the second pope to take a name different from his own, after John II in 533, who had been called Mercury) and became one of the most venal and immoral popes in history.* He was said to have held orgies in St. Peter's and died of a stroke in bed with a married woman.

---

*The custom of adopting a new name became the norm starting in the late tenth century, when Pope John XIV (983–984) became the fourth pope to change his name, the first to do so because his baptismal name was Peter. It was—and is—considered bad form to take the name of the greatest apostle.

Roman families of wealth and aristocratic lineage played a large role in papal elections from this period through the Renaissance. Also, the Holy Roman emperors nominated and vetoed candidates, including one Bruno, the noble German-born bishop of Toul, who accepted Emperor Henry III's nod only on condition of proper election by the clergy and people of Rome. He came to Rome in pilgrim's clothing, took the name Leo IX (1049–1054), and inaugurated a period of reform in the papacy and papal elections. He recruited like-minded advisers (including the monk Hildebrand who would later become pope himself) to help him hold a series of synods throughout Europe to push his campaign against simony (paying for religious favors) and clerical unchastity. For the remaining years of the eleventh century, many of his successors continued the reform program. It is important to note, also, that in 1054 the schism between the eastern and western churches became final, with mutual excommunications.

In 1059, Pope Nicholas II promulgated a momentous decree that forever changed the nature of papal elections, though his legislation was not fully implemented after his passing (as was often the case with such reforms). *In nominee Domini* (in the name of the master) provided that the cardinal bishops (from the suburban dioceses that surrounded Rome) would consult among themselves and then elect the pope; afterwhich, the election would then be ratified by the acclaim of the lower clergy and the people of Rome. As we have seen, the local clergy had consolidated their power and prestige from the third or fourth century, until the honorific of "cardinal" ("hinge man") became formalized as an office in service to the pope and the church of Rome. In the elections, there was a nod to imperial approval as well, but not without condition and not forever.

Gregory VII was born of humble means and elected pope by popular acclaim on April 22, 1073, the day after the death of his predecessor, Alexander. (He was consecrated as bishop of Rome on June 30, 1073.) As the monk known as Hildebrand, he had been an archdeacon and an adviser and friend to three popes. He would surprise no one when he went on to become one of the greatest pontiffs, always involved in one conflict or controversy or another.

He died in exile, in Salerno on May 25, 1085. Gregory VII kept the flames of reform and the monarchical authority of the papacy alive, both of which burned brightly before they were extinguished in later centuries. His elliptical decrees on the papacy, known as the *Dictatus Papae* (dictates of the pope) pushed the limits of spiritual and civic authority for the papacy. He tried to influence his succession by endorsing a fruitless "short list" of three candidates, but a yearlong vacancy after his death resulted in the election of an abbot of the famous monastery of Monte Cassino.

For the next two hundred years, through the reign of twenty-seven more popes—until the death of the tenth pope named Gregory—the elections were alternately difficult to disastrous, occasionally simple and triumphant, but consistently problematic. The vacancies became scandalous; two lasted for a year or more, one for nearly three years. Following the death of Pope Hadrian IV on September 1, 1159, the disputed election of one man, who was forced to withdraw by imperial troops, and the election of Alexander III (1159–1181), there was an eighteen-year schism and four antipopes. Violence and politics influenced papal elections for decades to come.

The papacy achieved an incredible apex with the pontificate of Innocent III (1198–1216). Having been elected unanimously at the age of thirty-eight, Innocent was recognized by the faithful and by the royal rulers throughout Europe as a priest-emperor or a sort of Christian "pharaoh" in his own right, who (at times, not without resistance) chose and deposed kings and emperors. He codified many of his dogmatic and secular achievements in the canons of the Fourth Council of the Lateran (1215), solidified the political position of the Papal States, enriched the papal treasury, launched the fourth crusade in the east, and effectively, if harshly, put down heresy through military means. He died eight months after his Great Council (Fourth Lateran) on July 16, 1216, in Perugia. There, the people of the city, fearing a lengthy conclave and period of uncertainty, prevented the assembled cardinals from leaving—in fact locked them up—to force a quick decision. The nineteen cardinals were able to elect the new man, an aged and infirm cardinal who became Honorius III. But, illustrating how quickly human beings can revert to previous behaviors, two of the longest vacancies in the history of the Roman see occurred within the next two generations.

From 1241 to 1243 there was an eighteen-month vacancy before the election of Innocent IV (1243—1254), and from 1268 to 1271 there was another very lengthy *interregnum*. Also during this mid-thirteenth century period, the cardinals used the *per compromissum* (by committee) method to elect when they were dead-locked. In the papal elections of 1227 and 1271, for example, they assigned a two- or three-man committee to make the decision. The college of cardinals dwindled in number to as few as eight members by 1261 (and it still took them three miserable months over that summer to conduct the election).

The Origin of the Conclave: 1274–1303

From the rather murky origins of the principle of papal election, through centuries of scandals and vicissitudes (useful euphemisms in this context), and through a millennium of legislation by popes and councils, we have arrived at the ceremonial and secretive gathering of the cardinals known as the conclave. The derivation of "conclave" is refreshingly simple in a milieu freighted with seemingly obscure terminology: from the Latin *cum* (with) and *clavis* (key). The conclave is a meeting held "under lock and key" to prevent pernicious outside influences from infecting the work of the Holy Spirit.

The first conclave, as such, was held in 1276, to choose the successor of Pope Gregory X, who had been elected in 1271 after the second-lengthiest vacancy in history: two years, nine months (see chart on page 54). At the fifth session of the Second Council of Lyons, Gregory promulgated a strict new apostolic constitution, *Ubi periculum* (where there is danger), in which the term "conclave" is first connected to papal elections.

Ubi periculum required the cardinals to wait ten days after the death of a pope to allow the entire college of cardinals to gather.

Then they were to assemble in the papal palace where the pope had died, or the nearest city not under interdict (i.e., papal sanction) in that bishop's palace. Each cardinal was allowed a single servant or "conclavist" to accompany him. All electors and conclavists were to gather in a single room without any partitions and to live there in common for the duration. This room and one other chamber were to be closed off completely from the outside world. No cardinal could send out or receive any message, and food was admitted only through one small window. The custom of ratification by the lower clergy and the people of Rome somewhat fell into desuetude at this time.

In 1276, there were three conclaves. After the second, on July 11, the newly elected pope, Hadrian V, scrapped the strict conclave decree of Gregory X because of its "many intolerable and obscure provisions."[13] So much for election reform!

Not every papal election has been held in Rome. In fact, nearly thirty legitimate elections were conducted elsewhere, as well as a dozen or more that were not canonical (the election of antipopes). Historically, many of these ex-Roman elections have been significant in the shaping of today's election process. One example is the election of Celestine V in 1294.

By mid-1294, the throne of Peter had been unoccupied for more than two years. Deadlocks and delays were caused in large measure by intrigues among the prominent Roman families (especially the Orsini and the Colonna clans) for control of the papacy— as well as by intense pressure from the king of France. Cardinal Latino Malabranca, the bishop of Ostia, proposed the name of an elderly hermit, Peter of Murrone. He was elected by the squabbling cardinals, who hoped that a truly holy man might serve God's church in this time of division. This election, on July 5, 1294, was also held in Perugia.

As Pope Celestine V, the hermit Peter (to be canonized in 1313) never even made it to Rome, and, appalled and frightened by the unholy politics of the papal court, was allowed (some say actively persuaded by his soon-to-be successor, the canon lawyer Cardinal Benedetto Gaetani) to resign after only five months.

Gaetani, as Boniface VIII, held the former pontiff as a virtual prisoner until his death in the spring of 1296. Boniface himself, one of the most imperial of all popes, would die as the result of conspiracy, arrest, torture, and house imprisonment.

Celestine's election had proved both the value and the potential pitfalls in electing a compromise candidate. Holding such an election away from the Holy See (though within papal territories) left it open to local popular and political pressures that were different and sometimes more dangerous than Roman street violence. So, as the norms of the papal election took shape over the next seven hundred years, the popes would begin to consolidate their powers within the city of Rome, and eventually in the tiny but formidable Vatican City, an independent state within Rome. Like so many things regarding the election process, this took time—centuries—to iron out.

Leading up to these near debacles in the thirteenth century (in so many other ways the high point of the late middle ages, the age of Francis of Assisi, Thomas Aquinas, and Bonaventure, among others) were centuries of reform in the papal election process, such as Gregory X's dictum, interspersed with relapses of judgment and spirituality. This was the age of the crusades, the Inquisition, and lawyer-popes (of whom Innocent III was the best and brightest example). It may be argued that despite human sin and error, the apostolic succession was preserved by the Holy Spirit and by men and women of faith. And there was more testing and generations of corruption to come.

The college of cardinals became secularized, if not corrupt; some of its members became incredibly wealthy and wielded heavy influence in the conclaves. Its numbers dwindled during short pontificates. Only twelve cardinals participated in the two conclaves of 1241, and only eight cardinals elected Urban IV in 1261. Seven cardinal-electors took six months to choose John XXI's successor, being deadlocked three-to-three for two candidates. During this period the conclaves sometimes delegated their decisions to committees (e.g., in 1216, 1227, and 1271) of two or three cardinals.

Exile and Schism, Reformation and Revolution: 1303–1800

The end of Boniface signaled the beginning of a century that saw papal exile in Avignon, then schism. First, the college of cardinals split into pro-French and anti-French factions in a time when France was the premiere European power. The pro-French block won out in the conclave of 1305, in Perugia again, after which the papacy relocated to Avignon, in southern France, for seventy years. There were seven Avignon popes, the last of whom was Gregory XI who moved the papal administration back to Italy. Following his death, a conclave was held in Rome in April 1378, with sixteen cardinals present (there were six still back in France). For the last time to date, the cardinals elected a non-cardinal as pope. They chose the sixty-year-old archbishop of Bari amid an uproar in Rome. The Romans feared another Frenchman and the loss of the papacy again to Avignon, so there were riots that spilled into the Lateran Palace (the pope's Roman residence). The cardinals were cowed, and falsely announced the election of an old Roman cardinal to placate the mob; they only announced the true election result the next day when they felt secure from recrimination. They were pleased with their choice because the new pope, Urban VI, had a reputation for honesty, austerity, and competence as an administrator. However, he proved to be a disastrous choice.

Urban VI (1378–1389) possessed a singularly violent temper and lofty view of papal prerogatives, which he wielded indiscriminately among the Roman Curia, the very men who had elevated him. Within a few months, the cardinals, especially the French, determined that he was insane and declared the election invalid; a group of cardinals held another conclave and elected a second pope, expecting Urban to abdicate, which he did not. Thus began the Great Western Schism, a forty-year split in the church and the college of cardinals—resulting in three rival claimants to the papacy—that ended at the Council of Constance in 1417.

That council held an extraordinary papal election after it had deposed or accepted the resignation of each of the three simultaneous popes. Twenty-two cardinals and thirty representatives, all of them bishops or archbishops, of five nations (Italy, France, Germany, Spain, and England) met in a conclave for three days and elected Martin V (1417–1431). This was the last time that non-cardinals participated in the election of a pope.

The cardinals remained uncomfortable with absolute papal authority, as it had developed since Innocent III. They rebelled, as cardinals are wont to do sometimes, and in the election of March 3, 1431, they forced the winning candidate to acquiesce to an electoral pact: Eugene IV (1431–1447) agreed to convoke a new council, to accept the authority of the council, and to govern the church and the Papal States with full collaboration from the college of cardinals. He later revoked the agreement and was deposed by a faction at the Council of Basle. To counterbalance the autocratic tendencies of both Martin V and Eugene IV, the next conclave elected a compromise candidate: a scholar who proved to be an effective conciliator.

The cycle of compromise and reaction continued. In the conclave of 1464, the cardinals forged another election pact, attempting to limit the pope's powers and to expunge the practice of nepotism (specifically the frequent appointment of a "cardinal nephew" of the pope, many of whom eventually became popes themselves). Paul II (1464–1471), who was elected on the first ballot, agreed to, then later shelved the rules the cardinals had legislated.

Electioneering, intrigue, bribery, simony, and nepotism continued almost unabated for the next few generations, especially under the Borgia pope, Alexander VI (1492–1503), and the two Medici popes, Leo X (1513–1521) and Clement VII (1523–1534). Julius II, himself elected with the aid of promises and bribes on November 1, 1503, attempted to end the practices with his 1505 bull (decree) on papal elections. But long conclaves and the election of elderly cardinals who could be controlled by the Roman Curia were the rule throughout the remainder of the Renaissance period.

Disillusionment with popes, even reformers like Julius II (1503–1513) led to the breakaway of new "churches" during the Protestant Reformation led by Martin Luther, John Calvin, and others. The English church split off under King Henry VIII, and Lutheranism took root in northern Europe, especially in the German and Scandinavian countries. The popes dragged their bejeweled feet. It wasn't until the election of Paul III (1534–1549), who was the oldest cardinal and dean of the college when unanimously elected, that the challenge was met head-on. He knew that reform was necessary for the survival of the Catholic Church and the papacy; he convoked the Council of Trent in late 1545. The council held several sessions over the next eighteen years, through five pontificates. With the council, the church took a militant stance in matters of doctrine and liturgy that defined it for the world for the next four hundred years, until the Second Council of the Vatican (1962–1965).

In one eighteen-month period, from August 1590 to January 1592, there were five popes and four conclaves, most of which were heavily influenced by factional tensions and pressures from the great powers of Europe. The first Jesuit-trained pope was elected on February 9, 1621, as Gregory XV and he worked hard in his twenty-nine-month pontificate to institute internal reforms. Regarding papal elections, he issued two decrees (in 1621 and 1622) to reduce outside political influences and insure the secrecy of the ballot. His system has remained virtually unchanged to the present day.

Revolution, anti-clericalism, and atheism during the Age of Reason culminated in the election and ultimate coronation of Napoleon as emperor of France. Pope Pius VI (1775–1799), elected after a 134-day conclave, was unlucky enough to inherit a devalued papacy that had sunk to its lowest level of prestige and power over a century that saw the suppression of the Society of Jesus, wars in and around the Papal States, and a kind of theological siege mentality, putting the church on the defensive for a very long time. The French Revolution seemed to seal the fate of the church by overturning the established order of Europe in which church and states had often worked hand in glove; the Civil Constitution on the Clergy reorganized the French church under state control. Pius was powerless to prevent French occupation of the Papal States. He was imprisoned in Florence, then shipped across the Alps where he eventually died a broken man. Depleted of prestige, the Holy See was vacant, and many considered him "the last pope."

The Holy Father: 1800–1903

During this period, the men who were elected to serve as pope were morally upright and theologically orthodox to the extreme. From the age of Napoleon to the dawn of the twentieth century, the papacy changed little in its essential nature. It gradually began to take on new ecclesiastical powers such as the nomination of bishops, though it was buffeted by political setbacks, including the loss of the Papal States in 1870, which effectively ended the temporal powers of the pontiff (except his personal sovereignty over a city-state of 108 acres in the middle of Rome). The two longest-reigning popes served consecutively during this century, and the First Vatican Council defined the pope's teaching as infallible on matters of doctrine and morals.

Pius VII (1800–1823) was elected at Venice under the protection of the Austrian Empire, and he proved to be a gentle but stubborn pope who restored some of the credibility and prestige of the papacy through personal courage in the face of Napoleon's face-to-face abuse. Since the papal treasury had been taken by Napoleon, he was crowned in Venice with a papier-mâché tiara. Despite a very inauspicious beginning, he reigned for twenty-three years, another exceptionally long pontificate, like his immediate predecessor's.

The election and reign of Pius IX (1846–1878) is a watershed in the history of the Roman Catholic Church, for one particular reason, among a score: his was the longest pontificate ever, thirty-one years and eight months. We must look to our own time, to the pontificate of John Paul II, to find parallels to the length, depth, and scope of the influence of *Pio Nono* on the papacy. It is also illuminating to consider the expectations placed upon the man by the cardinals at the time of his election. J. N. D. Kelly, in the useful guide, *The Oxford Dictionary of the Popes*, wrote: "An indefatigable pastor, he was reputed a liberal because he advocated administrative changes in the [Papal States] and sympathized emotionally with Italian national aspirations."

In contrast, his predecessor, Gregory XVI (1831–1846), had been considered one of the most reactionary of popes. (He considered gas lamps and railroad trains the work of the devil.) The conclave that began on June 15, 1846, two weeks after Gregory's death, was sharply divided; there were forty-six cardinals in attendance (of a total of sixty-two eligible electors), and they were split between the so-called "intransigenti" and the "liberali." Each side had a favored candidate. The deadlocked conclave turned to a compromise choice, the progressive Cardinal Giovanni Maria Mastai-Ferritti, an experienced bishop, and at age fifty-four, young and vigorous. Pius IX was elected with a vote of thirty-six on the second day of the conclave and crowned on June 21, five days later. His pontificate began with great joy and promise among the liberal forces in the church and across Europe.

Over time, Pius IX embraced the concept of a centralized authority within the church, contrary to the expectation of many at his election. He is remembered for many actions, including further reforms in the rules of the papal election, but three actions stand out: 1) the definition of the Immaculate Conception of the Blessed Virgin Mary, which holds that she was born free of original sin; 2) the publication of the *Syllabus of Errors*, which condemned any number of modern academic and political theories as antithetical to the teachings of the Catholic Church; and 3) perhaps the most significant act of all, the convocation of the First Council of the Vatican (December 8, 1869 to July 18, 1870). At that council, the doctrine of papal infallibility was defined, capping the theological development of the papacy over the previous eighteen centuries.

Under the leadership of *Pio Nono*, the church became ever more closed to the modern world and defensive in its political and diplomatic stance, having lost the territories of the Papal States in 1870. The pope then became the self-proclaimed "prisoner of the Vatican." He died on February 7, 1878, deeply unpopular with the people of Rome (who years later tried to throw his body into the Tiber), but one of the most recognized and beloved figures among Catholics worldwide—one of, if not the very first, cults of personality—thanks to the explosion of mass communications from the mid-nineteenth century onward.

Expectations were again shattered by the next papal election. Cardinal Gioacchino Pecci was an experienced scholar, diplomat and bishop of Perugia (and enemy of Pius IX's conservative secretary of state, Cardinal Giacomo Antonelli, who was also known as the "red pope"). He was also sixty-eight years old and of fragile health, which argued for a "transitional papacy" of perhaps three to five years. Sixty of the sixty-four eligible cardinal-electors chose Pecci relatively quickly, on the third ballot of the conclave. (The first American-born cardinal, Archbishop John McCloskey of New York, was absent.) Upon his election as Leo XIII he said, "Since God wills that I assume the papacy, I will not contradict."[14]

Not only was he long-lived—he reigned for twenty-five years and five months—but he was an active, accomplished administrator, firmly in control throughout his pontificate, though more moderate and socially conscious than his predecessor, as well as his eventual successor. One of his most important accomplishments was the May 15, 1891, encyclical letter known as *Rerum novarum* (of new things), against socialism while promoting workers' rights and social justice. Leo established nearly 250 new dioceses in Africa, Asia, and the United Sates, required educated Catholics to study the scholastic theology of St. Thomas Aquinas, and tried to bring the church up to date in a modern, ever-changing world, while maintaining doctrinal integrity and traditional piety. He died at age ninety-three.

Modern Popes and the Papacy: 1903–2003

The next hundred years of the papacy saw a continuing conflict between modernism and conservatism in the church, as well as a steady increase in centralized authority, and influence on world events. The elections in this period were some of the most vivid ideological battles ever held within the electoral college of the cardinals, the conclave.

In 1903, after the lengthy pontificate of the somewhat more progressive Leo XIII, the college of cardinals desired a different style for the papacy. As the French curial Cardinal François–Desiré Matthieu said, "We wanted a pope who had never engaged in politics, whose name would signify peace and concord, who had grown old in the care of souls, who would concern himself with government of the church in detail, who would be above all a father and shepherd."[15]

The leading candidate going into the conclave of July 31–August 4 was forty-nine-year-old Mariano Rampolla del Tindaro, the longtime cardinal secretary of state. However, he was cut from the same diplomatic cloth as Leo XIII. In contrast, Giuseppi Melchiorre Sarto, the Patriarch of Venice, was nothing if not a pastor, a pious and emotional diocesan bishop, and a parish priest at heart. Cardinal Sarto's election in the conclave of 1903 would be a turning point in the history of the popes and papal elections.

On the third day of the conclave, Cardinal Kniaz Johan Puzyna de Kozielsko, the archbishop of Krakow, announced that Emperor Franz Joseph of Austria (the last imperial claimant to the last vestiges of the Holy Roman Empire) wished to exercise the veto, or *jus exclusivae* (right of exclusion), against Rampolla. Why remains a bit of a mystery. Perhaps Rampolla was perceived as too "liberal" or "pro-French" by Franz Josef's standards. Perhaps the rumors that Rampolla had argued against allowing Christian burial for Franz Josef's suicidal son, Crown Prince Rudolf, were in the emperor's mind. The conclave erupted angrily at this untoward imperial interference—and it would be the last time the veto was ever used. Rampolla peaked at thirty-five votes in the next scrutiny. Sarto steadily gained votes as it became clear that Rampolla's candidacy was effectively finished. The sixty-two cardinals continued voting, and on the seventh ballot gave fifty votes to the patriarch of Venice, who accepted with the words, "If this cup may not pass away from me, Thy will be done," and took the name Pius X.[16] He sincerely did not want the job.

On January 20, 1904, the new pope promulgated the apostolic constitution *Commissum nobis* (committed to us), forever abolishing the right of exclusion that had given three once-great Catholic monarchies—France, Spain, and Austria—the veto power over papal candidates.

During his pontificate, Pius reorganized and streamlined the Roman Curia, renovated the theological curriculum of Catholic schools, and undertook a thorough revision of canon law. He was concerned with rooting out liberal thought in all its forms, and he required an oath by all clergy to disavow modernism as heretical. He was deeply concerned with the spiritual life; he revised the missal, the laity's liturgical handbook and encouraged daily mass attendance and reception of Holy Communion. Pius continued the trend of centralizing ultimate church authority in the papacy. He was canonized by Pius XII on May 29, 1954—and remains the only pope in the past four hundred-plus years (since Pius V, who reigned 1566–1572) to be canonized as a saint.

What next? An intellectual—proving once again that the cardinals nearly always prefer to elect someone different than the deceased pontiff, keeping a natural balance in the office and the governance of the church. The conclave opened on August 31, 1914. From the husky, rustic Pius X, the cardinals turned to the tiny, frail, refined scholar-diplomat, Cardinal Giacomo della Chiesa (1914–1922). As archbishop of Bologna since 1907, he had received the cardinal's red hat only three months before his election as pope. Rampolla had died the year before, and nationalistic tensions were running high, which added to the crisis atmosphere. At the four-day conclave, fifty-seven electors (of the sixty-five eligible) made the surprise choice of della Chiesa on the tenth scrutiny with an exact two-thirds vote. One cardinal demanded that the ballots be checked to make certain the winning candidate had not voted for himself, which was against the conclave rules; he had not. After this humiliating moment, della Chiesa chose the name Benedict XV. Almost immediately, Pius X's secretary of state and chief enforcer of papal authority, the Spanish Cardinal Rafael Merry del Val was dismissed. It was rumored that on del Val's desk the new pope found a letter of denunciation of himself as a modernist, which had been intended for the previous pontiff's attention.

Benedict's pontificate was defined, even overshadowed, by World War I. He worked hard to bring peace and to secure the independence of Vatican City. He canonized Joan of Arc in 1920 (in part as a conciliatory gesture to the French), and he promulgated the new code of canon law that his predecessor had begun to revise. Benedict XV died at the relatively young age of sixty-seven, after a brief illness, on January 22, 1922.

Because of Benedict's sudden death, the fifty cardinals who assembled in the Sistine Chapel on Tuesday, February 2, were poorly prepared for the conclave (three others who were ill also voted). There were two major candidates who reflected the divided college of electors: one was Pietro Gasparri, the former secretary of state and, as camerlengo, the president of the conclave who was favored by partisans of the late pope. The other was Pietro La Fontaine, the rabid anti-modernist patriarch of Venice, against whom rumors were circulated among the electors. Two others were also contenders: Cardinal Merry del Val, still a curial power, and Pietro Maffi, archbishop of Pisa. But surprise, a hallmark of many modern conclaves, won out when, after a deadlock through fourteen ballots, a compromise candidate won. He was Cardinal Achille Ratti, archbishop of his native Milan for only six months. He had spent nearly his entire clerical career as a librarian! Upon accepting his election, he declared, "It must never be said that I refused to submit unreservedly to the will of God. No one shall say that I shrank before a burden that was to be laid on my shoulders. No one shall say that I fail to appreciate the votes of my colleagues. Therefore, in spite of my unworthiness, of which I am deeply conscious, I accept."[17]

The watchword in the Vatican under the new pontiff, who would be called Pope Pius XI became, simply, "obedience." Pius XI told the cardinals that he would give the traditional blessing *Urbi et Orbi* (on the city and the world) from the balcony overlooking St. Peter's Square—for the first time since the loss of the Papal States in the Franco-Prussian War of 1870. According to church historian

Eamon Duffy: "The instant announcement that he would use the balcony in the square for his blessing was characteristic of the decisiveness of the new regime, a decisiveness soon revealed as nothing short of dictatorial."[18]

Pius negotiated the famous Concordat with Mussolini's Italy (February 1929) that guaranteed the sovereignty of the Vatican, with a few extraterritorial holdings such as the Lateran Basilica and Castelgandolfo, the pope's country retreat. Despite indefatigable diplomacy, he could not save Europe from the coming conflagration. He denounced socialism and embraced Francisco Franco, the fascist dictator of Spain. He did not condemn the Italian invasion of Ethiopia in 1935. Pius XI did issue a controversial letter in Germany, condemning the Nazi regime's persecution of the church, but he feared communism more than fascism, distrusted democracies, and died before he could publish an encyclical denouncing anti-Semitism, *Humani Generis Unitas* (the unity of the human race). At his passing on February 10, 1939, seven months before the outbreak of war, governments and people around the world mourned him as a man of courage, though his long-term legacy was mixed. As evidenced by Pius's reign, the popes had begun to influence political and moral decisions beyond the neighborhood of Rome, extending their influence around the world as communications and transportation sped up and continued to develop with astounding rapidity throughout the twentieth century. But popes of this period could not—or did not—directly combat the rise of fascism and Nazism, and the twin evils of war and genocide rolled over Europe.

Italian politics under Mussolini and internal church policy were the chief considerations among the sixty-two electors who assembled to choose Pius's successor. The choice of Eugenio Pacelli, Pius XI's secretary of state and camerlengo of the Holy Roman Church (and as such chairman of the conclave), today seems inevitable. But there were more than a few uncertainties at the time, not only abroad in the world, but also within the hearts of the cardinals who entered the conclave. The doors of the

Apostolic Palace were sealed on the evening of March 1, and the voting began on the morning of Thursday, March 2, 1939.

Cardinal William Henry O'Connell of Boston had missed the prior two conclaves, in 1914 and 1922, but he made this one—at the very last moment. He was a Pacelli supporter going in, as were most "foreign," or non-Italian cardinals, though no cardinal holding curial office had been elected since Gregory XVI (1831). Francis A. Burkle-Young recounts a telling conclave anecdote that involved the two friends of forty years' standing, O'Connell, the aging American lion, and Pacelli, the austere consummate church diplomat:

> At two o'clock [after lunch] the bell rang once more, for the begin-
> ning of the afternoon session. At its sound, Pacelli turned to descend
> the three steps into the Sistine, lost his footing, and fell heavily onto
> the solid marble floor. O'Connell, whose sharp wit seldom missed an
> opportunity, quickly bent down to help Pacelli to his feet. "The Vicar
> of Jesus Christ—on earth," exclaimed the Bostonian.[19]

The world press had floated the idea of a non-Italian pope, but the cardinals did not seriously consider any such candidates. On the second ballot, Cardinal Pacelli received the exact two-thirds majority required by the current rules of the conclave. However, before the dean of the college of cardinals approached to ask whether he would accept, Pacelli requested another ballot. He did not want to accept the office in such troubled times by a bare minimum of votes. The cardinals agreed and adjourned to luncheon, reassembled in the afternoon, and this time Pacelli received forty-eight votes, six more than two-thirds. He took the name Pius XII as a tribute to his predecessor. He added, "Have pity on me, O God, according to Thy mercy."[20]

Pius XII restored prestige to the papal office and embodied the new image of the modern pope as an exemplar of civilized morality. Today, his policies and leadership skills are questioned by those who criticize him for doing much too little to oppose Adolph Hitler's Nazi regime and the horrific slaughter of Jews and others during World War II. The debate will continue, with advocates on both sides marshalling evidence and arguing the morality of what he did and did not do during those dark years.

One of Pius's most crucial acts in terms of the internal church governance was the consistory of January 31, 1946, in which he created thirty-two new cardinals (only four Italians)—the most since Leo X in 1517 (thirty-one) and not surpassed until 2001 by John Paul II (forty-four). More than anyone before him, he internationalized the college of cardinals, creating brand-new cardinals in residential sees that had previously not seen a red hat.

Pope Pius XII served for nearly two decades, though in the last several years he was slowed by failing health. On December 8, 1945, he had promulgated a new constitution to govern the conclave, titled *Vacantis Apostolicae Sedis* (during vacancies of the Apostolic See). He died on October 9, 1958, at Castelgandolfo.

Reflecting the growing internationalism of the college, of the fifty-one electors in the conclave of October 25–28, 1958, only seventeen were Italian—the lowest percentage within a conclave since 1455 (the election of Callistus III as a compromise candidate). At ninety-two, Cardinal José María Carlo Rodriguez of Santiago, Chile, was the oldest cardinal-elector. Angelo Giuseppi Roncalli, the patriarch of Venice, was no spring chicken at seventy-seven, nor was he the oddsmakers' favorite, though he had a core of supporters—as did then-archbishop (not yet cardinal) Giovanni Battista Montini of Milan. Two cardinals were unable to participate in the conclave because they were detained behind the Iron Curtain: Joseph Mindszenty, archbishop of Esztergom, Hungary, and Alojzije Stepinac, archbishop of Zagreb, Yugoslavia.

The favorites going in included the grandly named Cardinal Gregory Peter XV Agagianian, patriarch of Cilicia of the Armenians, a bearded sixty-three-year-old known to be close to Pius XII. Likewise an American, Cardinal Francis Joseph Spellman of New York, one of Pius's closest personal friends, was the very first of his nationality to be given even a slight chance of election. Another *papabile* (prominent candidate for pope), Giacomo Lercaro, archbishop of Bologna, would garner a handful of protest votes against the Roman Curia, who would eventually coalesce around Agagianian's candidacy.

This conclave turned into a tussle between conservatives and liberals, with the latter sticking with Roncalli, through ten ballots with no two-thirds-plus-one majority, and even a loss of some votes, which caused some to scramble for a compromise liberal to replace him. But when he doubled his vote tally on the tenth and penultimate ballot and came two votes shy of election, it became clear that the patriarch was the one. On the eleventh scrutiny Roncalli received thirty-eight votes to Agagianian's ten.

The pope-elect gave a lengthy dissertation on his choice of a name, John. The electors were surprised, some aghast, at the unusual style of the response, which augured John XXIII's intention to break tradition in more ways than one. Six weeks after his coronation, he created twenty-three new cardinals, including Archbishop Montini of Milan, his future successor. (Also on this list was Franz König, the then-archbishop of Vienna and a future "great elector" in the second conclave of 1978, and at ninety-seven years old, currently the longest-serving cardinal.)

Within just a few months he would call for a new ecumenical council of the church, the first since Vatican I in 1870. In fact, he shocked and appalled a group of curial cardinals to whom he announced his intention; they reacted with chilly silence. Just as his acceptance speech had not sat well with traditionalists, this decision—which was perfectly within his sphere of responsibility to take—upset those, like Cardinal Alfredo Ottaviani, prefect of the Holy Office, who thought Catholic teaching needed enforcement, not a new representation in and to the modern world. All the *papabili* of the 1958 conclave would play important roles in the Second Vatican Council, which opened on October 11, 1962.

By bringing together all the bishops of the world, about 2,500 at that time, the council focused the church and the non-Catholic world on issues of faith, peace, justice, dialogue among various Christian churches, and relationships between Christians and members of non-Christian religions. Over its four sessions (1962–1965), the council hammered out documents that wrought immense changes in the way contemporary Catholics worship (the mass in local vernacular rather than Latin, for one) and relate to their church.

After a pontificate of less than five years, in which he forever changed the direction of the Catholic Church by convoking the council, John XXIII died on June 3, 1963, in his apartment in the Apostolic Palace. His death followed a lingering battle with cancer that was apparent even during the first session of the council. On more than one occasion during his reign, Pope John remarked that Cardinal Montini should be his successor and "expressed the opinion that he would make a good pope," an opinion he had held since before his own election when he had told some of his relatives, "the only thing left for me now is to become pope, but that will not happen, because the next pope will be your archbishop [Montini]."[21] He strongly felt that Montini would best govern the council and keep alive the flame of *aggiornamento*, that is, the spirit of renewal that John had initiated with the council.

Eighty cardinals entered the conclave on the evening of June 19, with a solemn understanding of their task. The college was sharply divided between conservatives who would prefer to suspend the work of the council (about one-third of the total, enough to block a progressive candidate) and the liberals who yearned for a pontiff to assume Pope John's mantle of reform. Fourteen of the cardinal-electors were over eighty, some of them very infirm. Only ten were under sixty. Cardinal Montini himself was a healthy, mentally acute sixty-five, probably the perfect age for a candidate in this conclave. The conservative bloc was more or less united behind the recently elevated Vatican diplomat, Cardinal Ildebrando Antoniutti, sixty-five years old. Another liberal, Lercaro, who had received a handful of votes in the previous conclave, was an active candidate. But on the morning of Thursday, June 20, in the first scrutiny, Montini led the pack with twenty-eight votes, to Antoniutti's twenty-four and Lercaro's twenty-two. Fifty-four votes were required for election.

The ultra-conservative cardinals Alfredo Ottaviani, curial veteran and head of the Holy Office, and Giuseppe Siri, archbishop of Genoa, held the anti-council bloc together the best they could, but eventually some of the more moderate curial cardinals saw the writing on the wall and voted for Montini. On the sixth ballot he achieved fifty-seven votes and the Throne of St. Peter.

Pope Paul VI modernized the face and function of the papacy that set the stage for his successors. Inevitably, as television and other mass communications developed at a rapid pace, and the changes wrought by the council took effect, Paul felt the tensions between the church and the world at the very core of his being. A decent, intellectual, empathetic man, he made some fundamental structural changes in the college of cardinals and the Roman Curia, but defaulted to strict orthodoxy in matters of sexuality and morality, resulting in the deeply controversial encyclical on artificial birth control. He reaffirmed the church's age-old doctrine rather than open the door to any possible revision. This created a spiritual whipsaw for many Catholics, especially in the United States. Paul is famously considered a Hamlet-like character, ultimately a near tragic figure who left an ambiguous footprint in the sands of papal history.

His immediate successor was a surprise choice that delighted Rome, the world, and the college of cardinals itself. "God's choice," he was called. The conclave began on Friday, August 25, 1978, nineteen days after Pope Paul's death. Nearly a quarter-million people had attended the funeral in St. Peter's Square, and now 111 cardinals gathered within the Apostolic Palace to conduct the election, under the rule of Paul's constitution, *Romano Pontifici Eligendo* (October 1, 1975).

It was a conclave that would be filled with many historic firsts. Giovanni Benelli, the archbishop of Florence, and Carlo Confalonieri, dean of the college of cardinals, were determined to be "grand electors," though Confalonieri was too old to participate in the balloting— and they had just the candidate to put in front of their fellow cardinals. But Giuseppe Siri, the archbishop of Genoa-Bobbio, was equally determined to carry the conservatives' banner for the third time.

In fact, Siri captured the most votes (twenty-five) on the first ballot, but he fell far short of the two-thirds-plus-one requirement, and

Albino Luciani, the patriarch of Venice and Benelli's man, was close behind (with twenty-three). Luciani promised to put a friendly, pastoral face on the policies of Paul VI, and he had a reputation for dealing with communists in a firm but Christian style. At sixty-five, he was in poor health, which was either not discussed or covered up by the few who knew the truth. A seismic shift occurred on the next ballot, as Luciani more than doubled his total (fifty-three) and Siri lost one vote. Needing seventy-five votes to win, he received ninety-two on the third ballot. Luciani had been elected pope in a single day, the shortest conclave ever (since 1276).[22] But it was not yet over.

In his apparent modesty, Cardinal Luciani demurred when asked whether he accepted election. Like Pius XII before him, though for a very different reason (because he really did not want the papacy), he asked for another ballot. Like the brevity of the conclave, this lack of clear acceptance was monumental in the history of papal elections. So, the cardinals held a fourth scrutiny. This time the vote was overwhelming: 102 of 111 for Luciani. The new pope shattered yet another precedent when he chose to be called by two names "John Paul." No other pope in history had been so named. Finally, he would make history by declining to be crowned with the cumbersome triple tiara of his predecessors, accepting instead a simpler installation ceremony.

In their euphoria, most of the cardinals were relieved at the swiftness and seeming rightness of their choice of a great pastor, rather than a politician or administrator, as their Holy Father. The series of surprises that had brought the church its Smiling Pope (so-called by the press and the populace alike because of his friendly demeanor) put the entire world at ease. But the seeds were planted for the Siri-Benelli confrontation of October, when, after the sudden death of John Paul, the cardinals met in the second conclave of this "year of three popes."

The second conclave of 1978 witnessed a momentous breakthrough with the election of a "foreign pope"—archbishop of Krakow, Karol Wojtyla—for the first time since 1523. Could this choice have been foreseen? Yes, according to some church historians. Cardinal

Franz König of Vienna played the great elector in the October conclave, with a purpose and vision of just such a result. Wojtyla was his candidate from the beginning, and he effectively laid the groundwork for the swing to the Polish cardinal when, as he strongly suspected, neither of the two more extreme parties could sustain their candidates. Cardinal John Krol of Philadelphia, a Polish-American, had also fixed on the young (fifty-eight-year-old) archbishop from Poland and helped to bring his fellow Americans on board. König deliberately teased Cardinal Stefan Wyszynski, the primate, or senior archbishop, of Poland toward an understanding of the need—if not the inevitability—of Wojtyla's election. Wyszynski was Wojtyla's senior in power and prestige. The younger cardinal was more charismatic than his elder colleague, and more skilled in skirting the restrictions placed on the Polish church by the communist regime; Wojtyla maintained a respectful but reserved relationship with the primate. At the eleventh hour it was Wyszynski who told Wojtyla that he must accept election "for Poland." Some in the conclave later reported seeing the younger cardinal in tears after this conversation with his primate.

Cardinal König's political maneuvering, sometimes subtle, sometimes overt, which he intensified on Sunday night, October 15, 1978, and Monday, October 16, proved out in spades. The long line of Italian popes had been broken, and the Catholic Church now had a leader who represented a changed church in a changed time. Morris West's 1962 novel about the surprise election of a Slavic cardinal as pope, *The Shoes of the Fisherman*, had suddenly come to be prophetic. By the sixth ballot, "Wojtyla had taken eleven votes from [Cardinal Giovanni] Benelli in the most surprising shift in the history of modern conclaves."[23]

Unlike his immediate predecessor, Karol Wojtyla did not hesitate when asked by the dean of the college of cardinals, Jean Villot, whether he accepted his election. He said, "In the obedience of faith before Christ my Lord, abandoning myself to the Mother of Christ and the church, and conscious of the great difficulties, *accepto*, I accept." He also shattered precedent when he chose to greet his colleagues, the cardinals who had elected him, standing rather than sitting on the makeshift throne in front of the altar. He embraced Cardinal Wyszynski with special, bittersweet emotion. The two men were now united as they had never been, and their roles had shifted dramatically.

The Polish pope today reigns as the Universal Pastor and the Servant of the Servants of God, harkening back to the very earliest days of the papacy and the papal elections that had sometimes produced choices that startled the Christian world. During his pontificate he has appointed nearly all of the men who will choose his successor. On February 21, 2001, he shattered Pius XII's record elevation of thirty-two new cardinals (itself the largest number in 450 years) with the elevation of forty-four cardinals, thirty-seven of whom were eligible to be electors.

John Paul II has also written the new rules by which the next conclave will be conducted, setting the stage for another historic, tension-filled gathering of the cardinals of the Holy Roman Church to fulfill their most solemn and important duty. Like perhaps none of the previous 250 or so elections of the pope, the next will be anticipated by billions (not millions or even hundreds of millions) of people in every corner of the planet, Catholics and non-Catholics alike. Thanks to his own surprise election and astoundingly long and significant pontificate, Pope John Paul has captured the world's attention and raised the bar to a dizzying new level for his successor, the 262nd Successor of Peter.

PART II

The Rules of the Papal Election

- The Apostolic Constitution: *Universi Dominici Gregis*

- THE VACANCY OF THE APOSTOLIC SEE

  - The Death of the Pope

  - The Powers of the College of Cardinals during the *Sede Vacante*

  - The Government of the Church during the Vacancy

  - The Congregations of the Cardinals in Preparation for the Election

  - Funeral Rites of the Roman Pontiff

- THE ELECTION OF THE ROMAN PONTIFF

  - The Electors: Who They Are; Rights and Responsibilities

  - The Conclave and Who May Be Admitted

  - The Election Begins

  - The Observance of Secrecy Regarding the Election

  - The Election Procedure

  - "Matters to Be Observed or Avoided" in the Election Process

  - Acceptance and Proclamation of the New Pope

The Rules of the Papal Election

The Apostolic Constitution:
Universi Dominici Gregis

An apostolic constitution is a decree by the pope in his capacity as chief legislator of the government of the church, as an exercise of his "apostolic authority." John Paul II's apostolic constitution, which will govern the procedures for the next papal election, is known by its Latin title taken from the first line of text: *Universi Dominici Gregis*, meaning "the shepherd of the Lord's whole flock." The introduction of this document, which was promulgated on February 22, 1996, outlines the theological and historical basis for the rules or "norms" of the election of the Roman Pontiff. Part One deals with the vacancy of the Holy See and Part Two with the actual election process. We will examine *Universi Dominici Gregis* (*UDG*) in depth; refer to Appendix D for the full text.

John Paul II's constitution supersedes the previous set of rules by Paul VI, which had been issued on October 1, 1975, under the title *Romano Pontifici Eligendo*, meaning simply the election of the Roman Pontiff. The more recent constitution is nearly a mirror reflection of the prior document, but with some significant divergences and new features that make it unique. Both apostolic constitutions seek to base the election norms upon tradition and precedence, as established by previous popes throughout the ages.

In a masterful understatement, John Paul introduces his new constitution by saying: "It is therefore understandable that the lawful apostolic succession in this See, with which 'because of its great preeminence every Church must agree,' has always been the object of particular attention." In other words, this is very important stuff—so, pay attention! Of special significance is the quotation from St. Irenaeus, second-century bishop and theologian, "because of its great preeminence every Church must agree," which reiterates the papal claims of direct apostolic succession and primacy.

Popes throughout history—and John Paul specifically cites twentieth-century popes Pius X, Pius XI, Pius XII, John XXIII, and Paul VI—have monitored the process and legislated various changes as they have seen fit. The last four popes have all sought both to increase the size of the college of cardinals and to diversify its composition to reflect the true face of the church in the contemporary world. Paul cites John XXIII's actions and Pius XII's Great Consistory of 1946 as modern improvements upon ancient practices:

> This is what Pius XII did, for example, when he added a number of Fathers to the College of Cardinals so that it might be more representative of the various nations and Churches of the Catholic world. John XXIII had the same end in view when he increased the number of members in the College and decreed that they should all receive the rank of bishop.[1]

Further, Pope Paul increased the maximum number of electors to 120, in order to expand the college and allow for a broader international membership, and dictated that all electors must be under the age of eighty to ensure a more forward-looking conclave. He got what he asked for in 1978. John Paul II confirms the same canonical maximum, yet he blew through that ceiling with his last consistory in February 2001, at which he named forty-four new cardinals and increased the number of eligible electors—at that time—to more than 135. In the past two years, the number of electors has dwindled, and now hovers closer to 110. As time passes, it becomes increasingly likely that Pope John Paul will call yet another consistory in 2003, though it is unlikely that he will name as many as forty-four new members of the sacred college.

As with his predecessors throughout history, the current pope has put his indelible stamp on the election rules, attempting to address potential problems and to streamline cumbersome practices, while retaining the sacred traditions of the past eight centuries. A simple breakdown of the content of *Universi Dominici Gregis* reveals the following major provisions, many of which are John Paul's changes from the previous rules, which we will highlight and examine in greater detail:

❖ During the vacancy of the Apostolic See, the college of cardinals has no power of jurisdiction in matters which pertain to the Supreme Pontiff during his lifetime or in the exercise of his office.

❖ During the vacancy the cardinals are to wear the usual black cassock with piping and the red sash, with skullcap, pectoral cross, and ring.

❖ At the death of the pope, all heads of the departments of the Roman Curia (called dicasteries) cease to exercise their office except for the camerlengo (or chamberlain) of the Holy Roman Church and the major penitentiary. Likewise the cardinal vicar general for the Diocese of Rome continues in office.

❖ The right to elect the Roman Pontiff belongs exclusively to the cardinals of the Holy Roman Church, with the exception of those who have reached their eightieth birthday before the day of the Roman Pontiff's death or the day when the Apostolic See becomes vacant.

❖ The maximum number of cardinal electors must not exceed 120.

❖ A cardinal who has been created and published before the college of cardinals thereby has the right to elect the pope, even if he has not yet received the red hat or the ring or sworn the oath.

❖ From the moment the Apostolic See is vacant, the cardinal electors must wait fifteen full days before beginning the election; they may wait a maximum of twenty days before beginning the conclave.

❖ The conclave shall take place within the territory of Vatican City.

❖ During the conclave the cardinal electors shall reside in the *Domus Sanctae Marthae*.

❖ The following persons shall also be admitted: the secretary of the college of cardinals who acts as the secretary of the conclave; the papal master of ceremonies along with two masters of ceremonies and two religious attached to the papal sacristy; an ecclesiastic chosen to assist the cardinal dean or the cardinal taking his place; confessors; and two medical doctors, cooks, and housekeepers.

❖ The election is to take place in the Sistine Chapel of the Apostolic Palace.

❖ Election by acclamation, inspiration, or by compromise is eliminated. Two-thirds of the votes, calculated on the basis of the total number of electors present, are required for election. If it is impossible to divide the number of electors into three equal parts, one additional vote shall be required for election.

❖ There shall be two ballots in the morning and two ballots in the afternoon.

❖ After a prescribed period of time and number of ballots (about thirty), the cardinals may decide, by majority vote, to waive the two-thirds rule and elect the pope by a simple majority of fifty per cent plus one.

❖ The crime of simony shall not invalidate or nullify the election.

❖ Civil authorities may not veto any candidate.

❖ Anyone may be elected; membership in the college of cardinals is not required.

❖ After his acceptance, the person elected, if he has already received episcopal ordination, is immediately bishop of the church of Rome, true pope and head of the college of bishops. He thus acquires and can exercise full and supreme power over the universal church.

❖ If the newly elected Supreme Pontiff is not already a bishop, his episcopal ordination shall be carried out by the dean of the college of cardinals or, in his absence, by the subdean or, should he too be prevented from doing so, by the senior cardinal bishop.

❖ The senior cardinal deacon announces that the election has taken place and proclaims the name of the new pope.

❖ The coronation of the new pope is replaced by the ceremony of the solemn inauguration of his pontificate.

Some of these rules may seem rather legalistic or formalistic to an outsider, but each has a basis in the history of the papacy and papal elections. In its essence, this election constitution would be familiar to cardinals in the thirteenth century. Yet there are several important new provisions that definitively make it a document for the papacy of the twenty-first century. For example, the elimination of election by acclamation or compromise is new, as is the provision for the cardinals to live outside the Apostolic Palace in the comfortable (but not fancy) St. Martha's Residence, from which they will be transported to the Sistine Chapel by bus. Most importantly, the new constitution allows for an election of the new pope by a simple majority if the cardinals feel that they have reached a deadlock after thirty or so ballots (in a prescribed formula outlined later in this section).

In this section of the book, we examine in detail these provisions that determine what will happen in the fifteen-to-twenty-day period after the pope dies, looking at how the election constitution differs with previous practice, as well as how it conforms to centuries-old traditions and protocols. We will follow the outline of the apostolic constitution, *Universi Dominici Gregis*, in more or less chronological order to trace the step-by-step progress of the conclave.

The Vacancy of the Apostolic See

Nothing creates as much anxiety and uncertainty within the Catholic Church as the death of a pope and the period of mourning and preparation for the conclave, which follow. In the modern era—really for the past two hundred years—there has been no long-term vacancy in the Holy See. Upon the death of the exiled and imprisoned Pope Pius VI in France on August 29, 1799, there was a gap of six months before the election of Cardinal Luigi Barnabà Chiaramonti as Pius VII. That was during the church's dark days, after the French Revolution and during the ongoing conflict with Napoleon, which only worsened in subsequent years.

The seventh century became known as the century of the long *interregna*, with several long vacancies, one of eleven months, three of a year or more. During this period, the see of Rome was vacant, on average, for eight months between each of the twenty-three pontificates of the time—including two periods of more than a year and a half (see chart on page 54)! One reason for the lengthy vacancies was the need, based on tradition and political necessity, to receive the emperor's approbation of the election. Since the sole emperor lived in Constantinople (after the fall of the western empire in 476) and his exarch (a sort of viceroy) in Ravenna, there was no imperial governor in Rome itself. Some popes took office without the emperor's formal approval, but there was nearly always a respectful waiting period as envoys went out and brought the "good news" to the imperial court.

The longest recorded vacancy occurred in the early fourth century, at the death of Pope Marcellinus on October 25, 304. His successor, the similarly named Marcellus was not elected until May 27, 308, according to official Vatican records. What happened? The Roman emperor Diocletian initiated a new persecution against Christianity on February 23, 303, "ordering the destruction of churches, the handing over of sacred books, and the offering of sacrifice to the gods by those attending courts of law."[2] At some point in 304, it was reported that Marcellinus complied with elements of the edict, thus disgracing and disqualifying him as bishop of Rome. He may have abdicated or been deposed as pope. We cannot be certain.

As noted on the following chart, the second-longest vacancy, of two years and nine months, resulted in Gregory X creating a new system of election, the conclave, to address the problems of such protracted delays in filling the chair of Peter. However, the next two longest vacancies occurred within forty years of these new, strict rules: the election of Celestine V in July 1294 and the election of John XXII in August 1316.

Today, it is extremely unlikely that there would or could be a vacancy longer than a few weeks. Not only do the rules encourage relatively swift, efficient voting procedures (given the ceremonial requirements), but the cardinals are motivated to come to a decision as quickly as possible and the Catholic world now expects such a decision from its leadership.

SIGNIFICANT VACANCIES (of one year or more)

3 years 7 months:	Marcellinus died October 25, 304— Marcellus I elected May 27, 308
2 years 9 months:	Clement IV died November 29, 1268— Gregory X elected September 1, 1271*
2 years 4 months:	Clement V died April 20, 1314— John XXII elected August 7, 1316
2 years 3 months:	Nicholas IV died April 4, 1292— Celestine V elected July 5, 1294
1 year 11 months:	Sixtus II died August 6, 258— Dionysius elected July 22, 260
1 year 10 months:	Eusebius died August 17, 309— Melchiades elected July 2, 311
1 year 7 months:	Honorius I died October 12, 638— Severinus elected May 28, 640
1 year 7 months:	Agatho died January 10, 681— Leo II elected August 17, 682
I year 7 months:	Celestine IV died November 10, 1241— Innocent IV elected June 25, 1243
1 year 2 months:	Fabian died January 20, 250— Cornelius elected March 251
1 year	Gregory VII died May 25, 1085— Victor III elected May 24, 1086

*This vacancy prompted Gregory X to create a new system of election, the conclave.

The Death of the Pope

What happens when the pope dies? The procedure outlined in *Universi Dominici Gregis* requires the following steps:

1) As soon as the pope is declared dead by the attending physician, the camerlengo, or chamberlain, of the Holy Roman Church must then officially and canonically determine his passing: "As soon as he is informed of the death of the Supreme Pontiff, the camerlengo of the Holy Roman Church must officially ascertain the pope's death, in the presence of the Master of Papal Liturgical Celebrations, of the Cleric Prelates of the Apostolic Camera and of the secretary and chancellor of the same, the latter shall draw up the official death certificate." (*UDG*, article 17.)

2) The camerlengo, the highest-ranking curial official who automatically takes over as administrator of the Holy See, now enters the most important phase of his duties, carrying out a series of ceremonial acts:

❖ He must stand near the body of the deceased and call out his Christian name three times; the silence of the dead bears the answer that is sought.

❖ Next, tradition calls for the camerlengo to strike the forehead of the pontiff with a silver hammer that bears the pope's coat of arms (each pope, cardinal, archbishop, and bishop possesses an ecclesiastical coat of arms). Another ritual may be substituted for the hammer: placing a veil over the face. Then the camerlengo will declare, simply, "The pope is dead."

❖ The silver hammer is then used to smash the Ring of the Fisherman, which the pope rarely wears, signaling the end of his temporal powers. His own episcopal ring (which each bishop wears) is not destroyed, but will be buried with him.

❖ The camerlengo seals off the pontiff's study and bedroom, restricting access to these rooms by anyone and everyone until the new pope is elected. No areas within the private apartments of the pope are occupied during the period of vacancy. The dead pope's personal property is stored until his will is executed.

3) The camerlengo assumes temporary possession of the Apostolic Palace (which houses the papal apartments and offices),

the Lateran Palace and basilica (the former papal residence and current diocesan cathedral), and the residential complex outside Rome, Castelgandolfo (where Popes Pius XII and Paul VI died).

4) The camerlengo presides over the conclave itself. If the office of camerlengo is vacant, the dean of the sacred college of cardinals will assume his functions until the cardinals, when they gather in Rome and begin to meet in their congregations, elect a new camerlengo pro tem.

5) The cardinal vicar of Rome, who is the chief administrative officer of the diocese after the pope, informs the people of the church of Rome of the pope's death and declares the see vacant. He issues a special announcement to this effect after the camerlengo has completed his job. The cardinal vicar continues in his office throughout the vacancy.

6) The Apostolic Penitentiary, a major office under the cardinal prefect who is called the major penitentiary, continues to function with full authority during the vacancy. The Apostolic Penitentiary is a tribunal that grants absolution from grave sins, dispensations, and indulgences; it is kept active during this period for "emergency" appeals that may arise. Because it is under the seal of the confessional, we do not know but can only imagine the occasions in which this appeal is exercised.

NOVEMDIALES:

The Nine-Day Period of Mourning after the Pope's Death

DAY 1:

Camerlengo certifies pontiff's death; all leaders of curial departments relinquish their posts. First particular congregation is held (small group of four cardinals, presided over by camerlengo). Masses for the deceased pontiff are held every day.

DAY 2:

First general congregation is held, presided over by the dean of college of cardinals. The particular congregation meets.

DAY 3:

Cardinals from outside Rome begin to gather, attend congregations, and offer masses for the deceased.

DAYS 4–5:

Planning and decision-making intensify in the congregations of the cardinals as more continue to arrive.

DAYS 6–8:

Congregations continue to meet. All cardinals take oaths of secrecy, review rules of the conclave, set funeral date and approve ceremonies and expenses. Pope's body lies in state in St. Peter's for viewing by faithful.

DAY 9:

Funeral mass concelebrated by all cardinals; burial of the pontiff (usually in crypt below altar of St. Peter's).

The Powers of the College of Cardinals during the *Sede Vacante*

Without a pope—the presiding bishop of the church of Rome—the cardinals, who are the "clergy of Rome" and the advisers of the Supreme Pontiff, only partially fill the vacuum of power. During the *Sede Vacante*, vacancy in the Holy See, no one or group of persons (the cardinals) may exercise any power or jurisdiction that pertain to or derive from the pope's authority. The heads of all the curial departments, most if not all cardinals, automatically relinquish their positions upon the death of the pope; all powers of the cardinals to conduct business of dicasteries are suspended during the vacancy. There are several exceptions, the first three previously noted:

❖ The cardinal camerlengo

❖ The cardinal vicar of Rome

❖ The cardinal prefect of the Apostolic Penitentiary.

❖ The second-ranking officials, usually known as secretaries, remain in office to continue the day-to-day functions of their congregations, councils, tribunals, and agencies.

One of the most important second-level offices is that of the *sostituto* of the Secretariat of State for General Affairs. This division of the secretariat is responsible for, among other things, the preparation of papal documents and decrees, the Vatican Press Office, and the government of the Vatican city-state. The *sostituto*, an archbishop who functions as a chief of staff, reports directly to the cardinal Secretary of State, who is in most cases the pope's right-hand man. Cardinal Benelli, a grand elector and *papabile* (i.e., leading candidate for pope) during the conclaves of 1978, had been Paul VI's *sostituto*, and one of the most powerful in history. The *sostituto* and other secretaries of curial agencies remain in place during the vacancy.

The college of cardinals may conduct ordinary business, which cannot legitimately be postponed. But they must be careful not to change any papal law or to allow any "rights of the Apostolic See and of the Roman Church" to lapse or be endangered in any way. When they meet in congregations during the *Sede Vacante*, the cardinals exercise the prescribed powers that they do possess. They cannot, for example, convoke an ecumenical council or synod of bishops during this time. They cannot declare saints or issue any encyclical letters on matters of faith or morals, as would a pope. They can, and do, handle administrative affairs on a limited basis, such as planning for the coming conclave and approving expenditures for the funeral and the conclave.

During the period after the death of Pope Paul VI in August 1978, the cardinals faced a situation roughly similar to the one they will find at the next vacancy: the entropy of bureaucratic functions after a long pontificate. In effect, many of the curial offices are held by elderly cardinals, archbishops, and bishops, and substantive business, such as canonization of saints and diplomatic relations with other states, has slowed—but not ceased—during the long twilight of Pope John Paul II's reign. The vacancy will thus provide a punctuation mark after the lengthy sentence, rather than prove a period of shock, as after the all-too sudden demise of John Paul I.

If there is any doubt or dispute regarding the provisions of the election constitution itself or how it is to be implemented, the college of cardinals may interpret any "doubtful or controverted points," and resolve such a dispute by a simple majority vote.

The Government of the Church during the Vacancy

The Roman Curia is a unique animal in ecclesiastical history. It has developed over time and been reformed more than once throughout the centuries, most recently by Popes Pius X, Paul VI, and John Paul II, giving it the structure and nomenclature it has today. According to the astute Jesuit writer and editor Thomas J. Reese: "The organization and procedures of the Roman Curia are not static; they are evolving today just as they have continually changed throughout the church's history, responding to different popes and to different historical situations."[3] I commend Father Reese's book, *Inside the Vatican,* for a thorough explanation of the workings of the curia. Suffice it to say here that the structure of this bureaucratic organization can be bewildering to the layperson who wants to figure out what all these cardinals, bishops, priests, religious, and laity are up to. The work of the curial offices has wide-ranging implications for Catholics around the world.

For example, the pope himself chooses each bishop for each diocese around the world, some four thousand of them, about 250 in the United States alone. From the eleventh through the early twentieth centuries, there were intense conflicts with secular governments and monarchs about who had the right to appoint bishops (who were once elected by local clergy). This was not resolved until the twentieth century, when canon law was revised to provide for papal appointment of all bishops of the Latin rite (which excludes some of the Eastern Catholic rite churches). Nowadays, sitting bishops submit lists of candidates to the papal nuncio (the pope's ecclesiastical ambassador) in their country. The nuncio investigates and narrows the list, then forwards his short list to the curial department, the Congregation for Bishops. That department then recommends the final candidate to the pope, who makes the final decision, most often approving the nomination of the congregation.

See the organizational chart below for a somewhat condensed picture of the Roman Curia.

The Organization of the Roman Curia

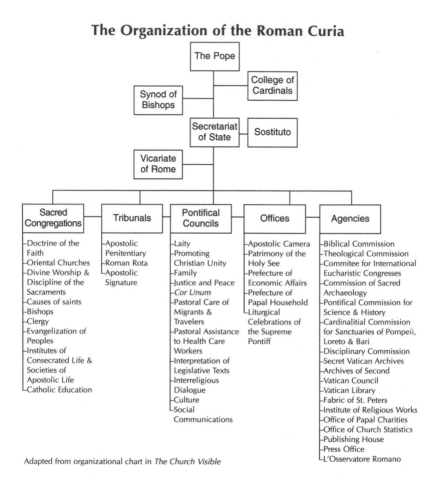

The Pope

Synod of Bishops

College of Cardinals

Secretariat of State — Sostituto

Vicariate of Rome

Sacred Congregations	Tribunals	Pontifical Councils	Offices	Agencies
‑Doctrine of the Faith	‑Apostolic Penitentiary	‑Laity	‑Apostolic Camera	‑Biblical Commission
‑Oriental Churches	‑Roman Rota	‑Promoting Christian Unity	‑Patrimony of the Holy See	‑Theological Commission
‑Divine Worship & Discipline of the Sacraments	‑Apostolic Signature	‑Family	‑Prefecture of Economic Affairs	‑Commitee for International Eucharistic Congresses
‑Causes of saints		‑Justice and Peace	‑Prefecture of Papal Household	‑Commission of Sacred Archaeology
‑Bishops		‑Cor Unum	‑Liturgical Celebrations of the Supreme Pontiff	‑Pontifical Commission for Science & History
‑Clergy		‑Pastoral Care of Migrants & Travelers		‑Cardinalitial Commission for Sanctuaries of Pompeii, Loreto & Bari
‑Evangelization of Peoples		‑Pastoral Assistance to Health Care Workers		‑Disciplinary Commission
‑Institutes of Consecrated Life & Societies of Apostolic Life		‑Interpretation of Legislative Texts		‑Secret Vatican Archives
‑Catholic Education		‑Interreligious Dialogue		‑Archives of Second
		‑Culture		‑Vatican Council
		‑Social Communications		‑Vatican Library
				‑Fabric of St. Peters
				‑Institute of Religious Works
				‑Office of Papal Charities
				‑Office of Church Statistics
				‑Publishing House
				‑Press Office
				‑L'Osservatore Romano

Adapted from organizational chart in *The Church Visible*

As noted earlier, the government of the church does not stop after the death of the pope, but the heads of all dicasteries of the Roman Curia—the departments known as prefectures, sacred congregations, and pontifical commissions—will cease to exercise their offices. Nothing that requires papal confirmation or discussion with the pope may be executed or approved during the vacancy.

The civil power of the pope, as sovereign of Vatican City, devolves to the college of cardinals during the vacancy. They may issue decrees or enter into agreements with other nation states in this period, with every such decision taken by a majority vote of the general congregation; however, the future pope must confirm any act of civil governance for it to remain valid. Just as in church matters, the cardinals derive their powers directly from and only from the pope himself.

The ordinary faculties, that is the ability of curial agencies to exercise certain powers, are to continue after the death of the pope. The day-to-day business of these agencies includes such mundane matters as payroll and pay raises, new publications or public announcements, and activity reports that must eventually be reviewed and approved by the Holy Father. And matters of special importance—"if such matters admit of no delay" (as in the case of dispensations which the Supreme Pontiff usually grants *in articulo mortis,* to those in danger of death)—may be delegated by the full college of cardinals to the one that had served as prefect of that dicastery until the pope's death, or to the group of cardinals who served with him. Again, any such decisions are only provisional, to be confirmed by the next pope.

The judicial branches of the Vatican—the Apostolic Penitentiary, the Supreme Apostolic Signatura (the Vatican's Supreme Court) and the Tribunal of the Roman Rota—continue to deal with cases during the *Sede Vacante,* per their papal and canonical charters.

The Congregations of the Cardinals in Preparation for the Election

During the vacancy, there are two kinds of congregations, that is, meetings of committees made up of cardinals, which meet regularly to carry out the ordinary business of the Holy See and to set plans for the conclave itself:

❖ The particular congregation: this is a smaller "steering committee" of four, which includes the camerlengo and three assistants (one from each order, see chart on page 69) chosen by lot from among the cardinals present in Rome. The three serve only for terms of three days, then are replaced by lot with a new group for the same term. The particular congregation handles housekeeping issues such as funeral and conclave preparations.

❖ The general congregation: this committee is comprised of *all* cardinals present in Rome (a "committee of the whole") and is run by the dean of the college of cardinals, so long as he is not over eighty years old. If neither he nor the subdean qualify, or if their offices are vacant, the cardinals elect a president of the general congregation. The general congregation deals with urgent business that may arise during the *Sede Vacante*, such as a financial or diplomatic matter that must be addressed before the new pope is chosen.

Those cardinals who are over eighty years of age have the option of attending or not attending the general congregations. But all cardinal electors are required to attend the meetings of the general congregation. As soon as a cardinal learns of the pope's death, he immediately prepares to leave for Rome, and most will arrive within a week of the pontiff's passing.

The general congregations are held daily, starting within a few days of the pope's death, including the *novemdiales*, the nine days of the funeral observations. During the first general congregation, the constitution *Universi Dominici Gregis* is to be distributed to all cardinals. The constitution is to be read aloud and discussed. The cardinals are required "to swear an oath to observe the prescriptions contained [therein] and to maintain secrecy." They "promise, pledge, and swear, as a body and individually, to observe exactly and faithfully all the norms" of the election constitution and "to maintain rigorous secrecy with regard to all matters in any way related to the election of the Roman Pontiff." This is the first of a series of oaths the cardinals will take regarding secrecy. Although all the cardinal electors may not be present for the first general congregation, each is expected, upon his arrival, to review the constitution and to swear the same oath on the Holy Gospels. The cardinals' schedules fill up with formal meetings (the congregations), as well as informal gatherings with other cardinals and curial officials (each cardinal serves in at least one of the curial departments), dinners, and social gatherings.

The agenda of the general congregation, as set by the apostolic constitution and the actions taken by the particular congregation, is full and rigorous. These are some of the "urgent decisions" the cardinals must make:

❖ To fix the day, hour, and manner in which the dead pope will be brought to St. Peter's Basilica for public mourning

❖ To approve arrangements for the funeral rites during the nine-day period of mourning, the *novemdiales*

❖ To make sure that the rooms of St. Martha's Residence are prepared for the cardinal electors, and that the Sistine Chapel is prepared for the election process to be held there

❖ To assign rooms by lot to the cardinal electors

❖ To assign two theologians to make "meditations" (presentations or homilies) to the cardinals on the problems facing the church and the need for "careful discernment in choosing the new pope"—also to set the times for these meditations

❖ To approve a budget of expenses for the period between the death of the pope and the election of the successor

❖ To read any document the pope left for the college of cardinals

❖ To arrange for the destruction of the Fisherman's Ring and the pope's lead seal (that is, the die of his seal) "with which Apostolic Letters are dispatched"

❖ To set the day and the hour for the beginning of the voting process

All issues are settled upon a majority vote of the cardinals in the general congregation. Verbal votes are not allowed but must be conducted "in a way which ensures secrecy." Any matter that the particular congregation cannot resolve and that requires "fuller examination," is submitted to the larger general congregation. One particular congregation may not revoke the actions of a previous one; only a general congregation can change such a decision by the lesser body.

Funeral Rites of the Roman Pontiff

Not to be forgotten amidst the bureaucratic minutiae and political maneuverings is the fact that the supreme head of the church has died and must be mourned. Even while the cardinals meet regularly in their congregations and hold informal dinners and greet colleagues from around the world, the dead pope is remembered for a prescribed nine-day period, called the *novemdiales*.

If the pope happens to die while away from the Vatican, he will be conveyed back to the Apostolic Palace, then to St. Peter's Basilica for the funeral rites. In this age of swift transportation and instant communications, it is unlikely that there would be any impediment to the dead pontiff's return if he happened to be on a foreign trip. However, if he were to be assassinated, that could create immense, unforeseeable difficulties, and tragic consequences would be felt worldwide. It would be a security nightmare as well as a political and diplomatic crisis, depending upon which country he was in when he died. (In 2002 it was revealed that there were assassination plots by the Al Qaeda terrorist organization against John Paul II, to be carried out when he traveled to the Philippines in the 1990s.)

There will be no autopsy performed upon the body of the pope, unless he has specifically given his permission before his death. Because there was no autopsy on John Paul I, mountains of speculation arose in the years following his death, with some journalists crying foul play. The fact remains that Albino Luciani was an ill man when he was elected, and this may have been one reason for his reluctance to accept his election as pope.

The constitution further provides: "No one is permitted to use any means whatsoever in order to photograph or film the Supreme Pontiff either on his sickbed or after death, or to record his words for subsequent reproduction. If after the pope's death anyone should wish to take photographs of him for documentary purposes, he must ask permission from the cardinal camerlengo of the Holy Roman Church, who will not however permit the taking of photographs of the Supreme Pontiff except attired in pontifical vestments." (*UDG*, article 30.)

The person of the dead pope, as head of state and head of the church, is considered more or less as a sacred relic to be venerated and buried with all due solemnity in the crypt below the high altar of St. Peter's, with 147 of his predecessors. It is not public knowledge where Pope John Paul II will be buried, whether within the basilica or in his native Poland. If the latter, it will be an extraordinary event in itself.

The pope's body will lie in state for three days in St. Peter's, and it is possible that up to a million people will see him at that time. His coffin will probably be a simple one, of wood, which will be encased in a lead liner, thence in a larger box of oak. The funeral mass will probably be held in St. Peter's Square, and virtually all of the cardinals, if they are present and physically able, will participate in the mass before hundreds of thousands of the faithful, as well as dignitaries and heads of state from around the world. The Swiss Guards will be present, as always for papal ceremonies, but more for show than for security, which will be provided by plainclothes Vatican officers, Italian carabinieri, and Italian national police. Because of previous assassination threats and the omnipresence of terrorism, the next papal funeral will be the most guarded in history—very different from the more open funerals of the two popes who died in 1978.

The Election of the Roman Pontiff

The second part of the election constitution addresses the actual election rules and procedures: who may be admitted into the conclave, how they are to carry out the balloting procedures, and what happens to the man who is elected pope. These rules date from ancient times, as we have seen in the Acts of the Apostles, and were further developed in the Roman Catholic Church throughout the centuries, always assuming participation in some form by the clergy and the people of Rome. That "clergy" eventually became the institution known as the sacred college of cardinals, the "people" at various times meant the citizens of the city or the senatorial families or imperial representatives, and the balance shifted back and forth until it settled about one thousand years ago firmly in the hands of the cardinals. (Though civil powers continued to interfere until 1903.) The conclave system itself was codified in 1274, after the nearly disastrous vacancy that ended in 1271 with the election of Gregory X. The system threatened to fall apart when the second pope so elected decided to dispose of it, but calmer, wiser heads prevailed and it was restored by Celestine V in 1294—and has been serving the church well ever since.

After the Renaissance and into the Age of Reason, the noble families eventually became non-players, as did the kings and emperors. However, from the time of Philip II of Spain (late sixteenth century) through the first election of the twentieth century, the right of exclusion was exercised by Spain, France, and Austria at various times. European politics had always affected the papal elections, sometimes indirectly, sometimes very directly indeed. Vigorous participation by Holy Roman emperors kept the cardinals on their toes. Simony, the buying and selling of ecclesiastical privileges and offices, was also a plague that waxed and waned through the ages. One of Martin Luther's chief protests was against such practices, as well as the selling of indulgences and the incontinency of the clergy.

The revolution in France chilled relations between the church and the state, and anticlericalism competed with Protestantism for priority as chief bane of the church hierarchy. Then, as tensions between sacred and secular purposes slowly faded in papal elections—especially since the loss of papal territories in 1870—the ritual of the election became almost an end in itself. Each rule not only served a spiritual purpose, but it was linked to history, which meant that echoes of conflicts past (sometimes violent) could still be heard, even into the twenty-first century.

THE CONCLAVE, DAY-BY-DAY

The cardinals must not begin the conclave until the fifteenth day after the death of the pope, and no later than the twentieth day.

DAY 1:
Mass *pro eligendo* (for electing the pope) is celebrated in St. Peter's Basilica. Cardinals go in procession to the Sistine Chapel where they are "locked in," then cast a single ballot in the morning. Lunch is followed by a brief rest period, then two more ballots in the afternoon.

DAY 2:
Cardinals depart their residence for the Sistine Chapel for two ballots in the morning and two in the afternoon. The winner must achieve two-thirds vote majority.

DAY 3:
Same as day 2; a maximum of four ballots is cast.

DAYS 4–6:
Same as day 3, with provision for breaks and consultations if balloting is inconclusive.

DAY 7:
After approximately thirty ballots, if no decision has been reached, cardinals may vote (by a simple majority) to allow for a winner to be chosen with a simple majority vote.

DAY OF ELECTION:
The winner accepts the vote of the cardinals, becomes bishop of Rome, greets the cardinals, and addresses "the city and the world" from the balcony of St. Peter's.

The Electors: Who They Are; Rights and Responsibilities

John Paul's constitution reaffirms the age-old prerogative of the college of cardinals, with Paul VI's age restriction: "The right to elect the Roman Pontiff belongs exclusively to the cardinals of the Holy Roman Church, with the exception of those who have reached their eightieth birthday before the day of the Roman Pontiff's death or the day when the Apostolic See becomes vacant."

The cardinals are a unique group whose history is somewhat shrouded in mystery because they emerged long after the apostolic age, unlike the scripturally based offices of bishop, deacon, and priest. Some scholars, however, argue that a group of the early church figures in the Acts of the Apostles, such as St. Stephen, were the equivalent of cardinals. It is clear that for the first several hundred years the cardinals were generally laymen, sometimes deacons (or archdeacons), often papal diplomats. The popes had secretaries and other assistants, and when the Papal States came into being, there arose the need for secular administration of the territories. These duties, of papal representative and pastor, are the same today for the cardinals who are residential archbishops, that is, those who live outside the vicinity of Rome.

By the ninth century, the three classes or orders of cardinals were established: cardinal bishops, cardinal priests, and cardinal deacons. Each order began to take on special tasks and ranks. All were tied directly to the pope and the papacy. By the twelfth century, the popes had begun to create cardinals outside Italy in residential sees across Europe, which helped them maintain eyes and ears in other nations and in the courts of distant rulers. As in so many aspects of protocol and procedure, the "orders" of cardinals come into play in the organization of the congregations and the functions within the conclave itself. There are three orders, listed according to precedence in the chart on page 69.

Each cardinal is assigned to one of the orders, and his "title" (from the Latin *titulus*)—that is, his Roman parish church or suburban diocese—is awarded at the time of his elevation to the cardinalate. Any cardinal may be promoted to a higher order during his career, at the discretion of the pope. There are few practical consequences of belonging to one order or another, except that in public processions at the Vatican and in the period of vacancy of the Holy See, the cardinal bishops and the dean of the college of cardinals (the most senior cardinal bishop) take precedence over the others, with cardinal priests second and cardinal deacons third in rank. In the conclave, each cardinal's vote is of equal value, no matter to what order he may belong. In the same way, each cardinal is required to respond to the call of the dean of the college to proceed to the election from wherever he may be and to participate in the election of the new pope.

ORDERS OF THE CARDINALS

CARDINAL BISHOPS:

There are, by tradition, the bishops of the seven dioceses that surround Rome, called "suburbicarian" (meaning suburban); by the mid-eleventh century the election of the pope was placed exclusively in their hands. The suburbicarian sees have periodically been reorganized. The cardinal bishops are the first-ranking order; the bishop of Ostia is, ex officio, the deacon of the college of cardinals.

CARDINAL PRIESTS:

These were the traditional twenty-five "pastors" of the principle parish churches of Rome (each, in turn, attached to one of the four major basilicas of Rome); these "titular" churches dated from the fifth century A.D. In recent centuries, this order has been widely expanded and new titles created, making it the largest of the three orders.

CARDINAL DEACONS:

The third rank of cardinals, these deacons were the original "servants" or "assistants" in Rome, serving from twelve to eighteen diaconal regions of Rome at different periods throughout history. For hundreds of years, the cardinal deacons were not ordained priests, and were highly influential relatives of the pontiffs, e.g., the "cardinal nephews." When non-residential bishops or theologians who are not bishops are named, they are quite often made cardinal deacons.

If any cardinal should refuse the call for any reason other than illness (as "attested to under oath by doctors and confirmed by the majority of electors"), the other cardinals may proceed with the election without waiting for him; if he changes his mind and wishes to join the conclave after it has begun, the cardinals will allow him to do so. As for illness, even a very sick cardinal will try his best to travel to Rome, unless his condition is so severe as to prevent him.

Obedience mixes with conscience in the role of the electors. If there is a council or synod of bishops under way when the pope dies, it must be adjourned and any cardinals who are participating must leave for Rome. Only the newly elected pope may order the meeting's resumption. No cardinal may be excluded from the election—even because of known crimes or sins—except by the age limit. (He may exclude himself by refusing to attend, though this is highly unlikely.) If the pope has elevated a cardinal but not yet presented him with the red hat and ring of his ecclesiastical office, he is eligible to vote. Only if the pope has deposed a cardinal or accepted a cardinal's resignation from that office, may such a cardinal not be admitted to the conclave. In 1998, Pope John Paul II accepted the resignation of Cardinal Hans Hermann Groër, the former archbishop of Vienna, who was an accused and acknowledged child molester; Groër relinquished all rights and privileges as a bishop and a cardinal, including his right to vote in the conclave.

The Conclave and Who May Be Admitted

The constitution *Universi Dominici Gregis* specifically states that the conclave must be held within the territory of Vatican City, with the balloting to be carried out specifically in the historic Sistine Chapel. The cardinals take residence in assigned rooms in St. Martha's Residence. Any cardinal who is ill may have a nurse in attendance, and special provisions are made to allow him to cast his ballot. "Due privacy and freedom" must be assured for the cardinals, including transportation between the residence and the Sistine Chapel. A special bus service will be provided for the cardinals for this short but open journey two or three times a day.

The cardinals need assistance in carrying out their duties in the conclave. In order to allow for smooth procedures and conduct of proper business, the following may be admitted to the conclave and lodged "in suitable areas":

❖ the secretary of the college of cardinals (who acts as secretary of the election itself)

❖ the master of papal liturgical celebrations, who helps with all the ceremonials that occur, especially when the new pope is chosen

❖ two masters of ceremonies who assist the above

❖ two religious attached to the Papal Sacristy, i.e., the sacristans who handle the vestments and sacred vessels

❖ an ecclesiastic assistant to the dean

❖ a number of priests from the regular clergy for hearing confessions in the different languages

❖ two medical doctors for possible emergencies. In virtually all recent conclaves (in the past one hundred years) there have been medical emergencies of some kind or another.

❖ a "suitable number" of persons to serve meals and maintain the residence for the cardinals. All such personnel must be authorized by the camerlengo and the particular congregation of cardinals.

These rules differ from past practice in which each cardinal was allowed a "conclavist," or a secretary-assistant to accompany him and attend to his needs while he was isolated in the Apostolic Palace. The new residence hall, St. Martha's Residence, will make life much easier for the electors in the next and future elections. All persons admitted to the conclave are required to maintain complete, perpetual confidentiality and secrecy, just as the cardinals themselves must. They, too, take an oath of secrecy that includes the following provision: "I likewise promise and swear to refrain from using any audio or video equipment capable of recording anything that takes place during the period of the election within Vatican City, and in particular anything which in any way, directly or indirectly, is related to the process of the election itself."

In Part Two, Chapter II of the election rules are the provisions that cut the cardinals off from any communication whatsoever with the outside world, or even with anyone who happens to be within Vatican City during the conclave. According to the constitution:

"The cardinal electors, from the beginning of the election until its conclusion and the public announcement of its outcome, are not to communicate—whether by writing, by telephone or by any other means of communication—with persons outside the area where the election is taking place, except in cases of proven and urgent necessity, duly acknowledged by the particular congregation." (*UDG*, article 44.)

The Election Begins

The election may not begin any sooner than the fifteenth day after the death of the pope, and no later than the twentieth day. Some ancient and medieval elections took place on the same day the pontiff died, or the next day. Emotions often ran high among the Roman community—anger, desperation, favor for one candidate over another—and the cardinals often wanted to get it over with as soon as possible. Alternatively, when they met outside of Rome, in Perugia or Avingnon, for example, other community pressures could cause them to rush or delay the process, depending on the political winds that might be blowing on a given day. Furthermore, European rulers often wanted either their national cardinals or personal representatives—or both—to be present for the election, which could cause delay in the convocation of the electors.

It is likely that every eligible elector will be present for the next conclave—with the total number being between 100 and 115. When all preparations have been made and it is fifteen days after the pope's death, the electors will celebrate a special mass, preferably in the morning, then assemble in the Pauline Chapel of the Apostolic Palace. There, vested in choir dress, they will proceed in a solemn procession to the Sistine Chapel, chanting the *Veni Creator Spiritus* (Come Creator Spirit). It is a spectacular picture that we probably will not see, unless special provision is made for photographs or film. (Although this scene was televised in 1978, it is not a binding precedent; that will be decided by the cardinals in the general congregation.)

Note that the rule calls for them to wear "choir dress." In a previous section of *Universi Dominici Gregis* referring to the dress code in the particular and general congregations, the rule holds that they should wear black cassocks in the congregations. With the exception of the red piping (lining around the edges), pectoral cross, and red skullcap, the cardinal looks very much like a regular priest. However, in their choir dress, the cardinals are quite unique and look very much like medieval prelates.

Choir dress is the description of the most formal vesture of bishops, archbishops, and cardinals, usually reserved for high liturgical occasions. The cardinal's color is a bright red, sometimes called scarlet, in contrast to the bishop's purple. Choir dress consists of the following elements:

❖ *Choir cassock and fascia*: The cassock is the familiar, traditional flowing vestment worn by priests throughout the ages; the cardinal's is vivid red, with the fascia, or sash, of watered silk worn high, above the belt line and beneath the breast. The fringed ends of the sash are worn long, down the cardinal's left leg.

❖ *Rochet*: The prelate's "foremost garment of choir dress,"[4] made of linen or lace, which reaches below the knee. The rochet is worn over the choir cassock and beneath the mozzetta; the neck is tied with a silk ribbon.

❖ *Mozzetta*: The short red cape that encircles the cardinal's shoulders, worn outside the rochet.

❖ *Zucchetto*: The familiar skullcap, bright red for cardinals.

❖ *Biretta*: Much less common now among priests than a couple of generations ago, the biretta is the square ecclesiastical cap with three peaks and a tuft, all black for priests. The cardinals' biretta is red, with a loop of scarlet silk instead of a tuft. The red silkmoiré biretta is the hat presented by the pope as a sign of the cardinalitial office.

❖ *Pectoral cross*: All bishops and cardinals wear a small cross made of gold or silver that hangs on a cord of red silk, intertwined with gold thread; the cross rests on the cardinal's breast, hence "pectoral."

Thus vested, the cardinal electors arrive within the Sistine Chapel where they will be seated in simple chairs with tables on which to write their ballots. In times past, when there were fewer cardinals, each sat upon a throne with an awning. After the election was concluded, all cardinals except the elected pope would lower their awnings.

The cardinal electors then take another secrecy oath, read aloud by the cardinal dean; when this has been completed, the master of papal liturgical celebrations will give the order "*Extra omnes!*" (everybody out!) The cardinal electors are then left alone to hear from one of the theologians previously chosen to preach to them "concerning the grave duty incumbent on them and thus on the need to act with right intention for the good of the Universal Church." The preacher then leaves and the dean asks the electors whether the election may begin, or whether there remains anything that must be clarified regarding the rules of the election. The rules, or the "norms and procedures" that govern the substantial part of the election process (such as the two-thirds rule) may not be changed, even by a unanimous vote.

At this point they are almost, but not quite, ready to begin the balloting.

The Observance of Secrecy Regarding the Election

It has been reiterated in this section, as it is throughout the election constitution, that the cardinals are required to maintain strict secrecy regarding every aspect of the conclave. In chapter IV, *Universi Dominici Gregis* states that the camerlengo and his three assistants on the particular congregation "are obliged to be especially vigilant in ensuring that there is absolutely no violation of secrecy with regard to the events occurring in the Sistine Chapel, where the voting takes place, and in the adjacent areas, before, as well as during and after the voting." In particular they will employ technicians to sweep the Apostolic Palace, and the Sistine Chapel itself, for recording or transmitting equipment. There will be "grave penalties" for anyone who tries to bug the sacred precincts of the conclave.

There is no equivocation in the rules regarding the need and requirement of secrecy. In fact, the cardinal-electors take several oaths of secrecy during the preparatory meetings and within the sealed conclave itself. There is nearly a millennium of history of conclaves, and throughout that time there have been attempts to control the outcome in one way or another, or to second-guess the voting of the cardinals and question the legitimacy of the election for one reason or another.

The cardinals must refrain from sending or receiving any messages outside the confines of Vatican City, upon pain of excommunication. The electors "are forbidden to reveal to any other person, directly or indirectly, information about the voting and about matters discussed or decided concerning the election of the pope." Nor can they bring any recording or writing instruments of any kind into the Sistine Chapel. This obligation of total secrecy applies also to those cardinals who cannot vote in the conclave (and are not admitted into the closed meeting) due to their age. The ultimate oath taken before the election, required of all cardinals, reads as follows:

We, the cardinal electors present in this election of the Supreme Pontiff promise, pledge and swear, as individuals and as a group, to observe faithfully and scrupulously the prescriptions contained in the Apostolic Constitution of the Supreme Pontiff John Paul II, Universi Dominici Gregis, *published on February 22, 1996. We likewise promise, pledge and swear that whichever of us by divine disposition is elected Roman Pontiff will commit himself faithfully to carrying out the* munus Petrinum *of Pastor of the Universal Church and will not fail to affirm and defend strenuously the spiritual and temporal rights and the liberty of the Holy See. In a particular way, we promise and swear to observe with the greatest fidelity and with all persons, clerical or lay, secrecy regarding everything that in any way relates to the election of the Roman Pontiff and regarding what occurs in the place of the election, directly or indirectly related to the results of the voting; we promise and swear not to break this secret in any way, either during or after the election of the new Pontiff, unless explicit authorization is granted by the same Pontiff; and never to lend support or favor to any interference, opposition or any other form of intervention, whereby secular authorities of whatever order and degree or any group of people or individuals might wish to intervene in the election of the Roman Pontiff.* [Each of the cardinal electors, according to the order of precedence, will then take the oath according to the following formula:] *And I, N. Cardinal N., do so promise, pledge and swear.* [Placing his hand on the Gospels, he will add:] *So help me God and these Holy Gospels which I touch with my hand.* (UDG, article 53.)

In the past, there have been serious as well as minor breaches of secrecy. During the conclave of 1724, one of the cardinals also held the position of ambassador of the court of Holy Roman Emperor Charles VI to the Holy See (a clear conflict of interest). The emperor wished to let the cardinal, already inside the conclave, know which candidates were not to his liking, and the written message was delivered to him by a young military officer who scaled the walls of the Vatican by using the iron bars of windows as a ladder. When he was unable to reach the window through which he had hoped to pass the letter to the waiting cardinal, he impaled the message on his sword and delivered it to the intended recipient that way.

During the election of Pius X in 1903, before the result could be announced at the traditional appearance of the new pope on the balcony of St. Peter's, a minor employee inside the conclave appeared at one of the windows facing the great piazza. He held a large pair of scissors in his hand and imitated the gesture of a tailor cutting cloth. The assembled Romans knew exactly what that meant. The name of the man elected was Giuseppe Sarto; *sarto* in Italian means "tailor." So, Cardinal Sarto was the new pope.

It has been reported that there were electronic transmissions to the news media in the conclaves of 1978. No doubt, there will be a Palm Pilot or two concealed among the cardinals' choir vestments during the next conclave, as well.

The Election Procedure

There is only one form of election allowed in John Paul II's constitution, which is known as *per scrutinium*, meaning by scrutiny. Two-thirds vote of the electors present is required for election (rather than the two-thirds-plus-one that Pius XII had imposed, following his own conclave experience, and which Paul VI also mandated in his election constitution of 1975). Election by compromise (that is, by a committee) or by acclamation (or "inspiration") are abolished in the pope's new rules. As outlined previously, when the dean asks for any questions about the election norms, after the final oath of secrecy, if there are none, the balloting may begin immediately.

According to *Universi Dominici Gregis*: "Should the election begin on the afternoon of the first day, only one ballot is to be held; then, on the following days, if no one was elected on the first ballot, two ballots shall be held in the morning and two in the afternoon." Thus, there will be a maximum of four ballots each day, starting on the second day of the conclave.

Paragraphs sixty-four through seventy-seven of the apostolic constitution outline the complex rules and ceremonies governing the balloting process in minute detail. These procedures have been followed for hundreds of years, and there is no substantial change in the outward process, but one crucial change in the ultimate number of votes needed for election if there occurs a deadlock in the election, which we will explore later in this section.

There are three phases in the voting process: the pre-scrutiny, the scrutiny proper, and the post-scrutiny.

1) **The pre-scrutiny phase** also has three parts. First, there is the preparation and distribution of the ballot papers; next, the choice by lot (by the most junior of the cardinal deacons) of the following:

❖ three men to serve as "scrutineers," who collect and count the ballots

❖ three men to serve as *infirmarii*, who distribute the ballots to cardinal electors who are sick

❖ three to serve as "revisers," who verify the election tallies

The first three names drawn will be scrutineers, the next three *infirmarii*, the last three revisers. If any of the names drawn are cardinals who cannot assume these tasks, other names will be drawn.

Immediately after the ballots are distributed, the non-cardinals are to leave the chapel. The junior cardinal deacon serves as doorkeeper to let them out, as well as to let the *infirmarii* carry ballots out to any sick cardinals and to bring them back.

The ballot paper is rectangular with the words *Eligo in Summum Pontificem* ("I elect as Supreme Pontiff") printed on the upper half, and on the bottom half room to write a name. Each cardinal will write, "as far as possible in handwriting that cannot be identified as his," the name of his candidate. The name must be legible in order to be counted properly. By tradition, a cardinal may not vote for himself. He will then fold the ballot twice.

2) **The scrutiny proper** phase is then carried out. In order of precedence, senior cardinal bishop first, down to the junior cardinal deacon, each elector holds his folded ballot for all to see and walks to the altar where the three scrutineers stand and upon which is a receptacle, usually a large golden chalice covered by a plate. At the altar, the cardinal elector recites aloud yet another oath: "I call as my witness Christ the Lord who will be my judge, that my vote is given to the one who before God I think should be elected." He places the ballot on the plate, which he tilts into the chalice. Then he bows to the altar and returns to his place among the other electors. If any of the cardinal electors are unable to walk to the altar, a scrutineer retrieves the ballot and drops it into the chalice.

If there are cardinal electors who are confined to their rooms and unable to appear in the Sistine Chapel, the *infirmarii* who have been selected for the task go to the ailing cardinals with a box (which has been examined by the scrutineers) and blank ballots on a tray. (The *infirmarii* may cast their own ballots immediately after the senior cardinal, so as not to prolong the already lengthy voting process.) Each sick elector writes his choice in secret, folds the ballot, and drops it into the box after taking the same oath as quoted above. If a cardinal is too sick to write, he may ask one of the *infirmarii* to write his vote on the ballot. The box is returned to the chapel where the scrutineers open it and count the number of ballots and drop them into the chalice on the altar.

After all the ballots have been deposited in the receptacle on the altar, one scrutineer shakes it to mix the ballots and another counts them out in full view of the cardinals to make certain the number corresponds to the number of electors. If there is any discrepancy, the ballots are burned and a second vote is taken immediately.

Assuming that the number is correct, the scrutineers take the ballots to a table where they sit and, one by one, open each ballot. The first scrutineer notes the name of the person on the ballot, passes it to the second, who does the same, then passes it to the third who reads the name aloud and writes it down on his own sheet. The third scrutineer puts a needle through each ballot (through the word *Eligo*) and places it on a thread, so that all ballots from this round of voting are preserved. After the names have been read aloud the ends of the thread are tied and the ballots placed in a receptacle on the table. All of this is done in full view and hearing of all the electors present in the Sistine Chapel.

3) **The post-scrutiny phase** involves counting the votes, checking the votes, and burning the ballots. The scrutineers add up all votes received by each individual, and if someone has received two thirds of the votes on that ballot, a canonical election has been accomplished; if, however, no one has obtained a two-thirds majority, the pope has not yet been elected. In either case, the revisers, the third group of election monitors chosen by lot, check the ballots and the notes made by the scrutineers to ensure the accuracy of the count. If all is well, the ballots are then burned by the scrutineers, with the help of the secretary of the conclave and the mas ters of ceremonies, "who in the meantime have been summoned by the junior cardinal deacon." If a second vote is to be taken immediately, the ballots from both votes will be burned together.

Pope John Paul II insists, in his constitution, "In order that secrecy may be better observed, I order each and every cardinal elector to hand over to the cardinal camerlengo or to one of the three cardinal assistants any notes which he may have in his possession concerning the results of each ballot. The notes are to be burnt together with the ballots." He further orders that at the end of the election the camerlengo prepare a document that contains the result of each balloting session to be given to the new pope, who will keep it in the archives, and which may be opened by no one except with his permission.

After the ballots have been counted and strung together, and the count verified and announced, the ballots are burned in a special stove just off the Sistine Chapel, which has been used for this purpose for more than a hundred years. The smoke from this ritual burning is released from a small chimney in sight of the crowds gathered in the piazza outside St. Peter's Basilica. When the vote has not produced a winner, it is burned with a chemical (in previous days, wet straw) that makes the smoke black; when a decision has been reached, the ballots are burned with a chemical (in previous days, dry straw) that makes the smoke white. The white smoke, *sfumata* in Italian, is the sign that observers look for, signaling that a pope has been elected.

So, the cardinals proceed in this way, two votes in the morning and two votes in the afternoon, until they reach a two-thirds total for one of the candidates. However—and the importance of this chance cannot be overemphasized—John Paul provides in paragraphs seventy-four and seventy-five a startling new rule. He allows that, if no one has been elected after three full days of balloting (i.e., seven ballots), the vote be suspended for a day of prayer and discussion; then after seven more ballots with no winner, there should be another pause for prayer and discussion; followed by another series of seven, then another series of seven. If, after all of these ballots an election still has not taken place, the camerlengo may call for a sense of the conclave "about the manner of proceeding." A majority of the cardinal electors may, at that point, decide to waive the two-thirds rule and accept a simple majority as the total needed for election. Alternatively, the majority may decide to keep only two names, the top two vote getters, under consideration (with the winner in that case also to be decided by a simple majority).

In the simplest terms: if, after twenty-eight ballots no one has achieved the two-thirds vote necessary for election, a majority of the cardinals may choose to go to a simple majority vote to elect the pope, or they may narrow the field to the two top candidates, with the same simple majority needed to win.

The possibility that a pope may be elected by anything less than a two-thirds majority vote changes the electoral dynamics in the most profound way since 1179, when the two-thirds requirement was first established! (See Appendix B.) This means that some group or voting bloc, if large enough, may hold out over several days until the conclave faces the option of going to a majority vote. Like the comfortable living quarters, the prospect of an election by a simple majority takes certain pressures off the cardinals that had been placed there originally to compel them to come to a wide consensus as quickly as humanly possible (under divine inspiration, of course).

"Matters to Be Observed or Avoided" in the Election Process

Harking back to historical precedent and experience, the election constitution of John Paul II declares that the commission of the crime of simony (he does not say by whom) is not reason to invalidate the election of the pope. This is a seemingly strange provision in a moral and spiritual document, but for practical reasons, the pope wishes not to impede his successor who could very well be unaware of such goings-on among his fellow electors. The crime (and sin) of simony itself is not pardoned in advance, however.

The cardinals are prohibited from making any plans or any deals or decisions regarding the election of the pope's successor. They are forbidden to enter into any kind of agreement or commitment regarding their vote, even under oath. They are exhorted to be guided by the Holy Spirit, and not by personal friendships or animosities in casting their votes in the election. As with the previous provision regarding simony, violation of these prohibitions can result in excommunication. But John Paul does not intend any of these restrictions to stop the "exchange of views concerning the election" that takes place during the *Sede Vacante*.

Section eighty forbids the exercise of the traditional right of exclusion by any civil power and threatens with excommunication any cardinal who may propose such a veto in the name of any outside interest. The pope goes on to state, "I intend this prohibition to include all possible forms of interference, opposition and suggestion whereby secular authorities of whatever order and degree, or any individual or group, might attempt to exercise influence on the election of the pope."

During the vacancy, and especially during the election itself, "the church is united in a very special way with her pastors and particularly with the cardinal electors" and must look to God, in prayer, for his grace to find the right man to serve as the Successor of Peter. John Paul invokes the union of Mary, the Mother of Jesus, with the "people of God" (a contemporary, post-Vatican II image of the church that means the church community):

> I therefore lay down that in all cities and other places, at least the more important ones, as soon as news is received of the vacancy of the Apostolic See and, in particular, of the death of the pope . . . humble and persevering prayers are to be offered to the Lord, that he may enlighten the electors and make them so like-minded in their task that a speedy, harmonious and fruitful election may take place. (*UDG*, introduction.)

He suggests, further, that the cardinals over the age of eighty, by virtue of their special position, lead the people in these prayers: "They will thereby participate in an effective and real way in the difficult task of providing a pastor for the universal church."

Finally, in this remarkable section of the apostolic constitution, the pontiff asks the one who is elected by his fellow cardinals not to refuse out of fear or uncertainty, promising that God will give him strength to carry out his responsibilities.

Acceptance and Proclamation of the New Pope

When the election has been successfully concluded, the dean of the college of cardinals, who is first in order (that is, a cardinal bishop) and seniority (that is, the bishop of Ostia, the senior suburbicarian see), approaches the man who has received the required majority. The constitution says he speaks "in the name of the whole college of electors" when he asks the consent of the one elected in the following words: "Do you accept your canonical election as Supreme Pontiff?" Traditionally, the pope-elect says, "*Accepto.*" (I accept.) At that moment, as long as he has been consecrated as a bishop, he becomes bishop of Rome, "true pope and head of the college of bishops. He thus acquires and can exercise full and supreme power over the universal church." If he has not received episcopal consecration, he will be so consecrated by the dean of the college of cardinals or, in descending order, the subdean or the senior cardinal bishop.

Immediately upon the acceptance, the cardinal dean asks, "By what name do you wish to be called?" The newly elected pontiff then responds with his choice of name: e.g., John, Paul, Pius, Gregory, or the like. The first pope to exercise the option of choosing a new name was Mercury, an elderly Roman presbyter, whose given name was that of a pagan god; he reigned as John II (533–535). The last pope to use his given name as his papal name was Marcellus II (1555), a zealous reformer who reigned for less than a month. Memorably, at the conclave of 1958, Angelo Roncalli gave a twenty-minute disquisition on his choice of "John," which shocked the cardinals who had anticipated that the seventy-seven-year-old would serve quietly for a few years.

For centuries it was the custom of the pope to remove his own cardinal's red zucchetto and put it on the head of the secretary of the conclave—which indicated he would later be elevated to the cardinalate. Most popes adhered to this custom, but when Leo XIII was elected in 1878, he absentmindedly forgot and put his red skullcap into his pocket. A few weeks later, he corrected his faux pas by making the forgotten secretary a cardinal.

The conclave ends immediately after the new pope accepts his election, "unless he should determine otherwise." John Paul II "determined otherwise," on October 16, 1978, when he asked the cardinals to stay together for another day of prayer and reflection before they dispersed to their homes around the world. Immediately after the new man agrees to his election, he may be approached by anyone who needs to discuss "matters of importance at the time." However, one can barely imagine an interruption of the new boss by an officious church bureaucrat at that sacred moment.

Oddly, as Leo XIII lay near death in 1903, the secretary of the conclave himself died. The college of cardinals had no right to appoint a new secretary (a papal prerogative), but they solved the problem by creating a new position, "pro-secretary," to which a brilliant young Spanish archbishop named Rafael Merry del Val was named. The newly elected Pius X did not forget to put his red zucchetto on the younger man's head, and shortly thereafter named Cardinal del Val to be his secretary of state and a future *papabile*.

The newly elected pontiff is whisked away into an adjoining sala, the so-called Room of Tears, to be temporarily vested with the appropriate robes, including the white silk simar (a special cassock) and skull cap and the red mozzetta (or shoulder cape), over which is placed an embroidered stole. Famously, there are three sizes of vestments prepared for this moment: John XXIII was too portly for any of them, so pins and tape were used liberally; for the diminutive Benedict XV, in 1914, there was none quite small enough.

The pope then returns to the Sistine Chapel, where he receives first the dean of the college of cardinals, then the camerlengo, then each of the cardinal electors one by one in order of precedence and seniority. The cardinals are expected to genuflect (for centuries they also kissed his shoe), then to embrace their new pontiff and to reverence his ring—the Ring of the Fisherman that he will wear on formal occasions (it's actually quite unwieldy) until his death.

It is usual practice for the newly elected pope to be presented to the people of Rome, and the world, and to offer his benediction upon them from the balcony of the Hall of the Benedictions, a huge, ornate Renaissance room on the upper level of St. Peter's Basilica. From that balcony the television cameras of the world's news agencies record the very first appearance of the new Holy Father, Supreme Pontiff, Pope, and Successor of St. Peter. This is one of the most dramatic moments of the entire election process, as the cardinal deacon recites the Latin formula, seeking the acclamation of the people. Those gathered in St. Peter's Square, and watching on television throughout the world, hang on the cardinal's every syllable:

Annuntio vobis gaudium magnum (I announce to you a great joy). *Habemus papam* (We have a pope)*! Eminentissimum ac Reverendissimum Dominum, Dominum* (His Most Eminent and Reverend Lord, Lord [here the baptismal or first name of the one elected]) . . . *Sanctae Romanae Ecclesiae Cardinalem* (Cardinal of the Holy Roman Church [here the surname]) . . . *qui sibi nomen imposuit* (who has chosen for himself the name of [here the new papal name]). . . .

In 1963, when the baptismal name "Giovanni Battista" was read, the people themselves filled in the last name, "Montini," because he was so familiar—and popular—a choice. However, after the second conclave of 1978, the name was unknown to the populace and sounded foreign; some thought he was an African: Karol Wojtyla. It was not until the new man appeared on the balcony that it began to dawn on the watchers that the cardinals had elected a Polish cardinal—for the first time ever!

If the cardinals have properly done their job, an awesome one at that, and followed the promptings of the Holy Spirit—keeping in mind the welfare of the Catholic Church and the world—then it is truly a joyful occasion when the new Roman pontiff is presented to bestow his apostolic blessing *Urbi et Orbi*, upon "the City and the World."

In a postscript to his election constitution, *Universi Dominici Gregis*, John Paul II lays down and prescribes that of these regulations and orders "no one shall presume to contest the present constitution and anything contained herein for any reason whatever. The constitution is to be completely observed by all, notwithstanding any disposition to the contrary, even if worthy of special mention. It is to be full and integrally implemented and is to serve as a guide for all to whom it refers." He further abrogates any and all previous constitutions pertaining to the election of the pope.

PART III

—•—

Challenges Awaiting
the Next Pope

—•—

◆ The Church Enters Its Third Millennium

◆ Crisis in the American Church

◆ The Question of Collegiality

◆ Gender, Globalization, and Ecumenism

◆ Who Will It Be?

Challenges Awaiting
the Next Pope

The Church Enters Its Third Millennium

The history of the Catholic Church is marked by theological, political, artistic, intellectual, and social achievements, as well as by holiness, folly, charity, and sin. In its divine institution, the church proclaims that it is guided and protected by the Holy Spirit. Other Christian communions look upon the Catholic Church with a peculiar admixture of skepticism, loathing, and longing. The non-Christian world, too, finds the Roman Catholic phenomenon problematic in many ways, both religiously and culturally. After two thousand years, there is a lot of "baggage" to be toted around by such an immense institution.

The current difficult issues that confront the church in the United States and, indeed, around the world, have been smoldering below the surface (occasionally flaring into the open) for decades, and in some cases, for centuries. In a sense, the scope and gravity of any of the Catholic Church's problems must be laid against its long history to gauge its importance and life span. Furthermore, many of the contemporary issues that face the current pope and the next pope are not new—but merely new manifestations of the same or similar problems that have arisen throughout history. The important question for the vast population of the faithful must be: will any of the current difficulties be cause for the church to rupture, or to sustain a wound from which it may not fully recover?

It is possible that these long-festering problems may prove so deeply damaging that the church is forever diminished—or split again by protest or schism. The great schism between the Orthodox east and the Catholic west that occurred with mutual excommunications in 1054 was only the final, visible split after many smaller but severe confrontations. (Paul VI and the ecumenical patriarch, Athenagoras I, lifted those mutual condemnations on December 7, 1965.) The so-called Great Western Schism—when the church had three popes simultaneously—lasted "only" forty years (from 1378 to 1417), and was considered an internal wound caused by stubborn and erratic behavior on the part of popes and cardinals. That schism was mended by a general council and by strong personalities committed to preventing a recurrence of such nonsense. However, it is the Protestant Reformation which resonates most strongly in today's difficulties, and which is the better, more apt example of what the church may face if internal reform and renewal are not undertaken by the bishops and the next pope.

The unrest that is abroad in the American Catholic Church is based not on doctrinal disagreements but on issues of church governance and accountability. Mixed in with the outrage among large segments of the laity at the child sexual abuse scandals is the long-running dissatisfaction among a strong minority about a variety of issues that are familiar to anyone who has observed the church since the 1960s: contraception, abortion, clerical celibacy, women priests, social justice, and the critique of the church's relationship to capitalism. This litany of protest and disagreement has waxed and waned for decades, and now the voices of protest have gained new vigor along with a new issue, a new scandal on which to focus. It is interesting—and somewhat ironic—that the Holy Father and the American bishops have often been more outspokenly "liberal" in promoting disarmament, civil justice, and redistribution of wealth; yet at the same time they have been very "conservative" (doctrinally orthodox) in hewing to the established teachings on reproductive issues, priestly celibacy, and the impermissibility of women priests. Add a dose of scandal, lay outrage at the way many bishops have handled (i.e., *mis*handled) the problem of priest-abusers and their victims, and bake it all in a pie of missed opportunities and a public-relations hash, and you have a recipe for continued anger and unrest in the American church.

High-level mea culpas, committee reports, lay commissions, and remedial actions aside, the secular media and some lay Catholic protest groups are now seeking episcopal resignations—and will not be satisfied with less than wholesale changes in the U.S. bishops' conference structure. Cardinal Bernard Law of Boston resigned in December 2002, capping the most explosive and visible series of abuse cases and allegations of diocesan cover-up. The documentation unearthed by legal actions and dogged press reporting became too overwhelming to defend or even to bear for the most powerful Catholic churchman in America. Now, some informed observers predict a domino effect of forced resignations of bishops—but, remember, any resignation must be accepted by the Holy See, the pope himself, in order to be valid.

In 2002, five U.S. bishops resigned in cases tied to the current scandals, and there are more on the horizon, despite Vatican efforts to staunch the hemorrhaging. Short of wholesale resignations, there have been further calls for administrative transparency and financial accountability on the parish and diocesan level. In the case of Boston, the threat of bankruptcy due to the volume of pending civil law suits created even more urgency around the tenuous status of the archbishop. Other dioceses (and some individual parishes) face similar financial straits; some disaffected Catholics have withheld contributions for fear that their monies will be used to settle complaints of abuse and cover-up by victims and families. It may take a substantial period of time to correct this volatile financial mess, and the Vatican will probably never approve a diocese filing for bankruptcy.

All of this will fall directly into the lap of the new pope and his curia. John Paul II has been as engaged as he can be, but his age and ill health have hampered his ability to respond with decisiveness. We cannot know, until the next election, what another pope may say or do to manage the growing crisis in the United States and around the world. But it will be a burning issue on his agenda.

He may face the possibility of a schism or new reformation movement that will be immensely difficult to manage. It will take some time for him to confront this unrest, but he will not have very much time: events have spiraled nearly out of control for him and for the bishops. The fact that these issues are now more acute in the United States than in the rest of the Catholic world complicates his task because of the relative importance of the American church in the overall scheme of things. If the new pope is more pastoral and less political in character (a tough, and admittedly somewhat artificial distinction), he will address the particular crisis in the U.S. church and the related issues in local churches across the globe with some focus and alacrity. Like an American president or any new parish priest, he will probably enjoy a brief (very brief) honeymoon period in which he can gain his bearings and grasp the helm of the huge vessel under his command.

Meanwhile, some among the clergy and the hierarchy—less so among the laity—continue to bitterly criticize the media, especially television networks and major-city newspapers (e.g., *The Boston Globe* and *The New York Times*) for fanning the flames of anti-Catholicism. Unlike with the scandals and schisms of the past, today's constant media frenzy—and instant availability of information through electronic communication—has brought the crisis to the center of the international stage. (Though the Protestant Reformation of the sixteenth century was fueled and supported by the newly invented printing press.) Protest groups such as Voice of the Faithful communicate with members largely, if not exclusively, online in instant response to new revelations and the actions of the bishops' conference.

Looking ahead to the other problems and opportunities for the church in the new millennium, the growth in the Catholic Church is happening in poorer countries in the southern hemisphere of the planet; whereas, in more affluent societies in the northern hemisphere, the church is well along into an age of decline. Yet in any given local church—on the level of diocese or parish—in the United States, there is ever a core of faithful adherents who attend daily mass and fervently love the Holy Father. And equally inevitable is the group or individual who freely criticizes the same pope, bishop, or pastor—perhaps with both love and exasperation. For this person, either the church is not what it once was or is not what it must be in the contemporary world.

The watershed event that defines and shapes both the anger and the constructive response to such a crisis is the Second Vatican Council. To this day, many American Catholics grumble about the loss of the Latin mass and other liturgical changes that they experience (or perceive) in daily or weekly mass. This conservative dissatisfaction has been somewhat muted by the recent scandals. Both conservatives and progressives are calling for changes in church governance.

It has ever been this way. The church has always had its critics (think of the bloody riots in second- and third-century Rome during papal elections) and always held many of those critics within its breast (the first antipope, Hippolytus, is a saint). Looking only at the history of the popes and the papal elections, which itself is just one course of the greater banquet, one can find every grotesque failing as well as every glorious aspiration known to humanity.

What are we to make of such a huge panorama of problems and potentialities? How are we to expect a group of one hundred men, most of them elderly celibates, to grapple with the realities faced by the "people of God"—a vast, diverse population united by a faith in Jesus Christ and the successors of his apostles, longing for salvation and comfort in this world and the next? Will the cardinals' choice of the next Supreme Pontiff have the spiritual significance sought by a billion souls in virtually every corner of the earth?

The sacred college of cardinals, a collection of elders, advisers, and servants, was designed to be charged with just this sort of sacred responsibility. Are they up to the task? Certainly most of them have the tools—education, faith, intellectual skills, prayer, spiritual and practical experience in the world—to construct and maintain the edifice of the church of Christ. As a group, the cardinals of the Holy Roman Church are quite formidable. Yet can they rise above their human limitations to seek the truth that lies beyond the grasp of most of us, that is: what does God will for his people in this age of omnipresent dangers and anxieties?

Again, I pose the question: Has it ever been different? I think not. Think back to the earliest days of the church in Rome, when Peter and Paul were hauled from the bosom of their fellow Christians to prison and martyrdom. What were the survivors to do? Not only did they stay alive, but they also kept the flame of the true faith burning and passed it on to the next generation of believers. Persecution became a way of life for hundreds of years, with occasional respites followed by ever more virulent recurrences. Then there were heresies, teachings that diverged from the jealously guarded apostolic traditions; at times more Christians were "heretics" than "Catholics," including emperors and bishops. Violence often greeted the election or prospect of election of a new pope, and sometimes the "winner" did not survive. In the case of John VIII, in 882, he was eliminated by his one-time supporters; he had apparently outlived his usefulness. Reformers dotted the landscape.

Take the case of Gregory VII, whose famous *Dictatus Papae* (1075) codified the privileges and prerogatives of the pope, including that his feet must be kissed by emperors and kings, but who fled Rome and died in exile in Salerno. Pius IX became a "prisoner" within the Vatican when he lost the papal states to Italy in 1870, yet the First Vatican Council had, only days before, confirmed the definition of papal infallibility. The specters of modernism and world war loomed over several pontificates in the nineteenth and twentieth centuries, yet two of the very greatest of all the popes, John XXIII and John Paul II, emerged from the ashes of the battlefield and the evils of totalitarianism. Is ours such a unique age, then, on the cusp of the third millennium of Christianity? Are we any nearer the "end times" than was St. Peter himself?

The issues that the cardinals must grapple with in the coming conclave are many, but may be summarized as follows: 1) the scandal of the priests who have sexually abused minors and the bishops who have mishandled the scandal; 2) collegiality, as defined and urged by the Second Vatican Council, among pope, bishops, priests, and laity—but especially in the relationship between the pope and the bishops of the world; 3) sexuality and gender, including homosexuality, contraception, abortion, the role of women, the call for the ordination of women as priests (a complicated, contradictory, and controversial area that most cardinals probably do not want even to talk about, publicly or privately); 4) globalization, which is another broad category that covers the concerns of the local churches and their members around the world, including poverty, political oppression, and pluralism or diversity within the governance of the local churches; 5) ecumenism among non-Catholic Christian communities and relationships with non-Christian faiths, especially Judaism and Islam; and 6) the pastoral profile (orthodoxy, personality, communication, and administrative skills) of the new pope.

The cardinal electors at the next conclave will, to a greater or lesser degree, weigh the metaphysical and "metahistorical" questions and balance them with these immediate, practical considerations. They will seek a shepherd, a pastor to guide the far-flung flock of Christ through the uncertainties of the time with a firm hand, guided by the ancient certainties expressed in scripture and the apostolic tradition—one who is able to proclaim (like the stuttering prophet and patriarch Moses) the truth to a polarized, terrorized, secularized world. The cardinals will seek a mediagenic figure like Popes John Paul I and John Paul II—avoiding an overly harsh, ascetic, or intellectual "look." The church requires, in our time, not so much a pontiff (the papal crown having been eschewed following Paul VI) as a prophet (think of John Paul II's denunciations of the "culture of death" and the historical excesses of capitalism) and a martyr, in its original meaning of "witness to the faith."

The church awaits the next phase of its life with some misgivings, tempered by an abiding faith in the trinitarian God of its creed: "We believe in one God, the Father, the Almighty . . . we believe in one Lord, Jesus Christ, the only son of God . . . we believe in the Holy Spirit, the Lord, the giver of life. . . . " The new covenant, Catholics believe, is real—for everyone who professes this faith. Where, then, will God lead his covenant people?

Crisis in the American Church

For American Catholics, some of whom feel burned by the Vatican, this coming papal election will be a signal of the future direction their church will take regarding the recent crisis of sexual abuse of minors by priests and the mistakes and poor judgments of their hierarchical superiors. This is the thorn in the side of the faithful in the United States, and the primary reason for many who have questioned their faith to stay away from church or to withhold financial contributions to an institution they now simply cannot abide. Even among the most orthodox believers, the bishops as a whole have lost some measure of the credibility that was once assumed along with the miter and crozier.

Throughout its history, the clergy and the people of the American church have struggled to find the correct balance between their subordination in matters of faith to the pope and the spirit of liberty and democracy with which they forever threw off the shackles of the European powers. Catholics in this country were once a persecuted or ignored minority—tiny in number, but feared, despised, and excluded by legal and social sanctions for more than a century of national life. In New Jersey, for example, Catholics could not vote until the mid-nineteenth century—and after that, they became a power not to be ignored!

American Catholics can point to parallels between their experiences and those of Jews and African-Americans, for they were shunned, indentured, and legislated against, their houses of worship burned, their culture demeaned in popular media for many decades. But the first few generations rose rather swiftly above the prejudices and legal restrictions, primarily through a system of education that paralleled public schools and universities. Then many American Catholics of various ethnic backgrounds (such as Irish, Italian, and Polish) intermarried and became suburbanized and decentralized, diffused in the more general culture. Now the growth in the American church is to be found among immigrant groups of Asian, African, and Latin American origin.

So, Catholic identity in the United States has, in recent decades, evolved in directions unforeseen by the traditional parish priest or the rosary lady in the pew every day of the week. In sheer numbers (U.S. Catholics today number about seven million) the Catholic Church is the largest single denomination in North America, and therefore any issues it faces—such as the current sexual-abuse scandal—will reverberate through all of society and in all news media, reaching the kitchen tables of Catholics and non-Catholics alike.

When the American Catholic Church is rocked to its foundation by an earthquake-like scandal, the resulting crisis spills out into the world at large. This is a vast departure from the once-prevalent practice of washing one's dirty laundry out of public view. Lay organizations such as Voice of the Faithful have sprung up or been reactivated by a minority of Catholics who seek a role in reform; needless to say, the response from the American hierarchy has been mixed. One recent online press release illustrates the conundrum:

In January [2002], Voice of the Faithful was no more than a few devoted Catholics meeting in the basement of a church in Wellesley, Massachusetts. Today we are a growing, vibrant organization of 25,000 members, with over 100 affiliates worldwide. In less than a year, we have become a recognized leader in the future of lay involvement in the Catholic Church. In the past week alone, VOTF was featured in three articles on the front page of *The New York Times*.

But this effort is not a sprint—it is a marathon. We need to be a reminder to our bishops and to the world that the whole Church must be accountable and collaborative—today and tomorrow. This means that we need a sufficient and sustained level of resources to do the Spirit-driven work we are called to do.[1]

What was not said in the release was that some bishops have prohibited the group from meeting on church-owned properties (the proverbial church basement) because it is felt that the group has a much deeper, semi-hidden agenda to push unacceptable reforms such as the ordination of women as priests; some bishops feel that this lay group is, in fact, anti-Catholic.

"Good Catholics," the ones who attend church regularly and support their parishes and dioceses with prayer, volunteer time, and financial contributions, have been burned badly and are still recovering from the hurt. They want to follow their bishops in good conscience, but they will not abrogate their spiritual faculties and free will. They believe deeply what their church teaches, they participate fully in the sacramental life of their church, and they yearn for clear, authoritative leadership among the clergy and hierarchy. They have winced as the scandal has become a cultural phenomenon that has mushroomed far beyond the Catholic coffee klatch or meeting of the Rosary Society. At the same time, many of these "good Catholics" have reached out to their priests, sought the company and the friendship of embattled local clergy who are not in any way involved in the criminal misbehavior of the few (in both number and percentage) serial abusers and those who covered their tracks.

Forgotten or largely marginalized in the scandal and subsequent measures taken to contain the scandal (as well as in the press reports), are the victims of sexual abuse and their families. It will be incumbent upon the new pope to remember and to consider these, the "least," the "children" (now adults, most of them), the "lambs" who suffered lifelong damage to their persons and to their faith. It is also important for the lay and clerical activists who have been politicized by the crisis to remember and to comfort the victims.

From whatever source it will come, now is the time for reform and renewal in the church. The scandals have raised issues long dormant within the American church. Many have known for decades that pedophiles and child abusers have been allowed to remain in holy orders and have been shuffled from parish to parish as a matter of course; treatment has been sought for some of these criminal abusers, but legal action has been avoided—in order to avoid just the sort of ugly scandal that erupted across the country in 2002. Even though strict guidelines for dealing with abusers—legally and canonically—were adopted by the national conference of bishops in 1993 (providing for victim protection, proper reporting to local law enforcement, and removal of abusers) the rules were not enforceable by any one authority (such as the conference itself or the Vatican) because they were voluntary. In the United States each diocese is independently incorporated and run according to the laws of the particular state. The bishop is either the president of a myriad of parish and institutional corporations or the "corporation sole," a one-man owner with executive power. Thus empowered, these autonomous entities could, and did, act in any way they chose. Too many seemingly discarded the conference guidelines.

But after the revelations of early 2002, the bishops felt the pressure from the Catholic population and the public at large to do something—and I believe they were sincerely moved by the plight of victims and victims' families and their own consciences to act. The extraordinary meeting between John Paul II and the American cardinals during the spring of 2002 was followed by a close monitoring by the Vatican of how the U.S. bishops dealt with the moral and legal issues surrounding sex-abuse cases, past and future. The Vatican (that is, the Roman Curia with the approval of the pope) required the bishops to revise their guidelines, passed in June 2002, to conform to canon law and to protect the rights of accused priests. The American bishops have had to respond to outrage among Catholic laity, intense press scrutiny, and tough supervision from Rome. Also, some states, such as California, have kept the legal pressure on local dioceses with loosened statutes of limitation and renewed prosecutorial investigations.

The cardinals entering the conclave will be acutely aware of these issues as they affect the American church, and how the crisis has mushroomed over the past two years in other countries. They can neither afford to ignore this problem, nor to choose a pope who will turn away from it or delegate it—the new man must be able to confront this pastoral crisis directly, in word and deed. He may, as John Paul II has done, attempt to tighten priestly discipline and reaffirm the age-old norms of celibacy and episcopal authority. The cardinals—and the church as a whole—would be better served by a pontiff who is willing to demand internal and external justice for victims and appropriately strict punishment for serial abusers. Clergy and laity alike want clear, fair, firm, just remedies—all of which must flow to and from the top man.

The Second Vatican Council, which has set the course of ecclesiastical life for this and future generations, is very clear in its acknowledgment of sin and error within the church and its mandate to reform and renew through the healing power of Jesus. The electors in the next conclave will be men who were not old enough or of high enough rank to have attended the Second Vatican Council, yet they are products of the council in many ways, not the least of which is how and when they received their seminary training and were formed in their early years as priests. All Catholics believe that the light of Christ (the "light of all nations") shines upon the church, even in its sinfulness. It offers that honest self-appraisal to the rest of the world in the decrees of the Second Vatican Council, calling on other Christian communions and non-Christians to open their hearts to the truth of revelation. Therefore, internal reform will loom as a spiritual, as well as a practical, juridical issue in the minds of the men who will elect the pope. These considerations lie beyond any scandal (which, from the Greek, means "stumbling block"), which is only the symptom of underlying problems. Ultimately, the cardinals will seek a candidate who can incorporate a sense of history and a vision of the future that does not deny the gifts of the Spirit and the human gaffes of the past; a pastor and a historian, if you will—a huge order!

Finally, financial accountability has ever been a sore point in the government of the universal church as well as within the American church. It may be a vain hope that the next pope will require more transparency in the church's financial position. But in the United States, there will be increased demands for credible, complete reporting by dioceses for current and past expenditures that are related to settlements of sex-abuse claims. The American cardinals in the conclave will bring with them this burden of financial and moral accountability that has not yet been resolved in the United States. But it will not go away until further, deeper changes are implemented on the diocesan level.

It is possible to view the situation of the American church as a test case for the rest of the world. The cardinal-electors cannot avoid American concerns (and potential reforms) in the wake of recent revelations. The same concerns will inevitably occupy the attention of the new pope. Who would have imagined, even a year before it happened, that Pope John Paul II would accept the resignation of the most prominent churchman in the United States? The American bishops, the cardinals, and the papacy itself have assumed a defensive position vis-à-vis the American Catholic Church and are likely to remain in that position for at least another decade. They are concerned that the door has now been opened too widely for well-educated laity to walk into the corridors of ecclesiastical power. As for the laity, Catholics in this country have always incorporated uniquely American attitudes toward liberty—religious and social—in the practice of their faith. Unlike other parts of the world, we have never had a centuries-long tradition of monarchy or feudalism or the divine rights of rulers to contend with. Therefore the disconnect of American Catholicism with the Vatican sometimes seems extreme. The current crisis has only deepened and exposed this gap and caused the hierarchy and laity to become more skeptical of each other.

The Question of Collegiality

What is meant by collegiality among the bishops of the church, and how will it affect the next papal election? In *Conclave*, John L. Allen, Jr., of *The National Catholic Reporter*, states succinctly: "Collegiality is perhaps *the* leading issue heading into the next conclave."[2] Francis Burkle-Young provides a historical context:

> The huge centralization of authority achieved in Paul VI's revolution was not intended, most cardinals believe, to be turned into an autocratic establishment for the imposition of papal will, without consultation—but this is precisely what John Paul II has done with his inheritance of power by acquiescing to or encouraging the continued expansion of authority within the Roman Curia. The new pope must decide how much of the episcopal power that was reaffirmed by the Second Vatican Council will be returned to local ordinaries [i.e., bishops].[3]

There is a lot of theological meat and practical, political conflict involved in this issue. But there is no doubt that the cardinals are acutely aware of—some of them made acutely uncomfortable by—the lack of true collegiality in the day-to-day execution of the office of the papacy and Roman Curia.

Collegiality then becomes a term loaded with meaning, and as it shakes out in the pre-conclave discussions and in the minds of the cardinals, it will translate as reform of the papacy and, more specifically, reform of the curia. Collegiality also speaks to the core of the role of an individual bishop and the relationships among bishops throughout the world, within their own national or regional conferences, and with the pope.

At the Sunday celebration of mass, Catholics profess to believe in "one holy catholic and apostolic church." Each of those four marks or essential characteristics of the church—one, holy, catholic, and apostolic—says much about the institution, as it does about the believers. Is the church one—that is, unified? The

Roman Catholic Church claims preeminent but not exclusive title to the "true church" or "church of Christ," and acknowledges that other churches and Christian communities participate in that unity to a greater or lesser degree. Is the church truly holy? Well, yes, in its participation in the life of God through the sharing of his grace in its sacramental and liturgical life. The church embraces sinners among its members but remains holy in its divine institution.* And catholic? This has a range of meanings, the most familiar of which is "universal"—that is, the church is one and the same everywhere on earth; each local church, as it adheres to doctrine and discipline, is a part of the greater whole. Finally, what is the meaning of apostolic, and how can the church claim to be related to and derived from the apostles? In addition to maintaining the purity and completeness of the apostolic preaching from the earliest days of Christianity, the church claims that its bishops are direct successors of the apostles. We have seen that the pope has the title Successor of St. Peter, and each of the four thousand bishops around the world may trace his office back through time to the very beginning. A bishop is consecrated by other bishops who have themselves been canonically consecrated. (Some of the earliest controversies and schisms within the church can be traced to this idea of legitimate apostolic succession.)

As we have seen, the Holy Father presides over the college of bishops as the first among equals, in his role as Supreme Pontiff and bishop of Rome. But if all bishops are "apostles," and all derive their authority from the apostles (as commissioned by Jesus Christ himself), then ought they not consult with and guide each other in the same way as the earliest apostles did?

Most Catholics these days look to the Holy Father for spiritual and moral leadership, perhaps somewhat less so for pure governance in the secular sense, though that power has devolved to the pope over the course of many centuries. The see of Rome, from the time of Clement I (c. 90–100) down to our own day, has

---

*See the writings of St. Augustine for the development of this theological concept.

achieved and vigorously maintained its position of preeminence in Christianity. A complex machinery of government, both church and temporal, has grown up about the pope, and the number and importance of the cardinals has increased as well, over time. Today, from the tiny city-state known as the Vatican, the Holy See exercises a far-flung influence on the lives of a billion people throughout the world. That power of leadership and example is vigorously exercised by the current pope. How will it be with the next pope? What role will the cardinals and bishops seek in relation to the pontiff? Will they seek a revival of national and regional conferences and synods?

If the pope is the Successor of St. Peter, as the church proclaims him to be, it means many things besides simply the exercise of apostolic authority. Peter himself was a strong and faithful follower of Jesus, yet he was also prone to speak without thinking, to go his own way, and even to deny his Lord in the darkest crisis of his life and the life of the nascent church. Yet he emerged from that sin and disgrace to assume a position of leadership among the apostles, which is evidenced by the scriptural sources, especially the Acts of the Apostles. Even the chief of the apostles was a human being, flawed and fallible, yet respected and (arguably) obeyed by his peers in the early church.

The Catholic Church ties the Petrine ministry (as discussed in part I) directly to Christ, in a very direct and immediate way. For example, in the Decree on Ecumenism of Vatican II, *Unitatis Redintegratio*, (Restoration of Unity) the council fathers stated:

> It is through the faithful preaching of the gospel by the apostles and their successors—the bishops with Peter's successor at their head—through their administration of the sacraments, and through their loving exercise of authority, that Jesus Christ wishes his people to increase under the influence of the Holy Spirit. Thereby too, he perfects his people's fellowship in unity: in the confession of one faith, in the common celebration of divine worship, and in the fraternal harmony of the family of God.[4]

Further, trying to balance the good and true qualities of the other Christian churches, where the "separated brethren" worship, with the belief that the Catholic Church holds the fullness of truth and grace, the Vatican Council emphasized the apostolic succession:

> For it is through Christ's Catholic church alone, which is the all-embracing means of salvation, that the fullness of the means of salvation can be obtained. It was to the apostolic college alone, of which Peter is the head, that we believe our Lord entrusted all the blessings of the new covenant, in order to establish on earth the one Body of Christ into which all those should be fully incorporated who already belong in any way to God's people. During its pilgrimage on earth, this people, though still in its members liable to sin, is growing in Christ and is being gently guided by God, according to his hidden designs, until it happily arrives at the fullness of eternal glory in the heavenly Jerusalem.[5]

This conciliar document and others, taken with the accumulated two millennia of tradition, doctrine, and practice of the church, emphasize the pope's unique position within the church and among all Christians. Not all Christians accept this teaching and its implications, of course, but all faithful Catholics do. And Catholics, if they care to seek a full understanding of the implications of this doctrine, will key in on the meaning of collegiality, which is often emphasized by critics of the monarchical or super-centralized papacy.

So, collegiality, the proper balance of authority and responsibility between popes and bishops, will inform the votes in the next conclave. Each cardinal will weigh the theology and the reality of the past with the need—among the multi-various members and constituencies of the church—for leadership that is open, at the very least, to true fraternal cooperation among all the bishops of the world, including the pope. It may be that they want a pope who will revive the spirit of national and regional conferences of bishops. They will be aware of historical examples in the Middle Ages of popes who were elected with promises to consult with or even be answerable to the college of cardinals, only to default to imperial papal prerogatives. The issue of collegiality will be played out in subtle ways over the next few decades, but the coming conclave will point out the direction—progressive or conservative—that the new generation of church leadership will take.

Gender, Globalization, and Ecumenism

Each of the issues of gender, globalization, and ecumenism has an element of controversy in the political and theological realms; each is a bundle of thorns to be presented to the next Holy Father upon his installation as pope. The question remainins whether one or more will become a crown of thorns that will inflict pain on the man and his church.

Will women be ordained as priests in the Catholic Church under the next pope? No. Should women be ordained as priests in the Catholic Church? That question has been disallowed in any official forum, though theologians and lay people (especially in the United States) always seem to be raising the issue; it is a hot button topic in virtually every discussion I have had with non-Catholics over the past several years. On May 22, 1994, in his encyclical letter *Ordinatio Sacerdotalis* (On the Reserving of Priestly Ordination to Men Alone), Pope John Paul II declared the issue closed, stating that there is no scriptural or traditional basis for even talking about the prospect of women priests. Given that the Catholic Church operates in a hierarchical organizational structure and seeks to make such changes, if at all, in a consensus mode among the church fathers rather than a majority vote of the church membership, it simply is not going to happen. In fact, even if it were put to a vote or a poll were to be taken, it is unlikely that there would be a majority of worldwide Catholics who would favor women as priests.

However, feminist theologians and church historians, especially in the United States, are determined to keep the notion of women's ordination as priests in the forefront of discussion, despite the displeasure of the hierarchy. In *Papal Sin* (2000), author Gary Wills devotes an entire chapter to the topic, pointing to the exclusion of women in ordained ministries as counter to scriptural and early traditional roles of women. And while organized groups in the United States, such as the Leadership Conference of Women Religious, have been much quieted by John Paul's declaration, they continue to push for reform, especially in light of the current scandals in the American church. In a recent press release concerning sexual abuse, the LCWR called for increased inclusion of women and laity:

> We are convinced that the current crisis calls for systemic change, particularly in the exercise of ecclesial power. We call for the inclusion of laity, Catholic clergy, brothers and sisters in the formation of policies and in decision-making which will allow for collaborative renewal of our church.[6]

While the coming conclave will probably not deal directly with the issue of the ordination of women, the new pontiff will be called upon to give some response to such concerns about the role of women in the church.

Further, will married men be ordained as priests in the Catholic Church under the next pope? Maybe. In fact, there are married priests in the Roman Catholic communion today; some priests of the Eastern rite churches (a liberal branch of the Ukrainian Catholic Church, for example) and the Anglican communion have converted to Catholicism and been re-ordained as Catholic priests.

Celibacy for priests, i.e., the unmarried state, has been the rule of the church in the West for more than a thousand years, and a controversial rule during most of that time. There are sound spiritual and theological reasons to encourage priestly celibacy, and many priests say that this state is a grace or a gift from God to them, which allows them to be better, holier, more focused servants. In the 1960s and '70s, priests left holy orders in droves to marry, creating—along with fewer vocations—a crisis of numbers in the once-teeming profession. A. W. Sipe, in his groundbreaking work, *Sex, Priests, and Power: Anatomy of a Crisis* reveals some shocking statistics regarding the state of celibacy in the priesthood:

> At any one time, 20% of priests in good standing are involved in sexual relationships with women; 8% are experimenting sexually, approximately evenly divided between heterosexual and homosexual activity. . . . About 50% of both homosexual and heterosexual priests practice celibacy.[7]

In response to this deviation from the church's strong stance on priestly celibacy, Catholic seminaries are teaching courses in sensitivity and sexual awareness, and men are screened psychologically with more intensity than in previous generations. Enrollments in some seminaries have begun to climb, and in some dioceses more men are being ordained annually than the average of a decade ago. Yet this issue continues to be one of intense debate, especially given the current sexual abuse controversy. Some who believe the church should allow clergy to marry argue that marriage will mature priests sexually, thereby reducing the amount of child molestation that has recently been brought into the open. Yet those who oppose this point of view counter that pedophilia stems from graver psychological and moral causes—though the secrecy that cloaks the celibate life can cover criminals, and has.

After Vatican II, more married men were invited to serve as ordained deacons of the church, an office that had fallen into desuetude for centuries. The order of the diaconate has come alive again, and in many parishes the deacon plays an important role supporting the overextended pastor. However, whether married men will be able to serve as ordained priests remains an issue to be addressed by future pontiffs. Perhaps it will be an issue that a church council will one day decide.

Should homosexual men be ordained as priests in the Catholic Church under the next pope? Here is a potentially explosive subject that is often raised by very conservative Catholics who seek to purify the priesthood, to address the sex-abuse scandal, and to reaffirm the moral authority of the church, as they deem most appropriate. There is a reform impulse among the deeply orthodox and politically conservative to purge the priesthood and especially the seminaries of gay men. However, it is also a fact—confirmed by independent studies in recent decades—that there are many homosexual men currently serving in the priesthood. According to Sipe, about thirty percent of priests have a homosexual orientation, half of whom are celibate and half non-celibate.[8] This reality is confirmed in other studies, such as *Gay Priests*, edited by James G. Wolf (1989). It is likely that some of the bishops and cardinals, who set the policies of the church in local dioceses and on a universal level, are celibate homosexuals. Some have been exposed, in the recent past, as sexually active.

Many Catholics, and many among the public at large, equate homosexuals with pedophiles, but I believe it is vitally important to separate the two categories if there is to be a just solution to this horrendous problem of abuse of minors. The aforementioned studies delineate between gay priests and pedophiles—criminal predators who abuse children of both sexes. Sipe writes, "Pedophilia can be either homosexual or heterosexual, but apparently in the general population, attraction to girls is twice as common as attraction to boys; many pedophiles are sexually aroused by both young boys and girls."[9] This not a point I wish to belabor here, merely to point to the distinction between sexuality and sexual disorder that often becomes confused in the debate.

As priests themselves, the cardinal-electors in the conclave will want to know how each candidate feels about this issue: whether he is progressive, open to change, or more orthodox and traditionally biblical in his theological stance. It is likely that he will be the latter, though popes have been known to change their minds—to develop, if you will, once they are in office. Here is where the cardinals may be open to surprise. (One wonders how many of the cardinal-electors may be homosexuals themselves and whether or not this might influence their votes, consciously or subconsciously.) But there is no question that all of these matters of gender and sexuality among the Catholic clergy will not go away—for the priests, the bishops, the cardinals in conclave, or the next pontiff.

Globalization, as I have stated before, is a catchword or codeword for the notion of building and sustaining the church *universal*, especially when the greatest growth in baptisms and priestly vocations currently come from the once-called third world. The Catholic Church is rapidly changing color, becoming culturally much more diverse and much less European, shifting its geographical loci, thereby subtly shifting its theological tone. Many of these changes will play out over the next few generations, but the outline of the shifts is becoming clearer with each passing day.

John Paul II has raised the stakes in this area by becoming *sui generis*, the Supreme Pastor that others have only written about. He helped to end the Cold War, survived an assassination attempt, traveled to more countries and canonized more saints than any other pope in history, and was seen by more people than any human being in history. And, as of April 17, 2003, he will have served in the office longer than any but two others in the two thousand-year span that extends back to Peter the apostle. Through him, one person, the church extends its reach into the farthest corners of the world, to places where there are no priests or religious missionaries. It is unlikely that the next pontiff can measure up to such a high standard, but the cardinals will seek someone who is attractive in appearance and personality, who can hold his corner of the world stage with confidence, if not with the total mastery of his predecessor.

With more than fifty percent of the cardinals now coming from outside of Europe, and more than forty percent from the once-designated third world (specific breakdowns are provided later in this chapter), the euphemism of globalization will translate into something more immediate than a philosophical or theological concept for many of the electors. Globalization, for them, goes beyond a flirtation in the 1970s and '80s with liberation theology, which blended Marxist philosophy with liberal Christian theology and Scripture interpretation. It is the reality of the contemporary Roman Catholic Church—less Rome-centered, more local and culturally diverse, with new languages (perhaps strange to longtime veterans within the curia) and new ethical and moral questions about war and peace, human reproduction and cloning, science and reason to be asked and answered than ever before.

The electors will weigh the value of new cultural traditions vs. Euro-centric concerns to the future of Catholicism. They will want a pope who understands, as did John Paul II and Paul VI, in particular, the incredible reach that mass media has brought to the papacy and its potential impact on lives tens of thousands of miles from Rome. The imperial style of Roman administration will be put to the test. Because of the papacy's vast reach and experience, it could be a huge benefit for believers to have a centralized religious authority for evangelization, but the riskier, darker side of the equation brings control issues to the fore—a replay of history that reaches back to the earliest days of Christianity when the "churches" of the Mediterranean basin did not always fall in line behind the church of Rome.

A related issue, ecumenism, i.e., the relationship between the Catholic Church and other Christian churches—as well as the related issue of interreligious dialogue between Catholics and non-Christian faiths—looms as more important than ever in this new millennium. In the wake of the global threat of religious-based movements of terror and repression, Vatican expert John L. Allen has called the church "schizophrenic" on these issues, citing some of the most baffling—to outsiders—actions and developments within the Holy See since the 1990s.[10] It is true that Pope John Paul II has done more than any of his predecessors to reach out to Jews, to Orthodox Christians, and to Protestant Christians, but so many internal forces—curial resistance, ultraconservative bishops—seem to retard progress in these areas.

The pope even called for "open season" on the primacy in his encyclical letter *Ut Unum Sint* issued May 25, 1995, but few Christian leaders and fewer Catholic leaders have yet responded to this call to dialogue. He understands that the papal office is one huge stumbling block for Christians in many communities outside of Catholicism. Why? Probably because it seems strange for one of the strongest pontiffs in the history of the church to be calling for such a discussion. Can he be serious? Is there a hidden agenda? I think the answers to these questions are both yes and no. In his prophetic role, he is inviting criticism and serious debate about the primacy of the papal office, and he can see that the office itself may change in the years to come—in ways that no one can foresee.

The cardinals who will elect his successor are long familiar with the bureaucratic institutions that have grown up over the past forty years, and they no doubt appreciate the need for an institutional response to the "separated brethren," as Vatican II famously called the Protestant and Orthodox Christians. While it will not be the topmost priority in their minds when they vote, they will no doubt nod to the need for continuing discussion among these communities.

In their deliberations, the cardinals also cannot ignore the ongoing confrontation (a harsher situation) with Islam in the political and religious arenas. Yes, there is serious dialogue in this arena, as well, but it is more difficult, more highly charged than comparable discussions with Protestant leaders. What will their solution be? Is there a solution to be obtained in the election of the most visible religious leader in the world? Although the pope often speaks about war and injustice, preaching peace and reconciliation in his annual New Year's plea for peace, for example, the Holy See has had no discernable impact on international conflicts and terrorism. Despite John Paul II's vigorous attempts in recent years (trips to Central America, Cuba, Eastern Europe, and the Holy Land), he has had little success on the worldwide political scene since the fall of the Soviet empire. A new man will have to confront the politics as well as the theological implications of Islamic fundamentalism, evangelical Christian missions in Africa and Asia, and the Israeli-Palestinian war.

John Paul II gave special priority to relations with the Jewish communities of Rome and of the world. From his own unique experience as a child and young man in Poland—through the horrors of World War II and the Shoah—he developed a special affinity for Jews, on the personal as well as the theological level. History may record that one man has done more to set right the evils of the past and to set the church on the proper moral course than any other, yet how deeply has this imperative been felt within the ranks of the faithful around the world? Have the cardinals themselves truly accepted and absorbed the pope's teaching and his personal example?

In the conclave, there will be quiet discussions about the efficacy of all these political, inter-faith and Christian-to-Christian initiatives—and the search for a leader to stay the course that was set by John XXIII and continued by his immediate successors.

Who Will It Be?

Any male Catholic, whether in holy orders or not, may be elected pope. However, the days of secular influence or any compelling reason to reach outside the ranks of the cardinals is long gone. Until the announcement is made—"*Habemus papam!* We have a pope!"—and the new pope appears at the central balcony of St. Peter's Basilica overlooking the great piazza, to impart his first benediction, the world will not know for certain who the next pope will be. But speculation, informed and otherwise, is rife throughout Christendom and will not stop until the very moment the new man shows his face, surrounded by the senior cardinals and masters of ceremonies. It will no doubt be a moment of great spiritual joy for some of the faithful; skepticism or disappointment for others; surprise for most. The Christian and non-Christian worlds alike will probably issue a collective sigh of relief, then turn to the daily business at hand. The world will continue to turn. But the church will be changed, perhaps imperceptibly, perhaps radically, by the one elected.

One can analyze the breakdown of the college of cardinals in any number of ways, but the most useful categories include nationality, age, and consistory date (i.e., when he was elevated to the cardinalate). Some pertinent statistics: of the 112 cardinal-electors as of February 1, 2003, ten are from Africa (nine percent of the total), fourteen are from Asia/Oceania (thirteen percent), fifty-three from European countries (forty-seven percent), twenty-three from Latin America (twenty percent), and thirteen from North America (United States and Canada), comprising eleven percent of the total.* Looking at national and regional areas more closely: the largest bloc of electors from a single nation is still Italy at eighteen, but it's important to note that the United States is second with eleven eligible electors. (Cardinal Bernard Law, despite his resignation as archbishop of Boston, is still an elector—he's only seventy-one years old.) The third largest group is from Germany (six) and the fourth is from Poland (five). There are fourteen cardinal-electors from Eastern Europe, and twenty-one from Western and Northern Europe (excluding Italy). There would be more from Africa than the current ten, but age has caught up with some of the men who have represented that continent to the Holy See, including Cardinal Bernardin Gantin of Benin, the dean of the college of cardinals, who turned eighty in 2002.

The age breakdown is also telling. The average age of a cardinal-elector is seventy-two and one-third years; the average among all cardinals is seventy-six years. There are only seven electors who are age sixty or younger: Vinco Puljic of Bosnia (fifty-seven), Christoph Schönborn of Austria (fifty-seven), Polycarp Pengo of Tanzania (fifty-eight), Juan Luis Cipriani Thorne of Peru (fifty-eight), Crescenzio Sepe of Italy (fifty-nine), Oscar Andres Rodríguez Maradiago of Honduras (fifty-nine), and Norberto Rivera Carrera of Mexico (sixty). These "kids" are close to the same age that Karol Wojtyla of Poland was when he was elected in 1978. Finally, only six of the total cardinal-electors were created cardinals by John Paul II's predecessor, Pope Paul VI (who died in 1978), which means that the current pope has named ninety-five percent of the electors who will choose his successor.

Scholars and journalists have long since either weighed in with their predictions or their reluctance to predict the unpredictable. Some strongly feel that the next pope will be an Italian, that John Paul's long reign has been an aberration not to be repeated any time soon. Others expect that the mold, now broken, will not be repaired, that a "foreign" pope is all but inevitable, given the overwhelming successes of the first non-Italian pontiff in 455 years. Rank and file Catholics, too, seem to want to continue the trend

---

*Throughout 2003, the population of eligible cardinal-electors will shrink unless new men are elevated to the college by the pope.

toward globalization, a theological-ecclesiastical buzzword that means, most simply, the inclusion of the seventy-five to eighty percent of the world that is neither affluent nor of European origin. As the previous statistics indicate, not only is the college of cardinals larger, more diverse, and less Euro-centric than ever before, but the most explosive growth in Catholicism in Asia, Africa, and Latin America is reflected to a greater degree than ever before.

As the list of eligible electors and non-eligible cardinals illustrates (see Appendix C), the internationalizing trend begun by Pius XII has continued apace through the pontificates of his four successors. John Paul II, in fact, has named more cardinals in more consistories than any pope in history: 201 cardinals, eight consistories. It is a far more international body than ever, but also a superconservative one, because Pope John Paul has elevated men of deep orthodoxy, both curial cardinals and residential ordinaries. Yet it is extremely unlikely that those men will attempt to elect a carbon copy of the current Holy Father. For one thing, this would be nearly impossible—a man like Karol Wojtyla is an extreme rarity, a true worldwide historical figure who was the right man at the right time, chosen by his fellow-cardinals, yet seemingly predestined or anointed from above.

The electors will chose a man they believe to be an accomplished pastor for the biggest pastorship in the world. In their minds he must be doctrinally orthodox (no wild card), yet open to consultation from the cardinals and the bishops in his decision-making and legislative responsibilities. Ultimately, the new man will have to be comfortable with the range and depth of his powers, which are considerable.

The new pope will be a bishop who has experienced—or confronted—papal authority as exercised by John Paul II and his curia. The winning candidate for pope rarely comes from within the ranks of the curia. The cardinals who head curial agencies and departments are the ultimate insiders and often the most resistant to change of any kind; often they are neither the most intellectual nor the most pastoral of prelates. A curial cardinal is, almost by definition, not *papabile*. Although Cardinal Joseph Ratzinger, the prefect of the Sacred Congregation for the Doctrine of the Faith—which used to be the

Holy Office, and before that the Inquisition—is a highly regarded theologian and intellectual; he is one of the least likely to be elected pope. And Pius XII (1939–1958), a high-born Roman, who had served his predecessor as secretary of state and knew the workings of the curia better than anyone, appointed no successor to himself as secretary of state, but was his own, thus diminishing curial influence for a while. The cardinals themselves are wary of clerical politicians and bureaucrats, per se, but prefer experienced pastors—men who have been bishops and archbishops of residential sees.

Further, the cardinals are likely to choose someone who will probably not reign for so long a period as John Paul II. Just as his very long pontificate has followed one of the shortest ever in papal history, the historical pattern has shown that the electors may desire a caretaker phase. The perfect candidate will be close to seventy years old, perhaps a shade younger or a few years older. That being said, all the other historical, political, practical, and spiritual considerations that we have previously outlined are sure to come to the surface, making for a volatile brew.

Going into the *prattiche*, which is the "informal preliminary negotiation" phase before the official opening of the conclave, the cardinals will likely have narrowed the field from more than one hundred to a half-dozen at most.[11] The long run-up to the conclave, in the years of Pope John Paul II's declining physical condition, has led many cardinals to inspect the pool of candidates (privately or quietly) and others to put themselves forward at informal dinner meetings, at consistories, and at the bishops' synods and other occasions. No overt campaigning is allowed, indeed it is forbidden by law and custom; it is considered bad taste. Personality counts, perhaps as much as policy considerations, and a candidate who can successfully navigate the waters of the pre-conclave period and find key supporters, without appearing to want the job too much, will be a top vote-getter in the initial balloting.

While it is unlikely that a liberal or reformer will be chosen (and there are not very many cardinals who fit either of those categories, anyway), it is also unlikely that a very strict conservative in the mold of John Paul II or Cardinal Ratzinger will be the cardinals' choice. Because of the atmosphere of crisis and conflict that pervades so much of the church today, they will seek a consensus-builder who will perhaps be open to some structural reforms in the way Paul VI was and in the way that the fathers of Vatican II were. Some of the same questions that arose in 1978 will recur in the next conclave, boiling down to one: will the next pope be a man true to the open, forward-looking, ecumenical spirit of Vatican II, or will he seek to turn back the clock on that watershed event?

The following chart highlights some of the most frequently mentioned contenders, their current status, with some reasons for and against each, listed in a speculative order of likelihood of election.

THE CONTENDERS

FRANCIS ARINZE: President of the Secretariat for Non-Christians, a Nigerian who converted from paganism to Catholicism as a child. Arinze, at age seventy, is widely talked about, always prominently featured in stories and interviews about the papacy and the next election. The election of a black African pope would electrify the world.

LUBOMYR HUSAR: Recently elected archbishop major of Lviv of the Ukrainians (that is, head of the Ukrainian Greek Catholic Church, with some six million members), elevated in the consistory of 2001, and thus a new cardinal. At seventy, he is just the right age. But is he Wojtyla redux as an Eastern European? And how about that American passport? (His parents emigrated when he was a youth and he holds dual citizenship.)

DIONIGI TETTAMANZI: Archbishop of Genoa (thus a successor to the oft papal bridesmaid Giuseppi Siri) and theologian, possibly the leading Italian candidate since Cardinal Martini (see next page) stepped off center stage in 2001. He is a conservative favorite of the Opus Dei movement, which he has supported.

OSCAR ANDRES RODRÍGUEZ MARADIAGO: A Salesian, first ordained as a bishop at age thirty-six, now archbishop of Teguciagalpa, Honduras, age sixty. Maradiago is the leading Latin American *papabile*. "He gets more conservative every day," a clerical insider once told me. Perhaps he sees some writing on a wall somewhere.

JEAN-MARIE LUSTIGER: Archbishop of Paris with a strong reputation as pastoral leader and a "priests' priest" in the traditional hotbed of anti-clericalism. He is one of the most intriguing potential choices, since he is a Jew who lost his mother at Auschwitz. Now seventy-five, he is at the upper age range, but can the cardinals pass up such a historic opportunity?

GODFRIED DANEELS: Archbishop of Mechelen-Brussels for more than two decades, age sixty-nine. Often quoted in the European press, he is blunt, collegial, and perceived as liberal. When the bishops and cardinals gather, Daneels is often the center of attention, appreciated for his wit and intellect. His health may be in question, however; he had a heart attack several years ago.

CHRISTOPH SCHÖNBORN: The second-youngest member of the college of cardinals (age fifty-eight), the archbishop of Vienna, and on virtually every list of serious contenders. Time has dimmed the glow once associated with this aristocratic scion, and he is probably too young for most of the electors.

CARLO MARIA MARTINI: The Jesuit former archbishop of Milan, once the darling of the liberal-moderate group within the college of cardinals and a media star, now seventy-five. Since his announcement that he has Parkinson's disease, Martini has all but admitted that his time has come and gone; but his intellect and open pastoral style still appeal to many.

GIOVANNI BATTISTA RE: Named archbishop of Milan, succeeding Martini, after a lengthy career as a curial official—including more than ten years as *sostituto* and a stint as president of the influential Congregation for Bishops. Was his appointment to such a visible Italian see a positioning for possible election to the papacy?

JAIME LACHICA SIN: One of the longest-serving current cardinal-electors (since his elevation in 1976), has been archbishop of Manila since 1974. As the leading churchman of the Philippines, he has seen the fall and rise of governments, all the while keeping a properly pastoral profile and remained liked within the Vatican and abroad. A pope named Sin?

JULIUS RIYADI DARMAATMADJA: Archbishop of Jakarta, Indonesia, and the darkest of dark horses. He is also a Jesuit, which militates against his election. However, Darmaatmadja has a stellar record as pastor, seminary rector, Jesuit provincial, military ordinary (bishop for military forces), and was previously archbishop of Semarang, a smaller diocese.

All things being equal—which they most certainly are not—and the Holy Spirit cooperating, the cardinals will probably not choose an Italian in the next conclave, though there will be some pressure to do so. The cardinals will most likely choose a Latin American, Asian, or African candidate as the next pope in order to signal their understanding of the new face of the church: younger, darker, less European, more global. Failing that, a bold choice (my sentimental favorite) that would win immense positive attention would be Cardinal Husar, the Ukrainian Catholic leader. At seventy, he is the perfect age and could make the double-edged sword of being an Eastern European who follows the first Eastern European work for the church in its ecumenical outreach to the Orthodox communion. (He is also a naturalized U.S. citizen.) Because of the recent crisis in the American Catholic church, and the cardinals' seeming lack of a unified, coherent response—as well as the traditional reluctance to invite secular political issues into the Vatican by electing a man from a superpower state—there is little to no chance that an American will be elected pope now or any time in the foreseeable future.

When the cardinals enter the Sistine Chapel, two weeks after the death of the pope, there will be an entire planet awaiting the result of their balloting. The world's news and media organizations have already reserved prime real estate for their coverage. Catholics have long since begun evaluating possible successors. And the cardinals themselves are acutely aware of the awesome responsibility that rests upon their shoulders.

From the shores of the Sea of Galilee in the first century to the rooms of the Apostolic Palace of the Vatican in the twenty-first . . . the papacy has been the longest-lived dynasty of leaders in any realm of human endeavor. Of course, the popes and their fellow believers would insist that theirs is an endeavor that is divinely instituted, and that triune God's hand has kept the church and the papacy in existence as instruments of his economy of salvation. What will happen? Who will it be?

The rules are laid out, and the clergy of Rome will make the choice, to be affirmed by the people, under the inspiration, they believe, of the Holy Spirit, the Lord and giver of life, he who has spoken, in ages past, through the prophets. What message will he try to convey to the cardinals of the Holy Roman Church, to the universal church—and to the world?

Notes

Introduction

1. Cf. Matthew 16: 18, 19 and John 21: 15–18 New Jerusalem Bible.

Preface

1. Francis A. Burkle-Young, *Passing the Keys: Modern Cardinals, Conclaves, and the Election of the Next Pope* (Lanham, Maryland: Madison Books, 1999), p. 284.
2. *Rosarium Virginis Mariae*, Chap II, §19.
3. Peggy Noonan, "John Paul the Great," *The Wall Street Journal*, 4 October 2002.
4. Lord Macaulay, *The Complete Writings* (New York: Brampton Society, 1898), 4:336.
5. See the Introduction to Pope John Paul II's Apostolic constitution *Universi Dominici Gregis (UDG)*, reprinted in its entirety in Appendix D. Copyright ©1996 by Libreria Editrice Vaticana.
6. Ibid.

Part I. History and Development of Papal Elections

1. Friedrich Gontard, *The Chair of Peter: A History of the Papacy*, trans. A. J. and E. F. Peeler (New York: Holt, Rinehart and Winston, 1964), p. 258.
2. Eamon Duffy, *Saints and Sinners: A History of the Popes* (New Haven: Yale University Press, 1997), p. 52. Duffy is quoting from Gregory I's influential treatise entitled *Pastoral Care*.
3. Acts 2: 5–11 NJB.
4. Matthew 16: 13–20 NJB.
5. Acts 2: 37–41 NJB.
6. Acts 6: 1–6 NJB.
7. Eusebius, *The History of the Church from Christ to Constantine*, trans. G. A. Williamson (New York: Penguin Books, 1965), p. 267–268.
8. Alexander Roberts and James Donaldson, eds., *The Ante-Nicene Fathers* (New York: Charles Scribner's Sons, 1925), 3:228. This particular quotation is from *Treatise Against the Heresies* by St. Irenaeus.
9. Duffy, p. 15.
10. Eusebius, book VI, article 29.
11. J. N. D. Kelly, *The Oxford Dictionary of Popes* (Oxford: Oxford University Press, 1986), p. 58.
12. P. G. Maxwell-Stuart, *Chronicle of the Popes* (London: Thames and Hudson,

Ltd., 1997), p. 48. Maxwell-Stuart is quoting from Gregory I's official collection of letters, *Registrum Epistularum*, 1.5.

13. Kelly, p. 200.

14. Burkle-Young, p. 4.

15. Duffy, p. 245.

16. Burkle-Young, p. 9.

17. Ibid., p. 25.

18. Duffy, p. 255.

19. Burkle-Young, p. 54.

20. Ibid., p. 55.

21. Ibid., p. 150.

22. Ibid., p. 256.

23. Ibid., p 286.

Part II. The Rules of the Papal Election

1. *Romano Pontifici Eligendo,* introduction.

2. Richard McBrien, *Lives of the Popes: The Pontiffs from St. Peter to John Paul II* (San Francisco: HarperCollins, 1997), p. 54.

3. Thomas J. Reese, *Inside the Vatican: The Politics and Organization of the Catholic Church* (Cambridge: Harvard University Press, 1996), p. 106.

4. See James-Charles Noonan, Jr., *The Church Visible: The Ceremonial Life and Protocol of the Roman Catholic Church* (New York: Viking Press, 1996), for detailed descriptions of all.

Part III. Challenges Awaiting the Next Pope

1. See http://www.votf.org

2. John L. Allen, Jr., *Conclave: The Politics, Personalities, and Process of the Next Papal Election* (New York: Doubleday, 2002), p. 42.

3. Burkle-Young, p. 411.

4. *Unitatis Redintegratio,* Chap I, § 2.

5. Ibid., Chap I, § 3.

6. See press release on sexual abuse posted on August 24, 2002, on the Leadership Conference of Women Religious Web site: http://www.lcwr.org

7. Margaret R. Miles, Ph.D., foreword to *Sex, Priests, and Power: Anatomy of a Crisis,* by A. W. Richard Sipe (New York: Brunner/Mazel, 1995), p. ix.

8. Ibid.

9. Ibid., p. 32.

10. Allen, p. 47.

11. Burkle-Young, p. 37

Glossary

Abdication: the renunciation of his office and powers by a monarch, in this case the pope. Although it is highly unusual, a pope may abdicate, though there is no canonical provision for what to do with a former pope.

Antipope: one whose election is not deemed canonical, or legal.

Apostle: a special, authorized messenger from God or from "the churches." Apostolic refers to a place (such as the see of Rome) founded by an apostle.

Apostolic authority: the authority of a bishop or pope that derives from the apostles.

Apostolic constitution: an official proclamation by the pope, such as the constitution that governs the conclave, *Universi Dominici Gregis.*

Apostolic succession: the lineal descent from the apostles to the present pope, conveyed by the laying on of hands by one bishop upon another; includes the apostolic authority.

Apostolic Palace: the apartments and offices of the pope within the Vatican, includes the Sistine Chapel.

Archbishop: a bishop who presides over an archdiocese, usually larger than a diocese, and who has limited jurisdiction over neighboring dioceses in an ecclesiastical province. (See also metropolitan.)

Bishop: the office of "overseer" (from the Greek *episkopoi*), also an "ordinary," that is, one with power to ordain, and preside over a diocese. Bishops reside in a city, and the diocese takes its name from that city, for example, the Diocese of Belleville, Illinois.

Bull: derives its name from *bulla* (Latin for "seal of lead"), used to validate the document. Papal bulls are the most formal and solemn documents, used, for example, to announce the canonization of a saint.

Camerlengo: the chamberlain or second-ranking member of the papal household, after the pope. The camerlengo presides over the conclave and holds limited powers during the vacancy.

Canon law: church law. A canon is one such law.

Cardinal: a title of great honor and preeminence granted by the pope. A cardinal is one of the chief advisers to the pope, and is often an archbishop, resident in the archdiocese; also a cardinal may be resident in Rome, as prefect or president of a key curial department. The chief duty of a cardinal (at least until age eighty) is to elect the pope in conclave.

Cathedra: the bishop's physical chair as well as his office (from the Latin for "chair").

College of bishops: the body of all the bishops of the world as constituted under church law and the apostolic succession.

College of cardinals: the body of all the cardinals together, the group of senior churchmen who advise and elect the pope.

Collegiality: the relationship between and among the pope and the bishops of the world.

Conclave: the system of election of the pope, also the name of the secret election meeting itself.

Congregation: in context of the conclave, a meeting of the cardinals; the *general congregation* is a meeting of all the cardinals to conduct necessary business during the period of vacancy, and the *particular congregation* is a smaller committee of cardinals under the camerlengo who formulate the agenda for the larger group.

Consistory: a meeting of the college of cardinals, presided over by the pope. An *ordinary consistory* is the meeting during which new cardinals are elevated; an *extraordinary consistory* is a special meeting called by the pope to discuss particular issues or problems within the church.

Council: a meeting of the bishops of the church, more formally called a general or ecumenical council, e.g., the Second Vatican Council (1962–1965).

Curia: (properly Roman Curia) the collection of departments (see dicastery), known as prefectures, that form the pope's "cabinet" or administrative bodies. Headed by cardinals or bishops, the curia carries out the complex work of consultation and administration.

Deacon: the office of "servant" (from the Greek *diakonos*), designating one who assists the priest or bishop. Throughout history the office of deacon has been more and less prominent; it is currently regaining a status that had eroded over time.

Dean: the senior member of the college of cardinals, holds title to the suburbicarian See of Ostia.

Dicastery: a department of the curia, known also as a prefecture, commission, council, tribunal, or congregation. Some examples include the Sacred Congregation for the Doctrine of the Faith (the senior congregation of the curia, charged with maintenance of the truth of all church teachings), the Apostolic Penitentiary (the agency that provides absolution from sin in the name of the pope), the International Theological Commission (a forum for discussion among theologians from around the world).

Diocese: the basic unit of local church government, also called the "local church," presided over by the bishop.

Domus Sanctae Marthae: also called St. Martha's Residence, the comfortable modern residence within the Vatican that will house the cardinals in conclave; takes the place of the makeshift cells that were used for centuries.

Episcopate/episcopacy: From the Greek *episkopos* (bishop), relating to the jurisdiction and office of a bishop.

Exarch: the representative of the eastern Roman emperor (sixth through ninth centuries), usually resident in Ravenna, Italy.

Holy See: another name for the papacy or the Vatican, often employed in diplomatic circles.

Major penitentiary: the head of the Apostolic Penitentiary, who keeps his office during the *Sede Vacante*; has the power to hear petitions for the forgiveness of sins.

Master of ceremonies: a priest who assists the president of the assembly (bishop or pope) in carrying out the ceremonies and rites for which he is responsible; also head of the papal office for liturgical celebrations.

Metropolitan: the title of an archbishop who heads a large diocese and leads the other bishops of his region.

Nepotism: giving favor to relatives; once a problem in papal administration, when the pope appointed and rewarded relatives (children, siblings, etc.) with papal offices. The cardinal nephew became a key papal office in the Middle Ages, later developed into the office of secretary of state.

Novemdiales: the nine-day period of mourning for the deceased pope.

Pallium: the distinctive white lamb's wool stole (with black crosses) that is worn by a metropolitan archbishop (including the pope) as a sign of his office; only worn within his own jurisdiction, except by the pope who may wear it anywhere.

Papabile: one who is considered a serious or prominent candidate for the papacy in the conclave. Plural is *papabili.*

Papal nuncio: The pope's chief ambassador and representative in a given country.

Patriarch: an ecclesiastical office higher than primate or archbishop. Many patriarchs are also cardinals. The patriarchal office is usually associated with a local church that was founded by one of the apostles, such as the ancient patriarchates of Antioch, Alexandria, and Rome (the pope); other patriarchates have been created throughout history, such as Venice.

Petrine ministry: derived from or referring to St. Peter, describes the office, mission, and ministry of the papacy.

Pontiff: from the Latin *pontifex* ("bridge builder"), which was the title of the presiding priest of the college of pontiffs. The pope is called the Supreme Pontiff or Roman Pontiff.

Prelate: a high-ranking churchman or dignitary, usually refers to the rank bishop or above, but may include others such as monsignori.

Province: a regional grouping of a religious congregation or order (such as the Jesuits) or a grouping of dioceses under the informal jurisdiction of a metropolitan archbishop.

Right of exclusion: the traditional veto power by civil authorities— specifically the monarchies of Spain, France, and Austria—between the sixteenth and twentieth centuries, in which they could disallow consideration of a candidate for the papacy. Also called *jus exclusivae,* or simply the "veto." Last exercised in the conclave of 1903, now prohibited.

Ring of the Fisherman: In Latin, the *pescatorio,* the ceremonial ring worn by the pope and destroyed at his death; it refers to his Petrine ministry, since Peter the Apostle was a fisherman.

Roman Curia: see *curia.*

Sede Vacante: the period in which the Holy See is vacant, between the death of the pope and the election of a new pope.

See: another word for diocese, also from Latin, sedes for seat (in geographical terms).

Simony: the buying or selling of religious privileges and favors, such as indulgences (release from time in purgatory). A historical cause for scandal in the church, simony was one of the immediate causes of the Protestant Reformation in the sixteenth century.

Sostituto: meaning "substitute," an important office in the Secretariat of State; a key adviser to the pope on administrative affairs.

Synod: a meeting of bishops, usually on a regional basis. A general council of the church is a "super synod," but not all synods qualify as general councils.

Vatican City: the 108-acre nation, located within the city limits of Rome, governed by the pope; came into existence in 1929 with the Lateran Treaty between the pope and the government of Italy. The term "Vatican" is also shorthand for the pope or the papacy.

Vicar: the representative of a higher authority, such as the vicar general of a diocese (representative of the presiding bishop) or the Vicar of Christ, one of the titles of the pope.

Sources and Recommended Reading

There are scores of excellent books on the papacy, many of which incorporate invaluable information on papal elections. Here are some, which I used as sources for this book, and which I recommend for further reading for anyone interested in learning more about the subject. These are listed in alphabetical order by title.

The Chair of Peter: A History of the Papacy, by Friedrich Gontard, translated by A. J. and E. F. Peeler (New York: Holt, Rinehart and Winston, 1964). This book is somewhat outdated now, forty years after original publication, but wonderfully written as a narrative history of the papacy, and provides invaluable chronological information.

The Church Visible: The Ceremonial Life and Protocol of the Roman Catholic Church by James-Charles Noonan, Jr. (New York: Viking Press, 1996). Full of facts found nowhere else about the vestments and ceremonial of the Catholic Church, this reference is for the purist and the demonic fact-checker.

Conclave: The Politics, Personalities, and Process of the Next Papal Election by John L. Allen, Jr. (New York: Doubleday, 2002). A wonderfully lucid and digestible report by a highly respected young journalist with impeccable credentials and access, Conclave gives mini-biographies of all the cardinals and *papabili,* as well as unique insights. Allen is Rome bureau chief for *The National Catholic Reporter.* Nobody does it better.

Ecumenical Councils of the Catholic Church by Hubert Jedin (New York: Herder and Herder, 1960). This handbook for church history buffs presents concise histories of each council, with exact dating and contextual notes.

Inside the Vatican: The Politics and Organization of the Catholic Church by Thomas J. Reese (Cambridge, Mass.: Harvard University Press, 1996). This is probably the most authoritative single contemporary book on the inside workings of the papacy, written by the editor of *America* magazine. Reese is a longtime observer of the Vatican and of the college of bishops throughout the world.

Lives of the Popes: The Pontiffs from St. Peter to John Paul II by Richard P. McBrien (San Francisco: HarperCollins, 1997). Very lively and complete, well-written and scholarly, by one of the most quoted and esteemed American Catholic theologians of our day—this is the ultimate pope-by-pope (and antipope!) reference throughout the ages. Along with Kelly's *Oxford Dictionary*, this book was constantly open at my side during the research and writing of *Selecting the Pope*.

The Making of the Popes 1978: The Politics of Intrigue in the Vatican by Andrew M. Greeley (Kansas City: Andrews and McMeel, Inc., 1979). This book is the "inside scoop" on the conclaves of that year, from the renowned priest, sociologist, commentator, and author of numerous fiction and non-fiction bestsellers. Greeley gives his unique perspective on people and events.

The New Jerusalem Bible (New York: Doubleday, 1999). This edition is recommended for faithful Catholics and scholars alike.

The Oxford Dictionary of Popes by J. N. D. Kelly (Oxford: Oxford University Press, 1986). This comprehensive reference is the cornerstone of any research into popes and the papacy, with a surprising amount of detail for such brief entries.

Passing the Keys: Modern Cardinals, Conclaves, and the Election of the Next Pope by Francis A. Burkle-Young (Lanham: Madison Books, 1999). This masterful study of the conclave system offers a helpful focus on the last century, the conclaves since 1903. The author provides not only facts and anecdotes about conclaves, but also gives a clear-eyed appraisal of the current college of cardinals and prospects for the next election.

Saints and Sinners: A History of the Popes by Eamon Duffy (New Haven: Yale University Press, 1997). By many estimates this is the best single-volume historical survey of the papacy from St. Peter to John Paul II. Full of wonderful facts and magisterial interpretation, Duffy's history will stand for decades as an invaluable resource.

Three key Web sites, which I used for both historical reference and constant up-to-date information, are listed below.

The Cardinals of the Holy Roman Church:
http://www.fiu.edu/~mirandas/cardinals.htm

> This site provides an inexhaustible source of information for private use and research (not available for publication) about the college of cardinals and conclaves throughout history. Valuable links to other sites can be found here, as well.

Cardinals of the Catholic Church:
http://www.catholic-pages.com/hierarchy/cardinals_list

> Part of the catholic-pages.com site, this list provides frequently updated information about the cardinals, especially deaths and birthdays, as they effect who will be electors in the next conclave.

Vatican: The Holy See:
http://www.vatican.va

> Available in several languages, this site can be difficult to navigate unless you know exactly what you are looking for.

Appendix A:
The Chronology of the Popes

Beginning date of pontificate is usually the date of consecration as bishop of Rome (if known), which may vary
from date of election.

Italics indicate an antipope (i.e., one whose election was
non-canonical).

Asterisk indicates abdication, resignation, deposition,
or assassination of a pope.

St. = Canonized a saint

Bl. = Proclaimed blessed

	Name	Dates of pontificate
1.	St. Peter the Apostle	died circa A.D. 64 or 67
2.	St. Linus	c. 66–78
3.	St. Anacletus [Cletus]	c. 78–88
4.	St. Clement I	c. 88–97
5.	St. Evaristus	c. 97–105
6.	St. Alexander I	c. 105–115
7.	St. Sixtus I	c. 115–125
8.	St. Telesphorus	c. 125–136
9.	St. Hyginus	c. 136–140
10.	St. Pius I	c. 140–155
11.	St. Anicetus	c. 155–166
12.	St. Soter	c. 166–175
13.	St. Eleutherius	c. 175–189
14.	St. Victor I	189–198
15.	St. Zephyrinus	198/199–217
16.	St. Callistus I	217–222
	St. Hippolytus	*217–235*
17.	St. Urban I	222–230
18.	St. Pontian	July 21, 230–September 28, 235*
19.	St. Anterus	November 21, 235–January 3, 236

20.	St. Fabian	January 10, 236–January 20, 250
21.	St. Cornelius	March 251–June 253
	Novatian	*251–258*
22.	St. Lucius I	June 25, 253–March 5, 254
23.	St. Stephen I	May 12, 254–August 2, 257
24.	St. Sixtus II	August 30, 257–August 6, 258
25.	St. Dionysius	July 22, 260–December 26, 268
26.	St. Felix I	January 5, 269–December 30, 274
27.	St. Eutychian	January 4, 275–December 7, 283
28.	St. Gaius [Caius]	December 17, 283–April 22, 296
29.	St. Marcellinus	June 30, 296–October 25, 304*
30.	St. Marcellus I	May 27/June 26, 308–January 16, 309
31.	St. Eusebius	April 18, 309/310–October 21, 309/310
32.	St. Miltiades	July 2, 311–January 11, 314
33.	St. Sylvester [Silvester] I	January 31, 314–December 31, 335
34.	St. Mark [Marcus]	January 18–October 7, 336
35.	St. Julius I	February 6, 337–April 12, 352
36.	Liberius	May 17, 352–September 24, 366
	Felix II	*355–November 22, 365*
37.	St. Damasus I	October 1, 366–December 11, 384
	Ursinus	*September 366–November 367*
38.	St. Siricius	December 384–November 26, 399
39.	St. Anastasius I	November 27, 399–December 19, 401
40.	St. Innocent I	December 22, 401–March 12, 417
41.	St. Zosimus	March 18, 417–December 26, 418
42.	St. Boniface I	December 28, 418–September 4, 422
	Eulalius	*December 27, 418–April 3, 419*
43.	St. Celestine I	September 10, 422–July 27, 432
44.	St. Sixtus III	July 31, 432–August 19, 440
45.	St. Leo I	September 29, 440–November 10, 461
46.	Hilarus	November 19, 461–February 29, 468
47.	St. Simplicius	March 3, 468–March 10, 483
48.	St. Felix III	March 13, 483–March 1, 492
49.	St. Gelasius I	March 1, 492–November 21, 496
50.	Anastasius II	November 24, 496–November 19, 498
51.	St. Symmachus	November 22, 498–July 19, 514
	Lawrence	*November 22, 498–February 499 (501–505)*
52.	St. Hormisdas	July 20, 514–August 6, 523
53.	St. John I	August 13, 523–May 18, 526
54.	St. Felix IV	July 12, 526–September 22, 530
55.	Boniface II	September 22, 530–October 17, 532

	Dioscorus	*September 22–October 14, 530*
56.	John II	January 22, 533–May 8, 535
57.	St. Agapitus I	May 13, 535–April 22, 536
58.	St. Silverius	June 1 or 8, 536–November 11, 537*
59.	Vigilius	March 29, 537–June 7, 555
60.	Pelagius I	April 16, 556–March 4, 561
61.	John III	July 17, 561–July 13, 574
62.	Benedict I	June 2, 575–July 30, 579
63.	Pelagius II	August 579–February 7, 590
64.	St. Gregory I	September 3, 590–March 12, 604
65.	Sabinian	September 13, 604–February 22, 606
66.	Boniface III	February 19–November 12, 607
67.	St. Boniface IV	August 25, 608–May 8, 615
68.	St. Deusdedit [Adeodatus I]	October 19, 615–November 8, 618
69.	Boniface V	December 23, 619–October 25, 625
70.	Honorius I	October 27, 625–October 12, 638
71.	Severinus	May 28–August 2, 640
72.	John IV	December 24, 640–October 12, 642
73.	Theodore I	November 24, 642–May 14, 649
74.	St. Martin I	July 5, 649–June 17, 653*
75.	St. Eugene I	August 10, 654–June 2, 657
76.	St. Vitalian	July 30, 657–January 27, 672
77.	Adeodatus II	April 11, 672–June 17, 676
78.	Donus	November 2, 676–April 11, 678
79.	St. Agatho	June 27, 678–January 10, 681
80.	St. Leo II	August 17, 682–July 3, 683
81.	St. Benedict II	June 26, 684–May 8, 685
82.	John V	July 23, 685–August 2, 686
83.	Conon	October 21, 686–September 21, 687
	Theodore	*687*
	Paschal	*687*
84.	St. Sergius I	December 15, 687–September 8, 701
85.	John VI	October 30, 701–January 11, 705
86.	John VII	March 1, 705–October 18, 707
87.	Sisinnus	January 15–February 4, 708
88.	Constantine	March 25, 708–April 9, 715
89.	St. Gregory II	May 19, 715–February 11, 731
90.	St. Gregory III	March 18, 731–November 28, 741
91.	St. Zacharias [Zachary]	December 10, 741–March 22, 752
92.	Stephen III†	March 26, 752–April 26, 757

†Stephen II was elected in late March 752 and died three days later, before he could be consecrated as pope.

93.	St. Paul I	May 29, 757–June 28, 767
	Constantine II	*July 5, 767–August 6, 768*
	Philip	*July 31, 768*
94.	Stephen IV	August 7, 768–January 24, 772
95.	Hadrian [Adrian] I	February 9, 772–December 25, 795
96.	St. Leo III	December 27, 795–June 12, 816
97.	Stephen V	June 22, 816–January 24, 817
98.	St. Paschal I	January 25, 817–February 11, 824
99.	Eugene II	May 824–August 827
100.	Valentine	August–September 827
101.	Gregory IV	March 29, 828–January 25, 844
102.	Sergius II	January 844–January 27, 847
	John	*January 844*
103.	St. Leo IV	April 10, 847–July 17, 855
104.	Benedict III	September 29, 855–April 17, 858
	Anastasius Bibliothecarius	*August–September 855*
105.	St. Nicholas I	April 24, 858–November 13, 867
106.	Hadrian [Adrian] II	December 14, 867–December 14, 872
107.	John VIII	December 14, 872–December 16, 882*
108.	Marinus I	December 16, 882–May 15, 884
109.	St. Hadrian III	May 17, 884–September 885
110.	Stephen VI	September 885–September 14, 891
111.	Formosus	October 6, 891–April 4, 896
112.	Boniface VI	April 896
113.	Stephen VII	May 896–August 897
114.	Romanus	August–November 897
115.	Theodore II	November/December 897
116.	John IX	January 898–January 900
117.	Benedict IV	February 900–July 903
118.	Leo V	August–September 903*
	Christopher	*September 903–January 904*
119.	Sergius III	January 29, 904–April 14, 911
120.	Anastasius III	June 911–August 913
121.	Lando	August 913–March 914
122.	John X	March/April 914–May 928
123.	Leo VI	May–December 928
124.	Stephen VIII	December 928–February 931
125.	John XI	March 931–December 935*
126.	Leo VII	January 3, 936–July 13, 939
127.	Stephen IX	July 14, 939–October 942
128.	Marinus II	October 30, 942–May 946

129. Agapitus II	May 10, 946–December 955
130. John XII	December 16, 955–May 14, 964*
131. Leo VIII	December 6, 963–March 1, 965
132. Benedict V	May 22–June 23, 964*
133. John XIII	October 1, 965–September 6, 972
134. Benedict VI	January 19, 973–July 974
Boniface VII	*June–August, 974 and August 984–July 20, 985*
135. Benedict VII	October 974–July 10, 983
136. John XIV	December 983–August 20, 984
137. John XV	August 985–March 996
138. Gregory V	May 3, 966–February 18, 999
John XVI	*February 977–May 998*
139. Sylvester [Silvester] II	April 2, 999–May 12, 1003
140. John XVII	May 16–November 6, 1003
141. John XVIII	December 25, 1003–July 1009
142. Sergius IV	July 13, 1009–May 12, 1012
143. Benedict VIII	May 18, 1012–April 9, 1024
Gregory	*May–December 1012*
144. John XIX	April 19, 1024–October 20, 1032
145. Benedict IX†	October 21, 1032–July 17, 1048*
146. Silvester III	January 20–March 10, 1045*
147. Gregory VI	May 5, 1045–December 20, 1046*
148. Clement II	December 25, 1046–October 9, 1047
149. Damasus II	July 17–August 9, 1048
150. St. Leo IX	February 12, 1049–April 19, 1054
151. Victor II	April 13, 1055–July 28, 1057
152. Stephen X	August 2, 1057–March 29, 1058
Benedict X	*April 5, 1058–January 1059*
153. Nicholas II	December 6, 1058–July 27, 1061
154. Alexander II	September 30, 1061–April 21, 1073
Honorius II	*October 28, 1061–May 31, 1072*
155. St. Gregory VII	June 30, 1073—May 25, 1085
Clement III	*June 25, 1080–September 8, 1100*
156. Bl. Victor III	May 19, 1087–September 16, 1087
157. B. Urban II	March 12, 1088–July 29, 1099
158. Paschal II	August 14, 1099–January 21, 1118
Theodoric	*September 1100–January 1101*
Albert	*1102*
Silvester IV	*November 18, 1105–April 12, 1111*
159. Gelasius II	March 10, 1118–January 28, 1119

†Benedict IX was elected three times and deposed three times during this period.

	Gregory VIII	*March 8, 1118–April 1121*
160.	Callistus II	February 2, 1119–December 13, 1124
161.	Honorius II	December 21, 1124–February 13, 1130
	Celestine	*1124*
162.	Innocent II	February 23, 1130–September 24, 1143
	Anacletus II	*February 14, 1130–January 25, 1138*
	Victor IV	*March–May 29, 1138*
163.	Celestine II	October 3, 1143–March 8, 1144
164.	Lucius II	March 12, 1144–February 15, 1145
165.	Bl. Eugene III	February 18, 1145–July 8, 1153
166.	Anastasius IV	July 12, 1153–December 3, 1154
167.	Hadrian [Adrian] IV	December 4, 1154–September 1, 1159
168.	Alexander III	September 20, 1159–August 30, 1181
	Victor IV	*September 7, 1159–April 20, 1164*
	Paschal III	*April 223, 1164–September 20, 1168*
	Callistus III	*September 1168–August 29, 1178*
	Innocent III	*September 29, 1179–January 1180*
169.	Lucius III	September 1, 1181–November 25, 1185
170.	Urban III	November 25, 1185–October 20, 1187
171.	Gregory VIII	October 25–December 17, 1187
172.	Clement III	December 19, 1187–March 1191
173.	Celestine III	April 14, 1191–January 8, 1198
174.	Innocent III	February 22, 1198–July 16, 1216
175.	Honorius III	July 24, 1216–March 18, 1227
176.	Gregory IX	March 19, 1227–August 22, 1241
177.	Celestine IV	October 25–November 10, 1241
178.	Innocent IV	June 28, 1243–December 7, 1254
179.	Alexander IV	December 12, 1254–May 25, 1261
180.	Urban IV	August 29, 1261–October 2, 1264
181.	Clement IV	February 5, 1265–November 29, 1268
182.	Bl. Gregory X	March 27, 1272–January 10, 1276
183.	Bl. Innocent V	January 21–June 22, 1276
184.	Hadrian V	July 11–August 18, 1276
185.	John XXI	September 8, 1276–May 20, 1277
186.	Nicholas III	December 26, 1277–August 22, 1280
187.	Martin IV	March 23, 1281–March 28, 1285
188.	Honorius IV	May 20, 1285–April 3, 1287
189.	Nicholas IV	February 22, 1288–April 4, 1292
190.	St. Celestine V	August 29–December 13, 1294*
191.	Boniface VIII	January 23, 1295–October 11, 1303
192.	Bl. Benedict XI	October 22, 1303–July 7, 1304

193.	Clement V	June 5, 1305–April 20, 1314
194.	John XXII	August 7, 1316–December 4, 1334
	Nicholas V	May 12, 1328–July 25, 1330
195.	Benedict XII	January 8, 1335–April 25, 1342
196.	Clement VI	May 7, 1342–December 6, 1352
197.	Innocent VI	December 18, 1352–September 12, 1362
198.	Bl. Urban V	November 6, 1362–December 19, 1370
199.	Gregory XI	January 4, 1371–March 27, 1378
200.	Urban VI	April 8, 1378–October 15, 1389
	Clement VII	September 20, 1378–September 16, 1394
201.	Boniface IX	November 9, 1389–October 1, 1404
	Benedict XIII	September 28, 1394–July 26, 1423
202.	Innocent VII	October 17, 1404–November 6, 1406
203.	Gregory XII	December 19, 1406–July 14, 1415*
	Alexander V	June 26, 1409–May 3, 1410
	John XXIII	May 17, 1410–May 29, 1415
204.	Martin V	November 21, 1417–February 20, 1431
	Clement VIII	June 10, 1423–July 26, 1429
	Benedict XIV	November 12, 1495
205.	Eugene IV	March 11, 1431–February 23, 1447
	Felix V	November 5, 1439–April 7, 1449
206.	Nicholas V	March 6, 1447–March 24, 1455
207.	Callistus III	April 8, 1455–August 6, 1458
208.	Pius II	August 19, 1458–August 15, 1464
209.	Paul II	August 30, 1464–July 26, 1471
210.	Sixtus IV	August 25, 1471–August 12, 1484
211.	Innocent VIII	August 29, 1484–July 5, 1492
212.	Alexander VI	August 26, 1492–August 18, 1503
213.	Pius III	October 1–18, 1503
214.	Julius II	November 1, 1503–February 12, 1513
215.	Leo X	March 17, 1513–December 1, 1521
216.	Hadrian [Adrian] VI	January 9, 1522–September 14, 1523
217.	Clement VII	November 19, 1523–September 25, 1534
218.	Paul III	October 13, 1534–November 10, 1549
219.	Julius III	February 8, 1550–March 23, 1555
220.	Marcellus II	April 10–May 1, 1555
221.	Paul IV	May 23, 1555–August 18, 1559
222.	Pius IV	December 25, 1559–December 9, 1565
223.	St. Pius V	January 7, 1566–May 1, 1572
224.	Gregory XIII	May 13, 1572–April 10, 1585
225.	Sixtus V	April 24, 1585–August 27, 1590

226.	Urban VII	September 15–27, 1590
227.	Gregory XIV	December 5, 1590–October 16, 1591
228.	Innocent IX	October 29–December 30, 1591
229.	Clement VIII	February 3, 1592–March 3, 1605
230.	Leo XI	April 1–27, 1605
231.	Paul V	May 16, 1606–January 28, 1621
232.	Gregory XV	February 9, 1621–July 8, 1623
233.	Urban VIII	August 6, 1623–July 29, 1644
234.	Innocent X	September 15, 1644–January 7, 1655
235.	Alexander VII	April 7, 1655–May 22, 1667
236.	Clement IX	June 20, 1667–December 9, 1669
237.	Clement X	April 29, 1670–July 22, 1676
238.	Bl. Innocent XI	September 21, 1676–August 12, 1689
239.	Alexander VIII	October 6, 1689–February 1, 1691
240.	Innocent XII	July 12, 1691–September 27, 1700
241.	Clement XI	November 30, 1700–March 19, 1721
242.	Innocent XIII	May 8, 1721–March 7, 1724
243.	Benedict XIII	May 29, 1724–February 21, 1730
244.	Clement XII	July 12, 1730–February 6, 1740
245.	Benedict XIV	August 7, 1740–May 3, 1758
246.	Clement XIII	July 6, 1758–February 2, 1769
247.	Clement XIV	May 28, 1769–September 22, 1774
248.	Pius VI	February 22, 1775–August 29, 1799
249.	Pius VII	March 14, 1800–August 20, 1823
250.	Leo XII	September 28, 1823–February 10, 1829
251.	Pius VIII	March 31, 1829–November 30, 1830
252.	Gregory XVI	February 2, 1831–June 1, 1846
253.	Pius IX	June 16, 1846–February 7, 1878
254.	Leo XIII	February 20, 1878–July 20, 1903
255.	St. Pius X	August 4, 1903–August 20, 1914
256.	Benedict XV	September 3, 1914–January 22, 1922
257.	Pius XI	February 6, 1922–February 10, 1939
258.	Pius XII	March 2, 1939–October 9, 1958
259.	John XXIII	October 28, 1958–June 3, 1963
260.	Paul VI	June 21, 1963–August 6, 1978
261.	John Paul I	August 26–September 28, 1978
262.	John Paul II	October 16, 1978–

Appendix B: Timeline
of History of Papal Elections

Date(s)	Election Event and/or Papal Decree
circa 64 or 67	Probable death of Peter the Apostle, considered the first "pope"
circa 66–100	Period of possible accession of Linus as a leader of church of Rome
circa 79	Possible accession of Anacletus as a leader of church of Rome
circa 88–97	Era of Clement as leading presbyter and "official correspondent" of church of Rome
circa 136	Telesphorus executed, only reliably documented martyrdom of second century pope
circa 150	"Mono-episcopacy" (rule by a single bishop) of Pius I at church of Rome
circa 180	Irenaeus, Bishop of Lyons, publishes list of first twelve successors of St. Peter as "bishops of Rome"
217 (month unknown)	First disputed papal election; Callistus I succeeds Zephyrinus but opposed by Hippolytus who becomes first "antipope"
September 28, 235	Pontian is first pope to abdicate
January 10, 236	Fabian elected by sign of the Holy Spirit; list of precise dates of elections is prepared (Liber Pontificalis)
March 251	Cornelius elected, ending vacancy of one year two months; election contested by Novatian, second antipope
July 22, 260	Dionysius elected after vacancy of nearly two years (during period of persecution)
304	Marcellinus abdicates or is deposed after apostasy (exact date uncertain), dies October 25, 304
May 27, 308	Marcellus elected after longest recorded vacancy, almost four years

May 20–July 25, 325	First Council of Nicea, pope represented by two presbyters
April 3, 419	First imperial intervention in papal elections by Emperor Honorius in favor of Boniface vs. Eulalius antipope
November 22, 498	Two elections held in same day
March 1, 499	*Ut si quis papa superstite*—oldest text concerning regulation of papal election—at synod of bishops in St. Peter's, banned all discussion of papal succession during pope's lifetime, but allowed him to nominate his successor, if he chose; participation of laity forbidden, role of clergy elevated
January 533	Legislation by king of Italy and senate of Rome (extend decree of Boniface II in 530)
607	Synod in Rome by Pope Boniface III, election reform forbids simony
March 23–25, 752	Stephen II: shortest "pontificate" (two days), not consecrated bishop
April 12, 769	Stephen III's Roman synod at which election of antipope Constantine declared invalid; only deacons and cardinal priests eligible to be elected pope; laity to have no vote in papal election
November 11, 824	Roman Constitution issued by Lothair (son of Emperor Louis I the Pious) restored tradition of lay electors in papal election
855–858	Supposed reign of Pope Joan, the first and only female pope, after pontificate of Leo IV (see also 1100)
December 16, 882	John VIII is the first pope to be assassinated
December 16, 882	Marinus I elected, first bishop from another diocese chosen as bishop of Rome (violation of canon law)
October 6, 891	Formosus elected, second bishop from another diocese chosen as bishop of Rome (later tried for crimes at "Cadaver Synod" of January 897)
898 and 904	Sergius, bishop of Caere elected twice, takes office officially on January 29, 904
April 2, 999	Sylvester, first Frenchman to be elected pope; forged close working relationship with Emperor Otto III

April 13, 1059	Nicholas II promulgates *In nominee Domini* at Lateran synod; provides cardinal bishops first consult and vote, then lower clergy and people acclaim election of pontiff
circa 1100	Alternative supposed reign of Pope Joan (see also 855–858)
1179	Alexander III's decree, *Licet de Vitanda*, at Third Lateran Council requires two-third majority vote of cardinals for election
September 1, 1271	Gregory X elected after vacancy of two years nine months
July 7, 1274	Gregory X promulgates *Ubi majus periculum* at Second Council of Lyons; important new election rules, establishes "conclave" as it has been known ever since, mandates strict rules, frugal meals
January 21, 1276	Innocent V elected at first conclave under new rules, held at Arezzo; first Dominican elected pope
July 11, 1276	Hadrian V elected; next day suspends election rules of Gregory X
December 10, 1294	*Constitutionem* of Celestine V restored legislation of Gregory X, allowing three forms of election: acclamation, compromise, and scrutiny
1295	Boniface VIII completely restores *Ubi majus periculum* and secures the seclusion of the conclave
October 22, 1303	First papal conclave held in the Vatican, Benedict XI elected unanimously
1311	*Ne romani* promulgated by Clement V at Council of Vienne, limits cardinals' powers during vacancy and extends electoral rights to cardinals previously suspended or excommunicated
December 5, 1351	*Licet in constitutione* issued by Clement VI allows for more comforts during conclave: cardinals allowed to bring two domestic servants, curtains to separate sleeping quarters in "dormitory," and more food
December 16–18, 1352	Conclave elects Innocent VI, twenty-five cardinals present legislate size of college of cardinals (not to exceed twenty-five), and require approval of new cardinals by college; also all revenues to be split between pope and cardinals

April 8, 1378	Election of Urban VI, last non-cardinal to be elected; second conclave held by schismatic cardinals, and first conclave held in Rome since 1303; beginning of Great Western Schism
November 11, 1417	End of Great Western Schism at Council of Constance; conclave held at council with twenty-three cardinals and twenty-five bishops (representing five nations: Italy, France, Germany, England, and Spain); last time non-cardinals have participated in papal election
1431	Eugene IV publishes bull shortly after election, accepting college of cardinals as co-governors of church and papal states
November 1, 1503	Julius II elected unanimously at one-day conclave, with aid of lavish promises and bribes
January 14, 1505	Bull (also Julius II) declares papal elections nullified by simony
July 1, 1517	"Grand Consistory" of Leo X, elevates record number of cardinals (thirty-one)
December 13, 1545– December 4, 1563	Council of Trent meets intermittently (also at Bologna), Counter-reformation response to Protestantism
December 1558	*Cum secundum Apostolum* decreed by Paul IV, prescribes severe penalties for secretly canvassing prior to death of the pope
November 19, 1561	Decree by Pius IV: if pope dies during ecumenical council, the cardinals, not council, are to choose his successor
October 9, 1562	*In eligendis* (also Pius IV) provides that a) conclave funds be restricted, b) conclave not responsible for debts of previous pope, c) cells for cardinals in conclave to be chosen by lot, and d) conclave under strict surveillance to insure secrecy and safety
1605	Leo XI appoints commission of cardinals to reform electoral process of conclave
November 15, 1621	Gregory XV's *Aeterni patris filius* restricts ability of rulers to interfere with conclave through *jus exclusivae* (right of exclusion, or civil veto by Austria, France, or Spain)
March 12, 1622	*Decet Romanum pontificem* decreed by Gregory XV, codifies the ceremonies to be observed in conclave

August 2, 1667	*Nos, volentes* by Clement IX, decree that granted privileges to conclavists, assistants to the cardinals in conclave
September 23, 1695	Innocent XII's *Ecclesiae Catholicae* forbids any and all promises or "capitulations" that would bind a future pope before his election (see practice begun in 1352)
October 4, 1732	*Apostolatus officium,* decree by Clement XII that regulates governing of the church during the *Sede Vacante*
December 24, 1732	*Avendo noi,* decree by Clement XII (completes document above) regarding expenses of the conclave
February 11, 1797	*Attentis peculiaribus praesentibus Ecclesiae circumstantis,* conclave legislation by Pius VI (for conclave during emergency conditions)
December 30, 1797	*Christi Ecclesiae regendae,* apostolic constitution by Pius VI governing conclave and vacancy period
November 13, 1798	*Quum nos superiore anno,* further constitution by Pius VI
October 30, 1804	Pius VII issues rules for conclave (on occasion of trip to Paris to crown Napoleon), not published
June 16, 1846	Election of Pius IX at two-day conclave (fifty electors)
December 4, 1869	Pius IX's *Cum Romanis pontificibus* provides that if the pope were to die during the First Vatican Council, the right to elect his successor is reserved exclusively to the cardinals, not the council
May 13, 1871	Italian Law of Guarantees enacted, provides for complete liberty and diplomatic immunity in papal conclaves
January 10, 1878	Pius IX issues regulations to be observed by college of cardinals during vacancy of Apostolic See
February 20, 1878	Election of Leo XIII on third ballot of two-day conclave (sixty electors)
May 24, 1882	*Praedecessores nostri* by Leo XIII lays out regulations for a conclave held during extraordinary circumstances
August 2, 1903	Emperor Franz Joseph of Austria employs right of exclusion against Cardinal Mariano Rampolla, secretary of state—last time *jus exclusivae* is employed
August 4, 1903	Election of Pius X on seventh ballot of four-day conclave (sixty-two electors)

September 3, 1914	Election of Benedict XV on tenth ballot of four-day conclave (fifty-seven electors)
February 6, 1922	Election of Pius XI on fourteenth ballot of five-day conclave (fifty-three electors)
March 2, 1939	Election of Pius XII on third ballot of one-day conclave (sixty-two electors)
February 18, 1946	"Grand Consistory" of Pius XII, elevates record number of cardinals (thirty-two)
October 28, 1958	Election of John XXIII on twelfth ballot of four-day conclave (fifty-one electors)
June 21, 1963	Election of Paul VI on fifth ballot of two-day conclave (eighty electors)
November 21, 1970	_Ingravescentem aetatem_, decree by Paul VI, restricts electors to cardinals under age of eighty at time of pope's death
October 1, 1975	_Romano Pontifici Eligendo_, apostolic constitution by Paul VI concerning election rules; confirmed age-limit of cardinal electors
August 26, 1978	Election of John Paul I on third ballot of one-day conclave (111 electors)
October 16, 1978	Election of John Paul II on eighth ballot of two-day conclave (111 electors; first non-Italian in 455 years
May 13, 1981	Pope John Paul II severely injured in assassination attempt in St. Peter's Square
May 25, 1995	_Ut unum sint_, encyclical letter on the primacy in relation to ecumenical dialogue, by John Paul II
February 22, 1996	_Universi Dominici Gregis_, apostolic constitution by John Paul II, sets out rules of next conclave; provisions include elimination of election by committee or by acclamation, and election by a simple majority after lengthy deadlock (thirty ballots)
2000	Holy Year declared by Pope John Paul II
February 21, 2001	"Grand Consistory" of John Paul II, elevates record number of cardinals (forty-four)
February 1, 2003	112 eligible electors

Appendix C:
The Sacred College of Cardinals

Only those cardinals under eighty years of age as of the date of the conclave are eligible to serve as electors, according to the Apostolic Constitution *Universi Dominici Gregis*. The following directory (as of February 1, 2003) is listed according to age, the youngest first.

Name/Position	Birth Date	Nationality	Consistory Date
VINCO PULJIC Archbishop of Vrhbosna since 1990	September 8, 1945	Bosnia	November 26, 1994
CHRISTOPH SCHÖNBORN, O.P. Archbishop of Vienna since 1995	January 22, 1945	Austria	February 21, 1998
POLYCARP PENGO Archbishop of Dar-es-Salaam since 1992	August 5, 1944	Tanzania	February 21, 1998
JUAN LUIS CIPRIANI THORNE Archbishop of Lima since 1999	December 28, 1943	Peru	February 21, 2001
CRESCENZIO SEPE Prefect of the Congregation for the Evangelization of Peoples since 2001	June 2, 1943	Italy	February 21, 2001
OSCAR ANDRÉS RODRÍGUEZ MARADIAGA, S.D.B. Archbishop of Tegucigalpa since 1993	December 29, 1942	Honduras	February 21, 2001
NORBERTO RIVERA CARRERA Archbishop of Mexico City since 1995	June 6, 1942	Mexico	February 21, 1998
WILFRID FOX NAPIER, O.F.M. Archbishop of Durban since 1992	March 8, 1941	South Africa	February 21, 2001
ZENON GROCHOLEWSKI Archbishop of Agropoli since 1991	October 11, 1939	Poland	February 21, 2001
AUDRYS JUOZAS BACKIS Archbishop of Vilnius since 1991	February 1, 1937	Lithuania	February 21, 2001
FRANCIS EUGENE GEORGE, O.M.I. Archbishop of Chicago since 1997	January 16, 1937	United States	February 21, 1998
JORGE MARIO BERGOGLIO, S.J. Archbishop of Buenos Aires since 1998	December 17, 1936	Argentina	February 21, 2001

NICOLÁS DE JESÚS LÓPEZ RODRIGUEZ Archbishop of Santo Domingo since 1981	October 31, 1936	Dominican Republic	June 28, 1991
JAIME LUCAS ORTEGA Y ALAMINO Archbishop of San Cristóbal de la Habana since 1981	October 18, 1936	Cuba	November 26, 1994
ANTONIO MARÍA ROUCO VARELA Archbishop of Santiago de Compostela since 1984	August 24, 1936	Spain	February 21, 1998
JEAN-CLAUDE TURCOTTE Archbishop of Montréal since 1990	June 26, 1936	Canada	November 26, 1994
KARL LEHMANN Bishop of Mainz since 1983	May 16, 1936	Germany	February 21, 2001
IVAN DIAS Archbishop of Bombay since 1997	April 14, 1936	India	February 21, 2001
JULIO TERRAZAS SANDOVAL,C.SS.R. Archbishop of Santa Cruz de la Sierra since 1991	March 7, 1936	Bolivia	February 21, 2001
ROGER MICHAEL MAHONY Archbishop of Los Angeles since 1985	February 27, 1936	United States	June 28, 1991
JOSÉ DA CRUZ POLICARPO Patriarch of Lisbon since 1998	February 26, 1936	Portugal	February 21, 2001
GEORG MAXIMILIAN STERZINSKY Bishop of Berlin since 1989	February 9, 1936	Germany	June 28, 1991
ALFONSO LÓPEZ TRUJILLO Archbishop of Medellín since 1979	November 8, 1935	Colombia	February 2, 1983
JULIUS RIYADI DARMAATMADJA, S.J. Archbishop of Semarang since 1983	December 20, 1934	Indonesia	November 26, 1994
CLÁUDIO HUMMES, O.F.M. Archbishop of São Paulo since 1998	August 8, 1934	Brazil	February 21, 2001
DIONIGI TETTAMANZI Archbishop of Milan since 2002	March 14, 1934	Italy	February 21, 1998
GIOVANNI BATTISTA RE Prefect of the Congregation for Bishops since 2000	January 30, 1934	Italy	February 21, 2001
JOACHIM MEISNER Archbishop of Cologne since 1988	December 25, 1933	Germany	February 2, 1983
GERALDO MAJELLA AGNELO Archbishop of São Salvador da Bahia since 1999	October 19, 1933	Brazil	February 21, 2001

FRANCISCO JAVIER ERRÁZURIZ OSSA Archbishop of Santiago de Chile since 1998	September 5, 1933	Chile	February 21, 2001
GODFRIED DANEELS Archbishop of Mechlin-Brussels since 1979	June 4, 1933	Belgium	February 2, 1983
JUAN SANDOVAL ÍÑIGUEZ Archbishop of Guadalajara since 1994	March 28, 1933	Mexico	November 26, 1994
SEVERINO POLETTO Archbishop of Turin since 1999	March 18, 1933	Italy	February 21, 2001
WALTER KASPER President of Pontifical Secretariat for the Promotion of Christian Unity since 2001	March 5, 1933	Germany	February 21, 2001
LUBOMYR HUSAR Archbishop Major of Lviv of the Ukrainians since 2001	February 26, 1933	Ukraine	February 21, 2001
FRANCIS ARINZE Prefect of Congregation for Divine Worship and the Discipline of the Sacraments since 2002	November 1, 1932	Nigeria	May 25, 1985
PEDRO RUBIANO SÁENZ Archbishop of Bogotá and Primate of Colombia since 1994	September 13, 1932	Colombia	February 21, 2001
CORMAC MURPHY-O'CONNOR Archbishop of Westminster since 2000	August 24, 1932	England	February 21, 2001
JAMES FRANCIS STAFFORD President of Pontifical Council for the Laity since 1996	July 26, 1932	United States	February 21, 1998
HENRI SCHWERY Retired Bishop of Sion since 1995	June 14, 1932	Switzerland	June 28, 1991
MILOSLAV VLK Archbishop of Prague since 1991	May 17, 1932	Czech Republic	November 26, 1994
EDWARD MICHAEL EGAN Archbishop of New York since 2000	April 2, 1932	United States	February 21, 2001
JOSÉ SARAIVA MARTINS, C.M.F. Prefect of the Congregation for the Causes of the Saints since 1998	January 6, 1932	Portugal	February 21, 2001
ADRIANUS JOHANNES SIMONIS Archbishop of Utrecht since 1983	November 26, 1931	The Netherlands	May 25, 1985
BERNARD FRANCIS LAW Archbishop Emeritus of Boston since 2002	November 4, 1931	United States	May 25, 1985

SERGIO SEBASTINI President of Prefecture for the Economic Affairs of the Holy See since 1997	April 11, 1931	Italy	February 21, 2001
WILLIAM HENRY KEELER Archbishop of Baltimore since 1989	March 4, 1931	United States	November 26, 1994
CAMILLO RUINI Vicar General for the Diocese of Rome and President of Italian Episcopal Conference since 1991	February 19, 1931	Italy	June 28, 1991
RICARDO J. VIDAL Archbishop of Cebu since 1982	February 6, 1931	Philippines	May 25, 1985
FRÉDÉRIC ETSOU-NZABI- BAMUNGWABI, C.I.C.M. Archbishop of Kinshasa since 1990	December 3, 1930	Congo	June 28, 1991
JANIS PUJATS Archbishop of Riga since 1991	November 14, 1930	Latvia	Feb 21, 1998
CHRISTIAN WIYGHAN TUMI Archbishop of Douala since 1991	October 15, 1930	Cameroon	June 28, 1988
MICHELE GIORDANO Archbishop of Naples since 1987	September 26, 1930	Italy	June 28, 1988
IGNACE MOUSSA I DAOUD Prefect of Congregation for the Oriental Churches since 2000	September 18, 1930	Syria	February 21, 2001
SALVATORE DE GIORGI Archbishop of Palermo since 1996	September 6, 1930	Italy	February 21, 1998
PAUL POUPARD President of Pontifical Council for Culture since 1988	August 30, 1930	France	May 25, 1985
THEODORE EDGAR MCCARRICK Archbishop of Washington, D.C., since 2000	July 7, 1930	United States	February 21, 2001
THOMAS STAFFORD WILLIAMS Archbishop of Wellington since 1979	March 20, 1930	New Zealand	February 2, 1983
ADAM JOSEPH MAIDA Archbishop of Detroit since 1990	March 18, 1930	United States	November 26, 1994
ALOYSIUS MATTHEW AMBROZIC Archbishop of Toronto since 1990	January 27, 1930	Canada	February 21, 1998
JÓZEF GLEMP Archbishop of Warsaw and Primate of Poland since 1981	December 18, 1929	Poland	February 2, 1983

DARIO CASTRILLÓN HOYOS Prefect of the Congregation for the Clergy since 1998	July 4, 1929	Colombia	February 21, 1998
MARIO FRANCESCO POMPEDDA Prefect of the Supreme Tribunal of the Apostolic Signatura since 1999	April 18, 1929	Italy	February 21, 2001
MICHAEL MICHAI KITBUNCHU Archbishop of Bangkok since 1973	January 25, 1929	Thailand	February 2, 1983
IGNACIO ANTONIO VELASCO GARCÍA, S.D.B. Archbishop of Caracas since 1995	January 17, 1929	Venezuela	February 21, 2001
HENRYK ROMAN GULBINOWICZ Archbishop of Wroclaw since 1976	October 17, 1928	Poland	May 25, 1985
JAIME LACHICA SIN Archbishop of Manila since 1974	August 31, 1928	Philippines	May 24, 1976
PETER SEIICHI SHIRAYANAGI Archbishop Emeritus of Tokyo since 2000	June 17, 1928	Japan	November 26, 1994
GIACOMO BIFFI Archbishop of Bologna since 1984	June 13, 1928	Italy	May 25, 1985
JAN PIETER SCHOTTE, C.I.C.M. General Secretary of the Synod of Bishops since 1985	April 29, 1928	Belgium	November 26, 1994
FRIEDRICH WETTER Archbishop of Munich and Freising since 1982	February 20, 1928	Germany	May 25, 1985
ANGELO SODANO Secretary of State of the Holy See since 1991	November 23, 1927	Italy	June 28, 1991
EDMUND CASIMIR SZOKA President of Pontifical Commission for Vatican City since 1997	September 14, 1927	United States	June 28, 1988
VARKEY VITHAYATHIL, C.SS.R. Major Archbishop of Ernakulam- Angamaly for Syro-Malabars since 1999	May 29, 1927	India	February 21, 2001
FRANCISZEK MACHARSKI Archbishop of Kraków since 1979	May 20, 1927	Poland	June 30, 1979
LÁSZLÓ PASKAI, O.F.M. Archbishop of Esztergom- Budapest and Primate of Hungary since 1987	May 8, 1927	Hungary	June 28, 1988

The Sacred College of Cardinals

JOSEPH RATZINGER Prefect of Congregation for the Doctrine of the Faith and President of Pontifical Biblical Commission and International Theological Commission since 1981; Dean of the College of Cardinals since 2002	April 16, 1927	Germany	June 27, 1977
EDUARDO MARTÍNEZ SOMALO Prefect of the Institutes of Consecrated Life and Societies of Apostolic Life since 1992; Camerlengo (Chamberlain) of the Holy Roman Church since 1993	March 31, 1927	Spain	June 28, 1988
CARLO MARIA MARTINI, S.J. Archbishop Emeritus of Milan since 2002	February 15, 1927	Italy	February 2, 1983
ADOLFO ANTONIO SUÁREZ RIVERA Archbishop Emeritus of Monterrey since 2003	January 9, 1927	Mexico	November 26, 1994
JORGE ARTURO MEDINA ESTÉVEZ Prefect Emeritus of the Congregation of Divine Worship and the Discipline of the Sacraments since 2002	December 23, 1926	Chile	February 21, 1998
EMMANUEL WAMALA Archbishop of Kampala since 1990	December 15, 1926	Uganda	November 26, 1994
WILLIAM WAKEFIELD BAUM Major Penitentiary Emeritus since 2001	November 21, 1926	United States	May 24, 1976
RICARDO MARÍA CARLES GORDÓ Archbishop of Barcelona since 1990	September 24, 1926	Spain	November 26, 1994
JEAN-MARIE LUSTIGER Archbishop of Paris since 1981	September 17, 1926	France	February 2, 1983
MARIAN JAWORSKI Archbishop of Lviv for Latins since 1991	August 21, 1926	Ukraine	February 21, 1998
AGOSTINO CACCIAVILLAN President Emeritus of Administration of the Patrimony of the Holy See since 2002	August 14, 1926	Italy	February 21, 2001
DESMOND CONNELL Archbishop of Dublin since 1988	March 24, 1926	Ireland	February 21, 2001
BERNARD AGRÉ Archbishop of Abidjan since 1994	March 2, 1926	Ivory Coast	February 21, 2001
MIGUEL OBANDO BRAVO, S.D.B. Archbishop of Managua since 1970	February 2, 1926	Nicaragua	May 25, 1985

José Freire Falcão Archbishop of Brasília since 1984	October 23, 1925	Brazil	June 28, 1988
Armand Gaétan Razafindratandra Archbishop of Antananarivo since 1994	August 7, 1925	Madagascar	November 26, 1994
Francisco Álvarez Martínez Archbishop of Toledo since 1995	July 14, 1925	Spain	February 21, 2001
Marco Cé Patriarch Emeritus of Venice since 2002	July 8, 1925	Italy	June 30, 1979
Antonio José González Zumárraga Archbishop of Quito since 1985	March 18, 1925	Ecuador	February 21, 2001
Alexandre do Nascimento Archbishop Emeritus of Luanda since 2001	March 1, 1925	Angola	February 2, 1983
Francesco Colasuonno Apostolic Nuncio in Italy since 1994	January 2, 1925	Italy	February 21, 1998
Giovanni Saldarini Archbishop Emeritus of Turin since 1999	December 11, 1924	Italy	June 28, 1991
Aloísio Lorscheider, O.F.M. Archbishop of Áparecida since 1995	October 8, 1924	Brazil	May 24, 1976
Serafim Fernandes de Araújo Archbishop of Belo Horizonte since 1986	August 13, 1924	Brazil	February 21, 1998
Edward Idris Cassidy President Emeritus of Pontifical Council for the Promotion of Christian Unity since 2001	July 5, 1924	Australia	June 28, 1991
Alexandre José Maria dos Santos, O.F.M. Archbishop of Maputo since 1974	March 18, 1924	Mozambique	June 28, 1988
Jozef Tomko President of Pontifical Committee for the International Eucharistic Congresses since 2001	March 11, 1924	Slovakia	May 25, 1985
Andrzej Maria Deskur President Emeritus of Pontifical Commission for Social Communications since 1984	February 29, 1924	Poland	May 25, 1985
Silvano Piovanelli Archbishop Emeritus of Florence since 2001	February 21, 1924	Italy	May 25, 1985

D. SIMON LOURDUSAMY Prefect Emeritus of Congregation for Oriental Churches since 1991	February 5, 1924	India	May 25, 1985
JÁN CHRYZOSTOM KOREC Bishop of Nitra since 1990	January 22, 1924	Slovakia	June 28, 1991
EDWARD BEDE CLANCY Archbishop Emeritus of Sydney since 2001	December 13, 1923	Australia	June 28, 1988
PIO TAOFINU'U, S.M. Archbishop Emeritus of Samoa-Apia since 2002	December 9, 1923	Samoa	March 5, 1973
PAUL SHAN KUO-HSI, S.J. Bishop of Kao-hsiung in Taiwan since 1991	December 3, 1923	Taiwan	February 21, 1998
ACHILLE SILVESTRINI Prefect Emeritus of Congregation for Oriental Churches since 2000; Grand Chancellor of Pontifical Oriental Institute since 1991	October 25, 1923	Italy	June 28, 1988
ANTHONY JOSEPH BEVILACQUA Archbishop of Philadelphia since 1988	June 17, 1923	United States	June 28, 1991

[The following are not eligible to be electors, as of February 1, 2003.]

MAURICE MICHAEL OTUNGA Archbishop Emeritus of Nairobi since 1997	January 31, 1923	Kenya	March 5, 1973
JORGE MARIÁ MEJÍA Archivist and Librarian of the Holy Roman Church since 1998	January 31, 1923	Argentina	February 21, 2001
ROGER ETCHEGARAY President of Central Committee for the Jubilee of the Holy Year 2000 since 1994 and papal envoy	September 25, 1922	France	June 30, 1979
ROSALIO JOSÉ CASTILLO LARA, S.D.B. President Emeritus of Pontifical Commission for the Vatican city-state since 1997	September 4, 1922	Venezuela	May 25, 1985
LUIS APONTE MARTINEZ Archbishop Emeritus of San Juan since 1999	August 4, 1922	Puerto Rico	March 5, 1973
LORENZO ANTONETTI President Emeritus of Administration of the Patrimony of the Holy See since 1998	July 31, 1922	Italy	February 21, 1998
GILBERTO AGUSTONI Prefect Emeritus of Supreme Tribunal of the Apostolic Signature since 1998	July 26, 1922	Switzerland	November 26, 1994

PIO LAGHI Prefect Emeritus of Congregation for Catholic Education since 1999	May 21, 1922	Italy	June 28, 1991
STEPHEN KIM SOU-HWAN Archbishop Emeritus of Seoul since 1998	May 8, 1922	South Korea	April 28, 1969
BERNARDIN GANTIN Prefect Emeritus of Congregation for Bishops and President Emeritus of Pontifical Commission for Latin America since 1998	May 8, 1922	Benin	June 27, 1977
DINO MONDUZZI Prefect Emeritus of Papal Household since 1998	April 2, 1922	Italy	February 21, 1998
VIRGILIO NOÈ Archpriest Emeritus of Patriarchial Vatican Basilica since 2002	March 30, 1922	Italy	June 28, 1991
CARLO FURNO Archpriest of Patriarchal Basilica of Santa Maria Maggiore since 1997	December 2, 1921	Italy	November 26, 1994
PAULO EVARISTO ARNS, O.F.M. Archbishop Emeritus of São Paulo since 1998	September 14, 1921	Brazil	March 5, 1973
PAULOS TZADUA Archbishop Emeritus of Addis Ababa since 1998	August 25, 1921	Ethiopia	May 25, 1985
ROBERTO TUCCI, S.J. President of Vatican Radio since 1986	April 19, 1921	Italy	February 21, 2001
ANTONIO MARÍA JAVIERRE ORTAS Prefect Emeritus of Congregation for Divine Worship and the Discipline of the Sacraments since 1996	February 21, 1921	Spain	June 28, 1988
HYACINTHE THIANDOUM Archbishop Emeritus of Dakar since 2000	February 2, 1921	Senegal	May 24, 1976
EUGÊNIO DE ARAÚJO SALES Archbishop Emeritus of São Sebastião do Rio de Janeiro since 2001	November 8, 1920	Brazil	April 28, 1969
JAMES ALOYSIUS HICKEY Archbishop Emeritus of Washington, D.C. since 2000	October 11, 1920	United States	June 28, 1988
JEAN HONORÉ Archbishop Emeritus of Tours since 1997	August 13, 1920	France	February 21, 2001

NASRALLAH PIERRE SFEIR Patriarch of Antioch for the Maronites since 1986	May 15, 1920	Lebanon	November 26, 1994
JOSÉ T. SÁNCHEZ Prefect Emeritus of Congregation for the Clergy since 1996	March 17, 1920	Philippines	June 28, 1991
SIMON IGNATIUS PIMENTA Archbishop Emeritus of Bombay since 1996	March 1, 1920	India	June 28, 1988
LEO SCHEFFCZYK Retired theologian (various positions in Germany and Rome)	February 21, 1920	Germany	February 21, 2001
STÉPHANOS II GHATTAS, C.M. Patriarch of Alexandria of the Copts since 1986	January 16, 1920	Egypt	February 21, 2001
HANS HERMANN GROËR, O.S.B. Resigned as Archbishop of Vienna in 1995	October 13, 1919	Austria	June 28, 1988
ANGELO FELICI Prefect Emeritus of Congregation for the Causes of Saints since 1995	July 26, 1919	Italy	June 28, 1988
ERNESTO CORRIPIO AHUMADA Archbishop Emeritus of Mexico City since 1994	June 29, 1919	Mexico	June 30, 1979
PAUL JOSEPH PHAM DÌNH TUNG Archbishop of Hanoi since 1994	June 15, 1919	Vietnam	November 26, 1994
RAÚL FRANCISCO PRIMATESTA Archbishop Emeritus of Córdoba since 1998	April 14, 1919	Argentina	March 5, 1973
GIOVANNI CHELI President Emeritus of Pontifical Council for the Pastoral Care of Migrants and Itinerant People since 1998	October 4, 1918	Italy	February 21, 1998
GIOVANNI CANESTRI Archbishop Emeritus of Genoa since 1995	September 30, 1918	Italy	June 28, 1988
SALVATORE PAPPALARDO Archbishop Emeritus of Palermo since 1996	September 23, 1918	Italy	March 5, 1973
AVERY DULLES, S.J. Theologian [not ordained as a bishop upon elevation to cardinalate]	August 24, 1918	United States	February 21, 2001
MARCELO GONZÁLEZ MARTÍN Archbishop Emeritus of Toledo since 1995	January 16, 1918	Spain	March 5, 1973

ÉDOUARD GAGNON President Emeritus of Pontifical Committee for International Eucharistic Congresses since 2001	January 15, 1918	Canada	May 25, 1985
LUIGI POGGI Archivist and Librarian Emeritus of the Holy Roman Church since 1998; Senior Cardinal Deacon	November 25, 1917	Italy	November 26, 1994
CAHAL BRENDAN DALY Archbishop Emeritus of Armagh since 1996	October 1, 1917	Ireland	June 28, 1991
ANGEL SUQUÍA GOICOECHEA Archbishop Emeritus of Madrid since 1994	October 2, 1916	Spain	May 25, 1985
FIORENZO ANGELINI President Emeritus of Pontifical Council for the Pastoral Care of Health Care Workers since 1996	August 1, 1916	Italy	June 28, 1991
JEAN MARGÉOT Archbishop Emeritus of Port-Louis since 1993	February 3, 1916	Mauritius	June 28, 1988
ANTONIO INNOCENTI President Emeritus of Pontifical Commission Ecclesia Dei since 1995	August 23, 1915	Italy	May 25, 1985
GIUSEPPE CAPRIO President Emeritus of Prefecture for the Economic Affairs of the Holy See since 1990	November 15, 1914	Italy	June 30, 1979
KAZIMIERZ SWIATEK Archbishop of Minsk-Mohilev	October 21, 1914	Belarus	November 26, 1994
JUAN FRANCISCO FRESNO LARRAIN Archbishop Emeritus of Santiago de Chile since 1990	July 26, 1914	Chile	May 25, 1985
ERSILIO TONINI Archbishop Emeritus of Ravenna- Cervia since 1990	July 20, 1914	Italy	November 26, 1994
AURELIO SABATTINI Prefect Emeritus of Supreme Tribunal of the Apostolic Signature since 1988	October 18, 1912	Italy	February 2, 1983
GERALD EMMETT CARTER Archbishop Emeritus of Toronto since 1990	March 1, 1912	Canada	June 30, 1979
JUAN CARLOS ARAMBURU Archbishop Emeritus of Buenos Aires since 1990	February 11, 1912	Argentina	May 24, 1976
LOUIS-ALBERT VACHON Archbishop Emeritus of Québec since 1990	February 4, 1912	Canada	May 25, 1985

PAUL AUGUSTIN MAYER, O.S.B. Archivist and Librarian Emeritus of the Holy Roman Church since 1988	May 23, 1911	Austria	May 25, 1985
OPILIO ROSSI President Emeritus of Commission of Cardinals for the Pontifical Sanctuaries of Pompeii, Loreto, and Bari since 1993	May 14, 1910	Italy	May 24, 1976
JOHANNES WILLEBRANDS President Emeritus of Pontifical Council for the Promotion of Christian Unity since 1989	September 4, 1909	The Netherlands	April 28, 1969
CORRADO URSI Archbishop Emeritus of Naples since 1987	July 26, 1908	Italy	June 26, 1967
FRANZ KÖNIG Archbishop Emeritus of Vienna since 1985	August 3, 1905	Austria	December 15, 1958
CORRADO BAFILE Prefect Emeritus of Congregation for the Causes of Saints since 1980	July 4, 1903	Italy	May 24, 1976

Glossary of Religious Orders of the Cardinals

C.I.C.M. (Congregation of Immaculate Heart of Mary – Missionaries of Scheut)

C.M.F. (Congregation of the Missionary Sons of the Immaculate Heart of Mary – Claretians)

C.SS.R. (Congregation of the Most Holy Redeemer – Redemptorists)

O.S.B. (Order of St. Benedict)

O.F.M. (Order of the Friars Minor – Franciscans)

O.M.I. (Oblates of Mary Immaculate)

O.P. (Order of Preachers – Dominicans)

S.D.B. (Salesians of Don Bosco)

S.J. (Society of Jesus – Jesuits)

S.M. (Society of Mary)

Appendix D

Apostolic Constitution

Universi Dominici Gregis
On the Vacancy of the Apostolic See and
The Election of the Roman Pontiff

Proclaimed by John Paul II, Supreme Pontiff, Bishop,
Servant of the Servants of God

Introduction

The Shepherd of the Lord's whole flock is the Bishop of the Church of Rome, where the Blessed Apostle Peter, by sovereign disposition of divine Providence, offered to Christ the supreme witness of martyrdom by the shedding of his blood. It is therefore understandable that the lawful apostolic succession in this See, with which "because of its great pre-eminence every Church must agree," has always been the object of particular attention.

Precisely for this reason, down the centuries the Supreme Pontiffs have deemed it their special duty, as well as their specific right, to establish fitting norms to regulate the orderly election of their Successor. Thus, also in more recent times, my Predecessors Saint Pius X, Pius XI, Pius XII, John XXIII, and lastly Paul VI, each with the intention of responding to the needs of the particular historical moment, issued wise and appropriate regulations in order to ensure the suitable preparation and orderly gathering of the electors charged, at the vacancy of the Apostolic See, with the important and weighty duty of electing the Roman Pontiff.

If I too now turn to this matter, it is certainly not because of any lack of esteem for those norms, for which I have great respect and which I intend for the most part to confirm, at least with regard to their substance and the basic principles which inspired them. What leads me to take this step is awareness of the Church's changed situation today and the need to take into consideration the general revision of Canon Law which took place, to the satisfaction of the whole Episcopate, with the publication and promulgation first of the Code of Canon Law and subsequently of the Code of Canons of the Eastern Churches. In conformity with this revision, itself inspired by the Second Vatican Ecumenical Council, I then took up the reform of the Roman Curia in the Apostolic Constitution *Pastor Bonus*. Furthermore, Canon 335 of the Code of Canon Law, restated in Canon 47 of the Code of Canons of the Eastern Churches, makes clear the need to issue and constantly update the specific laws regulating the canonical provision for the Roman See, when for any reason it becomes vacant.

While keeping in mind present-day requirements, I have been careful, in formulating the new discipline, not to depart in substance from the wise and venerable tradition already established.

It is in fact an indisputable principle that the Roman Pontiff has the right to define and adapt to changing times the manner of designating the person called to assume the Petrine succession in the Roman See. This regards, first of all, the body entrusted with providing for the election of the Roman Pontiff: based on a millennial practice sanctioned by specific canonical norms and confirmed by an explicit provision of the current Code of Canon Law (Canon 349), this body is made up of the College of Cardinals of the Holy Roman Church. While it is indeed a doctrine of faith that the power of the Supreme Pontiff derives directly from Christ, whose earthly Vicar he is, it is also certain that this supreme power in the Church is granted to him "by means of lawful election accepted by him, together with episcopal consecration." A most serious duty is thus incumbent upon the body responsible for this election. Consequently the norms which regulate its activity need to be very precise and clear, so that the election itself will take place in a most worthy manner, as befits the office of utmost responsibility which the person elected will have to assume, by divine mandate, at the moment of his assent.

Confirming therefore the norm of the current Code of Canon Law (cf. Canon 349), which reflects the millennial practice of the Church, I once more affirm that the College of electors of the Supreme Pontiff is composed solely of the Cardinals of the Holy Roman Church. In them one finds expressed in a remarkable synthesis the two aspects which characterize the figure and office of the Roman Pontiff: *Roman*, because identified with the Bishop of the Church in Rome and thus closely linked to the clergy of this City, represented by the Cardinals of the presbyteral and diaconal titles of Rome, and to the Cardinal Bishops of the suburbicarian Sees; *Pontiff of the universal Church*, because called to represent visibly the unseen Pastor who leads his whole flock to the pastures of eternal life. The universality of the Church is clearly expressed in the very composition of the College of Cardinals, whose members come from every continent.

In the present historical circumstances, the universality of the Church is sufficiently expressed by the College of one hundred and twenty electors, made up of Cardinals coming from all parts of the world and from very different cultures. I therefore confirm that this is to be the maximum number of Cardinal electors, while at the same time indicating that it is in no way meant as a sign of less respect that the provision laid down by my predecessor Pope Paul VI has been retained, namely, that those Cardinals who celebrate their eightieth birthday before the day when the Apostolic See becomes vacant do not take part in the election. The reason for this provision is the desire not to add to the weight of such venerable age the further burden of responsibility for choosing the one who will have to lead Christ's flock in ways adapted to the needs of the times. This does not however mean that the Cardinals over eighty years of age cannot take part in the preparatory meetings of the Conclave, in conformity with the norms set forth below. During the vacancy of the Apostolic See, and especially during the election of the Supreme Pontiff, they in particular should lead the People of God assembled in the Patriarchal Basilicas of Rome and in other churches in the Dioceses throughout the world, supporting the work of the electors with fervent prayers and supplications to the Holy Spirit and imploring for them the light needed to make their choice before God alone and with concern only for the "salvation of souls, which in the Church must always be the supreme law."

It has been my wish to give particular attention to the age-old institution of the Conclave, the rules and procedures of which have been established and defined by the solemn ordinances of my Predecessors. A careful historical examination confirms both the appropriateness of this institution, given the circumstances in which it originated and gradually took definitive shape, and its continued usefulness for the orderly, expeditious and proper functioning of the election itself, especially in times of tension and upheaval.

Precisely for this reason, while recognizing that theologians and canonists of all times agree that this institution is not of its nature necessary for the valid election of the Roman Pontiff, I confirm by this Constitution that the Conclave is to continue in its essential structure; at the same time, I have made some modifications in order to adapt its procedures to present-day circumstances. Specifically, I have considered it appropriate to decree that for the whole duration of the election the living-quarters of the Cardinal electors and of those called to assist in the orderly process of the election itself are to be located in suitable places within Vatican City State. Although small, the State is large enough to ensure within its walls, with the help of the appropriate measures indicated below, the seclusion and resulting concentration which an act so vital to the whole Church requires of the electors.

At the same time, in view of the sacredness of the act of election and thus the need for it to be carried out in an appropriate setting where, on the one hand, liturgical actions can be readily combined with juridical formalities, and where, on movements of the Holy Spirit, I decree that the election will continue to take place in the Sistine Chapel, where everything is conducive to an awareness of the presence of God, in whose sight each person will one day be judged.

I further confirm, by my apostolic authority, the duty of maintaining the strictest secrecy with regard to everything that directly or indirectly concerns the election process itself. Here too, though, I have wished to simplify the relative norms, reducing them to their essentials, in order to avoid confusion, doubts and even the eventual problems of conscience on the part of those who have taken part in the election.

Finally, I have deemed it necessary to revise the form of the election itself in the light of the present-day needs of the Church and the usages of modern society. I have thus considered it fitting not to retain election by acclamation *quasi ex inspiratione*, judging that it is no longer an apt means of interpreting the thought of an electoral college so great in number and so diverse in origin. It also appeared necessary to eliminate election *per compromissum*, not only because of the difficulty of the procedure, evident from the unwieldy accumulation of rules issued in the past, but also because by its very nature it tends to lessen the responsibility of the individual electors who, in this case, would not be required to express their choice personally.

After careful reflection I have therefore decided that the only form by which the electors can manifest their vote in the election of the Roman Pontiff is by secret ballot, in accordance with the rules set forth below. This form offers the greatest guarantee of clarity, straightforwardness, simplicity, openness and, above all, an effective and fruitful participation on the part of the Cardinals who, individually and as a group, are called to make up the assembly which elects the Successor of Peter.

With these intentions, I promulgate the present Apostolic Constitution containing the norms which, when the Roman See becomes vacant, are to be strictly followed by the Cardinals whose right and duty it is to elect the Successor of Peter, the visible Head of the whole Church and the Servant of the servants of God.

PART ONE:

The Vacancy of the Apostolic See

CHAPTER I – The powers of the College of Cardinals during the vacancy of the Apostolic See

1. During the vacancy of the Apostolic See, the College of Cardinals has no power or jurisdiction in matters which pertain to the Supreme Pontiff during his lifetime or in the exercise of his office; such matters are to be reserved completely and exclusively to the future Pope. I therefore declare null and void any act of power or jurisdiction pertaining to the Roman Pontiff during his lifetime or in the exercise of his office which the College of Cardinals might see fit to exercise, beyond the limits expressly permitted in this Constitution.

2. During the vacancy of the Apostolic See, the government of the Church is entrusted to the College of Cardinals solely for the dispatch of ordinary business and of matters which cannot be postponed (cf. No. 6), and for the preparation of everything necessary for the election of the new Pope. This task must be carried out in the ways and within the limits set down by this Constitution: consequently, those matters are to be absolutely excluded which, whether by law or by practice, come under the power of the Roman Pontiff alone or concern the norms for the election of the new Pope laid down in the present Constitution.

3. I further establish that the College of Cardinals may make no dispositions whatsoever concerning the rights of the Apostolic See and of the Roman Church, much less allow any of these rights to lapse, either directly or indirectly, even though it be to resolve disputes or to prosecute actions perpetrated against these same rights after the death or valid resignation of the Pope. All the Cardinals are obliged to defend these rights.

4. During the vacancy of the Apostolic See, laws issued by the Roman Pontiffs can in no way be corrected or modified, nor can anything be added or subtracted, nor a dispensation be given even from a part of them, especially with regard to the procedures governing the election of the Supreme Pontiff. Indeed, should anything be done or even attempted against this prescription, by my supreme authority I declare it null and void.

5. Should doubts arise concerning the prescriptions contained in this Constitution, or concerning the manner of putting them into effect, I decree that all power of issuing a judgment in this regard belongs to the College of Cardinals, to which I grant the faculty of interpreting doubtful or controverted points. I also establish that should it be necessary to discuss these or other similar questions, except the act of election, it suffices that the majority of the Cardinals present should concur in the same opinion.

6. In the same way, should there be a problem which, in the view of the majority of the assembled Cardinals, cannot be postponed until another time, the College of Cardinals may act according to the majority opinion.

CHAPTER II – The congregations of the Cardinals in preparation for the election of the Supreme Pontiff

7. While the See is vacant, there are two kinds of Congregations of the Cardinals: *General* Congregations, which include the whole College and are held before the beginning of the election, and *Particular* Congregations. All the Cardinals who are not legitimately impeded must attend the General Congregations, once they have been informed of the vacancy of the Apostolic See. Cardinals who, by virtue of No. 33 of this Constitution, do not enjoy the right of electing the pope are granted the faculty of not attending these General Congregations, should they prefer.

The Particular Congregation is made up of the Cardinal Camerlengo of the Holy Roman Church and three Cardinals, one from each Order, chosen by lot from among the Cardinal electors already present in Rome. The office of these Cardinals, called

Assistants, ceases at the conclusion of the third full day, and their place is taken by others, also chosen by lot and having the same term of office, also after the election has begun.

During the time of the election, more important matters are, if necessary, dealt with by the assembly of the Cardinal electors, while ordinary affairs continue to be dealt with by the Particular Congregation of Cardinals. In the General and Particular Congregations, during the vacancy of the Apostolic See, the Cardinals are to wear the usual black cassock with piping and the red sash, with skull-cap, pectoral cross and ring.

8. The Particular Congregations are to deal only with questions of lesser importance which arise on a daily basis or from time to time. But should there arise more serious questions deserving fuller examination, these must be submitted to the General Congregation. Moreover, anything decided, resolved or refused in one Particular Congregation cannot be revoked, altered or granted in another; the right to do this belongs solely to the General Congregation, and by a majority vote.

9. The General Congregations of Cardinals are to be held in the Apostolic Palace in the Vatican or, if circumstances demand it, in another place judged more suitable by the Cardinals. At these Congregations the Dean of the College presides or, should he be absent or lawfully impeded, the Subdean. If one or both of these, in accordance with No. 33 of this Constitution, no longer enjoy the right of electing the Pope, the assembly of the Cardinal electors will be presided over by the senior Cardinal elector, according to the customary order of precedence.

10. Votes in the Congregations of Cardinals, when more important matters are concerned, are not to be expressed by word of mouth but in a way which ensures secrecy.

11. The General Congregations preceding the beginning of the election, which are therefore called "preparatory," are to be held daily, beginning on the day which shall be fixed by the Camerlengo of the Holy Roman Church and the senior Cardinal of each of the three Orders among the electors, and including the days on which the funeral rites for the deceased Pope are celebrated. In this way the

Cardinal Camerlengo can hear the opinion of the College and communicate whatever is considered necessary or appropriate, while the individual Cardinals can express their views on possible problems, ask for explanations in case of doubt and make suggestions.

12. In the first General Congregations provision is to be made for each Cardinal to have available a copy of this Constitution and at the same time to have an opportunity to raise questions about the meaning and the implementation of its norms. The part of the present Constitution regarding the vacancy of the Apostolic See should also be read aloud. At the same time the Cardinals present are to swear an oath to observe the prescriptions contained herein and to maintain secrecy. This oath, which shall also be taken by Cardinals who arrive late and subsequently take part in these Congregations, is to be read aloud by the Cardinal Dean or by whoever else presides over the College by virtue of No. 9 of this Constitution, in the presence of the other Cardinals and according to the following formulas:

We, the Cardinals of the Holy Roman Church, of the Order of Bishops, of Priests and of Deacons, promise, pledge and swear, as a body and individually, to observe exactly and faithfully all the norms contained in the Apostolic Constitution Universi Dominici Gregis *of the Supreme Pontiff John Paul II, and to maintain rigorous secrecy with regard to all matters in any way related to the election of the Roman Pontiff or those which, by their very nature, during the vacancy of the Apostolic See, call for the same secrecy.*

Next, each Cardinal shall add: *And I, N. Cardinal N., so promise, pledge and swear.* And, placing his hand on the Gospels, he will add: *So help me God and these Holy Gospels which I now touch with my hand.*

13. In one of the Congregations immediately following, the Cardinals, on the basis of a prearranged agenda, shall take the more urgent decisions regarding the beginning of the election. In other words:

they shall fix the day, hour and manner in which the body of the deceased Pope shall be brought to the Vatican Basilica in order to be exposed for the homage of the faithful;

they shall make all necessary arrangements for the funeral rites of the deceased Pope, to be celebrated for nine consecutive days, determining when they are to begin, in such a way that burial will take place, except for special reasons, between the fourth and sixth day after death;

they shall see to it that the Commission, made up of the Cardinal Camerlengo and the Cardinals who had formerly held the offices of Secretary of State and President of the Pontifical Commission for Vatican City State, ensures that the rooms of the *Domus Sanctae Marthae* are made ready for the suitable lodging of the Cardinal electors, that rooms suitable for those persons mentioned in No. 46 of the present Constitution are also made ready, and that all necessary arrangements are made to prepare the Sistine Chapel so that the election process can be carried out in a smooth and orderly manner and with maximum discretion, according to the provisions laid down in this Constitution;

they shall entrust to two ecclesiastics known for their sound doctrine, wisdom and moral authority the task of presenting to the Cardinals two well-prepared meditations on the problems facing the Church at the time and on the need for careful discernment in choosing the new Pope; at the same time, without prejudice to the provisions of No. 52 of this Constitution, they shall fix the day and the time when the first of these meditations is to be given;

they shall approve – at the proposal of the Administration of the Apostolic See or, within its competence, of the Governatorato of Vatican City State – expenses incurred from the death of the Pope until the election of his successor;

they shall read any documents left by the deceased Pope for the College of Cardinals;

they shall arrange for the destruction of the Fisherman's Ring and of the lead seal with which Apostolic Letters are dispatched;

they shall make provision for the assignment of rooms by lot to the Cardinal electors;

they shall set the day and hour of the beginning of the voting process.

CHAPTER III – Concerning certain offices during the vacancy of the Apostolic See

14. According to the provisions of Article 6 of the Apostolic Constitution *Pastor Bonus*, at the death of the Pope all the heads of the Dicasteries of the Roman Curia – the Cardinal Secretary of State and the Cardinal Prefects, the Archbishop Presidents, together with the members of those Dicasteries – cease to exercise their office. An exception is made for the Camerlengo of the Holy Roman Church and the Major Penitentiary, who continue to exercise their ordinary functions, submitting to the College of Cardinals matters that would have had to be referred to the Supreme Pontiff.

Likewise, in conformity with the Apostolic Constitution *Vicariae Potestatis* (No. 2 § 1), the Cardinal Vicar General for the Diocese of Rome continues in office during the vacancy of the Apostolic See, as does the Cardinal Archpriest of the Vatican Basilica and Vicar General for Vatican City for his jurisdiction.

15. Should the offices of Camerlengo of the Holy Roman Church or of Major Penitentiary be vacant at the time of the Pope's death, or should they become vacant before the election of his successor, the College of Cardinals shall as soon as possible elect the Cardinal, or Cardinals as the case may be, who shall hold these offices until the election of the new Pope. In each of the two cases mentioned, election takes place by a secret vote of all the Cardinal electors present, with the use of ballots distributed and collected by the Masters of Ceremonies. The ballots are then opened in the presence of the Camerlengo and of the three Cardinal Assistants, if it is a matter of electing the Major Penitentiary; if it is a matter of electing the Camerlengo, they are opened in the presence of the said three Cardinals and of the Secretary of the College of Cardinals. Whoever receives the greatest number of votes shall be elected and shall *ipso facto* enjoy all the relevant faculties. In the case of an equal number of votes, the Cardinal belonging to the higher Order or, if both are in the same Order, the one first created a Cardinal, shall be appointed. Until the Camerlengo is elected, his functions are carried out by the Dean of the College or, if he is

absent or lawfully impeded, by the Subdean or by the senior Cardinal according to the usual order of precedence, in conformity with No. 9 of this Constitution, who can without delay take the decisions that circumstances dictate.

16. If during the vacancy of the Apostolic See the Vicar General for the Diocese of Rome should die, the Vicegerent in office at the time shall also exercise the office proper to the Cardinal Vicar in addition to the ordinary vicarious jurisdiction which he already holds. Should there not be a Vicegerent, the Auxiliary Bishop who is senior by appointment will carry out his functions.

17. As soon as he is informed of the death of the Supreme Pontiff, the Camerlengo of the Holy Roman Church must officially ascertain the Pope's death, in the presence of the Master of Papal Liturgical Celebrations, of the Cleric Prelates of the Apostolic Camera and of the Secretary and Chancellor of the same, the latter shall draw up the official death certificate. The Camerlengo must also place seals on the Pope's study and bedroom, making provision that the personnel who ordinarily reside in the private apartment can remain there until after the burial of the Pope, at which time the entire papal apartment will be sealed; he must notify the Cardinal Vicar for Rome of the Pope's death, whereupon the latter shall inform the People of Rome by a special announcement; he shall notify the Cardinal Archpriest of the Vatican Basilica; he shall take possession of the Apostolic Palace in the Vatican and, either in person or through a delegate, of the palaces of the Lateran and of Castel Gandolfo, and exercise custody and administration of the same; he shall determine, after consulting the heads of the three Orders of Cardinals, all matters concerning the Pope's burial, unless during his lifetime the latter had made known his wishes in this regard; and he shall deal, in the name of and with the consent of the College of Cardinals, with all matters that circumstances suggest for safeguarding the rights of the Apostolic See and for its proper administration. During the vacancy of the Apostolic See, the Camerlengo of the Holy Roman

Church has the duty of safeguarding and administering the goods and temporal rights of the Holy See, with the help of the three Cardinal Assistants, having sought the views of the College of Cardinals, once only for less important matters, and on each occasion when more serious matters arise.

18. The Cardinal Major Penitentiary and his Officials, during the vacancy of the Apostolic See, can carry out the duties laid down by my Predecessor Pius XI in the Apostolic Constitution *Quae Divinitus* of March 25, 1935, and by myself in the Apostolic Constitution *Pastor Bonus.*

19. The Dean of the College of Cardinals, for his part, as soon as he has been informed of the Pope's death by the Cardinal Camerlengo or the Prefect of the Papal Household, shall inform all the Cardinals and convoke them for the Congregations of the College. He shall also communicate news of the Pope's death to the Diplomatic Corps accredited to the Holy See and to the Heads of the respective Nations.

20. During the vacancy of the Apostolic See, the Substitute of the Secretariat of State, the Secretary for Relations with States and the Secretaries of the Dicasteries of the Roman Curia remain in charge of their respective offices, and are responsible to the College of Cardinals.

21. In the same way, the office and attendant powers of Papal Representatives do not lapse.

22. The Almoner of His Holiness will also continue to carry out works of charity in accordance with the criteria employed during the Pope's lifetime. He will be dependent upon the College of Cardinals until the election of the new Pope.

23. During the vacancy of the Apostolic See, all the civil power of the Supreme Pontiff concerning the government of Vatican City State belongs to the College of Cardinals, which however will be unable to issue decrees except in cases of urgent necessity and solely for the time in which the Holy See is vacant. Such decrees will be valid for the future only if the new Pope confirms them.

CHAPTER IV – Faculties of the Dicasteries of the Roman Curia during the vacancy of the Apostolic See

24. During the period of vacancy, the Dicasteries of the Roman Curia, with the exception of those mentioned in No. 26 of this Constitution, have no faculty in matters which, *Sede plena*, they can only deal with or carry out *facto verbo cum Sanctissimo* or *ex Audientia Sanctissimi* or *vigore spectalium et extraordinariarum facultatum* which the Roman Pontiff is accustomed to grant to the Prefects, presidents or Secretaries of those Dicasteries.

25. The ordinary faculties proper to each Dicastery do not, however, cease at the death of the Pope. Nevertheless, I decree that the Dicasteries are only to make use of these faculties for the granting of favors of lesser importance, while more serious or controverted matters, if they can be postponed, shall be exclusively reserved to the future Pope. If such matters admit of no delay (as for example in the case of dispensations which the Supreme Pontiff usually grants *in articulo mortis*), they can be entrusted by the College of Cardinals to the Cardinal who was Prefect until the Pope's death, or to the archbishop who was then President, and to the other Cardinals of the same Dicastery, to whose examination the deceased Supreme Pontiff would probably have entrusted them. In such circumstances, they will be able to decide *per modum provisionis,* until the election of the Pope, what they judge to be most fitting and appropriate for the preservation and defense of ecclesiastical rights and traditions.

26. The Supreme Tribunal of the Apostolic Signatura and the Tribunal of the Roman Rota, during the vacancy of the Holy See, continue to deal with cases in accordance with their proper laws, with due regard for the prescriptions of Article 18, paragraphs 1 and 3 of the Apostolic Constitution *Pastor Bonus.*

CHAPTER V – The Funeral rites of the Roman Pontiff

27. After the death of the Roman Pontiff, the Cardinals will celebrate the funeral rites for the repose of his soul for nine consecutive days, in accordance with the *Ordo Exsequiarum Romani*

Pontificis, the norms of which, together with those of the *Ordo Rituum Conclavis*, they are to observe faithfully.

28. If burial takes place in the Vatican Basilica, the relevant official document is drawn up by the Notary of the Capter of the Basilica or by the Canon Archivist. Subsequently, a delegate of the Cardinal Camerlengo and a delegate of the Prefect of the Papal Household shall separately draw up documents certifying that burial has taken place. The former shall do so in the presence of the members of the Apostolic Camera and the latter in the presence of the Prefect of the Papal Household.

29. If the Roman Pontiff should die outside Rome, it is the task of the College of Cardinals to make all necessary arrangements for the dignified and reverent transfer of the body to the Basilica of Saint Peter's in the Vatican.

30. No one is permitted to use any means whatsoever in order to photograph or film the Supreme Pontiff either on his sickbed or after death, or to record his words for subsequent reproduction. If after the Pope's death anyone should wish to take photographs of him for documentary purposes, he must ask permission from the Cardinal Camerlengo of the Holy Roman Church, who will not however permit the taking of photographs of the Supreme Pontiff except attired in pontifical vestments.

31. After the burial of the Supreme Pontiff and during the election of the new Pope, no part of the private apartment of the Supreme Pontiff is to be lived in.

32. If the deceased Supreme Pontiff has made a will concerning his belongings, bequeathing letters and private documents, and has named an executor thereof, it is the responsibility of the latter to determine and execute, in accordance with the mandate received from the testator, matters concerning the private property and writings of the deceased Pope. The executor will give an account of his activities only to the new Supreme Pontiff.

PART TWO:

The Election of the Roman Pontiff

CHAPTER I – The Electors of the Roman Pontiff

33. The right to elect the Roman Pontiff belongs exclusively to the Cardinals of the Holy Roman Church, with the exception of those who have reached their eightieth birthday before the day of the Roman Pontiff's death or the day when the Apostolic See becomes vacant. The maximum number of Cardinal electors must not exceed one hundred and twenty. The right of active election by any other ecclesiastical dignitary or the intervention of any lay power of whatsoever grade or order is absolutely excluded.

34. If the Apostolic See should become vacant during the celebration of an Ecumenical Council or of a Synod of Bishops being held in Rome or in any other place in the world, the election of the new Pope is to be carried out solely and exclusively by the Cardinal electors indicated in No. 33, and not by the Council or the Synod of Bishops. For this reason I declare null and void acts which would in any way temerariously presume to modify the regulations concerning the election or the college of electors. Moreover, in confirmation of the provisions of Canons 340 and 347 § 2 of the Code of Canon Law and of Canon 53 of the Code of Canons of the Eastern Churches in this regard, a Council or Synod of Bishops, at whatever point they have reached, must be considered immediately suspended *ipso iure*, once notification is received of the vacancy of the Apostolic See. Therefore without any delay all meetings, congregations or sessions must be interrupted, and the preparation of any decrees or canons, together with the promulgation of those already confirmed, must be suspended, under pain of nullity of the same. Neither the Council nor the Synod can continue for any reason, even though it be most

serious or worthy of special mention, until the new Pope, canonically elected, orders their resumption or continuation.

35. No Cardinal elector can be excluded from active or passive voice in the election of the Supreme Pontiff, for any reason or pretext, with due regard for the provisions of No. 40 of this Constitution.

36. A Cardinal of the Holy Roman Church who has been created and published before the College of Cardinals thereby has the right to elect the Pope, in accordance with the norm of No. 33 of the present Constitution, even if he has not yet received the red hat or the ring, or sworn the oath. On the other hand, Cardinals who have been canonically deposed or who with the consent of the Roman Pontiff have renounced the cardinalate do not have this right. Moreover, during the period of vacancy the College of Cardinals cannot readmit or rehabilitate them.

37. I furthermore decree that, from the moment when the Apostolic See is lawfully vacant, the Cardinal electors who are present must wait fifteen full days for those who are absent; the College of Cardinals is also granted the faculty to defer, for serious reasons, the beginning of the election for a few days more. But when a maximum of twenty days have elapsed from the beginning of the vacancy of the See, all the Cardinal electors present are obliged to proceed to the election.

38. All the Cardinal electors, convoked for the election of the new Pope by the Cardinal Dean, or by another Cardinal in his name, are required, in virtue of holy obedience, to obey the announcement of convocation and to proceed to the place designated for this purpose, unless they are hindered by sickness or by some other grave impediment, which however must be recognized as such by the College of Cardinals.

39. However, should any Cardinal electors arrive *re integra*, that is, before the new Pastor of the Church has been elected, they shall be allowed to take part in the election at the stage which it has reached.

40. If a Cardinal with the right to vote should refuse to enter Vatican City in order to take part in the election, or subsequently,

once the election has begun, should refuse to remain in order to discharge his office, without manifest reason of illness attested to under oath by doctors and confirmed by the majority of the electors, the other Cardinals shall proceed freely with the election, without waiting for him or readmitting him. If on the other hand a Cardinal elector is constrained to leave Vatican City because of illness, the election can proceed without asking for his vote; if however he desires to return to the place of the election, once his health is restored or even before, he must be readmitted.

Furthermore, if a Cardinal elector leaves Vatican City for some grave reason, acknowledged as such by the majority of the electors, he can return, in order once again to take part in the election.

CHAPTER II – The place of the election and those admitted to it by reason of their office

41. The Conclave for the election of the Supreme Pontiff shall take place within the territory of Vatican City, in determined areas and buildings, closed to unauthorized persons in such a way as to ensure suitable accommodation for the Cardinal electors and all those legitimately called to cooperate in the orderly functioning of the election.

42. By the time fixed for the beginning of the election of the Supreme Pontiff, all the Cardinal electors must have been assigned and must have taken up suitable lodging in the *Domus Sanctae Marthae*, recently built in Vatican City. If reasons of health, previously confirmed by the appropriate Congregation of Cardinals, require that a Cardinal elector should have a nurse in attendance, even during the period of the election, arrangements must be made to provide suitable accommodation for the latter.

43. From the beginning of the electoral process until the public announcement that the election of the Supreme Pontiff has taken place, or in any case until the new Pope so disposes, the rooms of the *Domus Sanctae Marthae*, and in particular the Sistine Chapel and the areas reserved for liturgical celebrations are to be closed to unauthorized persons, by the authority of the Cardinal

Camerlengo and with the outside assistance of the Substitute of the Secretariat of State, in accordance with the provisions set forth in the following Numbers.

During this period, the entire territory of Vatican City and the ordinary activity of the offices located therein shall be regulated in a way which permits the election of the Supreme Pontiff to be carried out with due privacy and freedom. In particular, provision shall be made to ensure that no one approaches the Cardinal electors while they are being transported from the *Domus Sanctae Marthae* to the Apostolic Vatican Palace.

44. The Cardinal electors, from the beginning of the election until its conclusion and the public announcement of its outcome, are not to communicate—whether by writing, by telephone or by any other means of communication—with persons outside the area where the election is taking place, except in cases of proven and urgent necessity, duly acknowledged by the Particular Congregation mentioned in No. 7. It is also the competence of the Particular Congregation to recognize the necessity and urgency of any communication with their respective offices on the part of the Cardinal Major Penitentiary, the Cardinal Vicar General for the Diocese of Rome and the Cardinal Archpriest of the Vatican Basilica.

45. Anyone not indicated in No. 46 below and who, while legitimately present in Vatican City in accordance with No. 43 of this Constitution, should happen to meet one of the Cardinal electors during the time of the election, is absolutely forbidden to engage in conversation of any sort, by whatever means and for whatever reason, with that Cardinal.

46. In order to meet the personal and official needs connected with the election process, the following individuals must be available and therefore properly lodged in suitable areas within the confines mentioned in No. 43 of this Constitution: the Secretary of the College of Cardinals, who acts as Secretary of the electoral assembly; the Master of Papal Liturgical Celebrations with two Masters of Ceremonies and two Religious attached to the Papal Sacristy;

and an ecclesiastic chosen by the Cardinal Dean or by the Cardinal taking his place, in order to assist him in his duties.

There must also be available a number of priests from the regular clergy for hearing confessions in the different languages, and two medical doctors for possible emergencies.

Appropriate provisions must also be made beforehand for a suitable number of persons to be available for the preparing and serving meals and for housekeeping.

All the persons indicated here must receive prior approval from the Cardinal Camerlengo and the three Cardinal Assistants.

47. All the persons listed in No. 46 of this Constitution who in any way or at any time should come to learn anything from any source, directly or indirectly, regarding the election process, and in particular regarding the voting which took place in the election itself, are obliged to maintain strict secrecy with all persons extraneous to the College of Cardinal electors: accordingly, before the election begins, they shall take an oath in the form and using the formula indicated in No. 48.

48. At a suitable time before the beginning of the election, the persons indicated in No. 46 of this Constitution, having been duly warned about the meaning and extent of the oath which they are to take, shall, in the presence of the Cardinal Camerlengo or another Cardinal delegated by him, and of two Masters of Ceremonies, swear and sign the oath according to the following formula:

I, N.N., promise and swear that, unless I should receive a special faculty given expressly by the newly elected Pontiff or his successors, I will observe absolute and perpetual secrecy with all who are not part of the College of Cardinal electors concerning all matters directly or indirectly related to the ballots cast and their scrutiny for the election of the Supreme Pontiff.

I likewise promise and swear to refrain from using any audio or video equipment capable of recording anything which takes place during the period of the election within Vatican City, and in particular anything which in any way, directly or indirectly, is related to the process of the election itself. I declare that I take this oath fully aware that an infraction thereof will make me subject to the spiritual and canonical penalties which the future Supreme Pontiff will see fit to adopt, in accordance with Canon 1399 of the Code of Canon Law.

So help me God and these Holy Gospels which I touch with my hand.

CHAPTER III – The beginning of the election

49. When the funeral rites for the deceased Pope have been celebrated according to the prescribed ritual, and everything necessary for the regular functioning of the election has been prepared, on the appointed day—and thus on the fifteenth day after the death of the Pope or, in conformity with the provisions of No. 37 of the present Constitution, not later than the twentieth—the Cardinal electors shall meet in the Basilica of Saint Peter's in the Vatican, or elsewhere, should circumstances warrant it, in order to take part in a solemn Eucharistic celebration with the Votive Mass *Pro Eligendo Papa*. This celebration should preferably take place at a suitable hour in the morning, so that in the afternoon the prescriptions of the following Numbers of this Constitution can be carried out.

50. From the Pauline Chapel of the Apostolic Palace, where they will assemble at a suitable hour in the afternoon, the Cardinal electors, in choir dress, and invoking the assistance of the Holy Spirit with the chant of the *Veni Creator*, will solemnly process to the Sistine Chapel of the Apostolic Palace, where the election will be held.

51. Retaining the essential elements of the Conclave, but modifying some less important elements which, because of changed circumstances no longer serve their original purpose, I establish and decree by the present Constitution that the election of the Supreme Pontiff, in conformity with the prescriptions contained in the following Numbers, is to take place exclusively in the Sistine Chapel of the Apostolic Palace in the Vatican. The Sistine Chapel is therefore to remain an absolutely enclosed area until the conclusion of the election, so that total secrecy may be ensured with

regard to everything said or done there in any way pertaining, directly or indirectly, to the election of the Supreme Pontiff.

It will therefore be the responsibility of the College of Cardinals, operating under the authority and responsibility of the Camerlengo, assisted by the Particular Congregation mentioned in No. 7 of the present Constitution, and with the outside assistance of the Substitute of the Secretariat of State, to make all prior arrangements for the interior of the Sistine Chapel and adjacent areas to be prepared, so that the orderly election and its privacy will be ensured.

In a special way, careful and stringent checks must be made, with the help of trustworthy individuals of proven technical ability, in order to ensure that no audiovisual equipment has been secretly installed in these areas for recording and transmission to the outside.

52. When the Cardinal electors have arrived in the Sistine Chapel, in accordance with the provisions of No. 50, and still in the presence of those who took part in the solemn procession, they shall take the oath, reading aloud the formula indicated in No. 53.

The Cardinal Dean, or the Cardinal who has precedence by order and seniority in accordance with the provisions of No. 9 of the present Constitution, will read the formula aloud; then each of the Cardinal electors, touching the Holy Gospels, will read and recite the formula, as indicated in the following Number.

When the last of the Cardinal electors has taken the oath, the Master of Papal Liturgical Celebrations will give the order *Extra omnes*, and all those not taking part in the Conclave must leave the Sistine Chapel.

The only ones to remain in the Chapel are the Master of Papal Liturgical Celebrations and the ecclesiastic previously chosen to preach to the Cardinal electors the second meditation, mentioned in No. 13 d), concerning the grave duty incumbent on them and thus on the need to act with right intention for the good of the Universal Church, *solum Deum prae oculis habentes*.

53. In conformity with the provisions of No. 52, the Cardinal Dean or the Cardinal who has precedence by order and seniority, will read aloud the following formula of the oath:

We, the Cardinal electors present in this election of the Supreme Pontiff promise, pledge and swear, as individuals and as a group, to observe faithfully and scrupulously the prescriptions contained in the Apostolic Constitution of the Supreme Pontiff John Paul II, Universi Dominici Gregis, published on February 22, 1996. We likewise promise, pledge and swear that whichever of us by divine disposition is elected Roman Pontiff will commit himself faithfully to carrying out the munus Petrinum of Pastor of the Universal Church and will not fail to affirm and defend strenuously the spiritual and temporal rights and the liberty of the Holy See. In a particular way, we promise and swear to observe with the greatest fidelity and with all persons, clerical or lay, secrecy regarding everything that in any way relates to the election of the Roman Pontiff and regarding what occurs in the place of the election, directly or indirectly related to the results of the voting; we promise and swear not to break this secret in any way, either during or after the election of the new Pontiff, unless explicit authorization is granted by the same Pontiff; and never to lend support or favor to any interference, opposition or any other form of intervention, whereby secular authorities of whatever order and degree or any group of people or individuals might wish to intervene in the election of the Roman Pontiff.

Each of the Cardinal electors, according to the order of precedence, will then take the oath according to the following formula:

And I, N. Cardinal N., do so promise, pledge and swear. Placing his hand on the Gospels, he will add: So help me God and these Holy Gospels which I touch with my hand.

54. When the ecclesiastic who gives the meditation has concluded, he leaves the Sistine Chapel together with the Master of Papal Liturgical Celebrations. The Cardinal electors, after reciting the prayers found in the relative Ordo, listen to the Cardinal Dean (or the one taking his place), who begins by asking the College of electors whether the election can begin, or whether there still remain doubts which need to be clarified concerning the norms and procedures laid down in this Constitution. It is not however

permitted, even if the electors are unanimously agreed, to modify or replace any of the norms and procedures which are a substantial part of the election process, under penalty of the nullity of the same deliberation.

If, in the judgment of the majority of the electors, there is nothing to prevent the election process from beginning, it shall start immediately, in accordance with the procedures indicated in this Constitution.

CHAPTER IV – Observance of secrecy on all matters concerning the election

55. The Cardinal Camerlengo and the three Cardinal Assistants *pro tempore* are obliged to be especially vigilant in ensuring that there is absolutely no violation of secrecy with regard to the events occurring in the Sistine Chapel, where the voting takes place, and in the adjacent areas, before, as well as during and after the voting.

In particular, relying upon the expertise of two trustworthy technicians, they shall make every effort to preserve that secrecy by ensuring that no audiovisual equipment for recording or transmitting has been installed by anyone in the areas mentioned, and particularly in the Sistine Chapel itself, where the acts of the election are carried out.

Should any infraction whatsoever of this norm occur and be discovered, those responsible should know that they will be subject to grave penalties according to the judgment of the future Pope.

56. For the whole duration of the election, the Cardinal electors are required to refrain from written correspondence and from all conversations, including those by telephone or radio, with persons who have not been duly admitted to the buildings set aside for their use. Such conversations shall be permitted only for the most grave and urgent reasons, confirmed by the Particular Congregation of Cardinals mentioned in No. 7.

It shall therefore be the duty of the Cardinal electors to make necessary arrangements, before the beginning of the election, for the handling of all non-deferrable official or personal business, so that there will be no need for conversations of this sort to take place.

57. The Cardinal electors are likewise to refrain from receiving or sending messages of any kind outside Vatican City; naturally it is prohibited for any person legitimately present in Vatican City to deliver such messages. It is specifically prohibited to the Cardinal electors, for the entire duration of the election, to receive newspapers or periodicals of any sort, to listen to the radio or to watch television.

58. Those who, in accordance with the prescriptions of No. 46 of the present Constitution, carry out any functions associated with the election, and who directly or indirectly could in any way violate secrecy—whether by words or writing, by signs or in any other way—are absolutely obliged to avoid this, lest they incur the penalty of excommunication *latae sententiae* reserved to the Apostolic See.

59. In particular, the Cardinal electors are forbidden to reveal to any other person, directly or indirectly, information about the voting and about matters discussed or decided concerning the election of the Pope in the meetings of Cardinals, both before and during the time of the election. This obligation of secrecy also applies to the Cardinals who are not electors but who take part in the General Congregations in accordance with No. 7 of the present Constitution.

60. I further order the Cardinal electors, *graviter onerata ipsorum conscientia*, to maintain secrecy concerning these matters also after the election of the new Pope has taken place, and I remind them that it is not licit to break the secret in any way unless a special and explicit permission has been granted by the Pope himself.

61. Finally, in order that the Cardinal electors may be protected from the indiscretion of others and from possible threats to their independence of judgment and freedom of decision, I absolutely forbid the introduction into the place of the election, under whatsoever pretext, or the use, should they have been introduced, of technical instruments of any kind for the recording, reproducing or transmitting of sound, visual images or writing.

CHAPTER V – The election procedure

62. Since the forms of election known as *per acclamationem seu inspirationem* and *per compromissum* are abolished, the form of electing the Roman Pontiff shall henceforth be *per scrutinium* alone.

I therefore decree that for the valid election of the Roman Pontiff two thirds of the votes are required, calculated on the basis of the total number of electors present.

Should it be impossible to divide the number of Cardinals present into three equal parts, for the validity of the election of the Supreme Pontiff one additional vote is required.

63. The election is to begin immediately after the provisions of No. 54 of the present Constitution have been duly carried out. Should the election begin on the afternoon of the first day, only one ballot is to be held; then, on the following days, if no one was elected on the first ballot, two ballots shall be held in the morning and two in the afternoon. The voting is to begin at a time which shall have been determined earlier, either in the preparatory Congregations or during the election period, but in accordance with the procedures laid down in Nos. 64ff of the present Constitution.

64. The voting process is carried out in three phases. The first phase, which can be called the *pre-scrutiny*, comprises: 1) the preparation and distribution of the ballot papers by the Masters of Ceremonies, who give at least two or three to each Cardinal elector; 2) the drawing by lot, from among all the Cardinal electors, of three Scrutineers, of three persons charged with collecting the votes of the sick, called for the sake of brevity *Infirmarii*, and of three Revisers; this drawing is carried out in public by the junior Cardinal Deacon, who draws out nine names, one after another, of those who shall carry out these tasks; 3) if, in the drawing of lots for the Scrutineers, *Infirmarii* and Revisers, there should come out the names of Cardinal electors who because of infirmity or other reasons are unable to carry out these tasks, the names of others who are not impeded are to be drawn in their place. The first three drawn will act as Scrutineers, the second three as *Infirmarii* and the last three as Revisers.

65. For this phase of the voting process the following norms must be observed: 1) the ballot paper must be rectangular in shape and must bear in the upper half, in print if possible, the words *Eligo in Summum Pontificem*; on the lower half there must be a space left for writing the name of the person chosen; thus the ballot is made in such a way that it can be folded in two; 2) the completion of the ballot must be done in secret by each Cardinal elector, who will write down legibly, as far as possible in handwriting that cannot be identified as his, the name of the person he chooses, taking care not to write other names as well, since this would make the ballot null; he will then fold the ballot twice; 3) during the voting, the Cardinal electors are to remain alone in the Sistine Chapel; therefore, immediately after the distribution of the ballots and before the electors begin to write, the Secretary of the College of Cardinals, the Master of Papal Liturgical Celebrations and the Masters of Ceremonies must leave the Chapel. After they have left, the junior Cardinal Deacon shall close the door, opening and closing it again each time this is necessary, as for example when the *Infirmarii* go to collect the votes of the sick and when they return to the Chapel.

66. The second phase, the *scrutiny* proper, comprises: 1) the placing of the ballots in the appropriate receptacle; 2) the mixing and counting of the ballots; 3) the opening of the votes. Each Cardinal elector, in order of precedence, having completed and folded his ballot, holds it up so that it can be seen and carries it to the altar, at which the Scrutineers stand and upon which there is placed a receptacle, covered by a plate, for receiving the ballots. Having reached the altar, the Cardinal elector says aloud the words of the following oath: *I call as my witness Christ the Lord who will be my judge, that my vote is given to the one who before God I think should be elected.* He then places the ballot on the plate, with which he drops it into the receptacle. Having done this, he bows to the altar and returns to his place.

If any of the Cardinal electors present in the Chapel is unable to go to the altar because of infirmity, the last of the Scrutineers goes to him. The infirm elector, having pronounced the above oath, hands the folded ballot to the Scrutineer who carries it in full view to the altar and omitting the oath, places it on the plate, with which he drops it into the receptacle.

67. If there are Cardinal electors who are sick and confined to their rooms, referred to in Nos. 41ff of this Constitution, the three *Infirmarii* go to them with a box which has an opening in the top through which a folded ballot can be inserted. Before giving the box to the *Infirmarii*, the Scrutineers open it publicly, so that the other electors can see that it is empty; they are then to lock it and place the key on the altar. The *Infirmarii*, taking the locked box and a sufficient number of ballot papers on a small tray, then go, duly accompanied, to the *Domus Sanctae Marthae* to each sick elector, who takes a ballot, writes his vote in secret, folds the ballot and, after taking the above-mentioned oath, puts it through the opening in the box. If any of the electors who are sick is unable to write, one of the three *Infirmarii* or another Cardinal elector chosen by the sick man, having taken an oath before the *Infirmarii* concerning the observance of secrecy, carries out the above procedure. The *Infirmarii* then take the box back into the Chapel, where it shall be opened by the Scrutineers after the Cardinals present have cast their votes. The Scrutineers then count the ballots in the box and, having ascertained that their number corresponds to the number of those who are sick, place them one by one on the plate and then drop them all together into the receptacle. In order not to prolong the voting process unduly, the *Infirmarii* may complete their own ballots and place them in the receptacle immediately after the senior Cardinal, and then go to collect the votes of the sick in the manner indicated above while the other electors are casting their votes.

68. After all the ballots of the Cardinal electors have been placed in the receptacle, the first Scrutineer shakes it several times in order to mix them, and immediately afterwards the last Scrutineer proceeds to count them, picking them out of the urn in full view and placing them in another empty receptacle previously prepared for this purpose. If the number of ballots does not corre-

spond to the number of electors, the ballots must all be burned and a second vote taken at once; if however their number does correspond to the number of electors, the opening of the ballots then takes place in the following manner.

69. The Scrutineers sit at a table placed in front of the altar. The first of them takes a ballot, unfolds it, notes the name of the person chosen and passes the ballot to the second Scrutineer, who in his turn notes the name of the person chosen and passes the ballot to the third, who reads it out in a loud and clear voice, so that all the electors present can record the vote on a sheet of paper prepared for that purpose. He himself writes down the name read from the ballot. If during the opening of the ballots the Scrutineers should discover two ballots, folded in such a way that they appear to have been completed by one elector, if these ballots bear the same name they are counted as one vote; if however they bear two different names, neither vote will be valid; however, in neither of the two cases is the voting session annulled.

When all the ballots have been opened, the Scrutineers add up the sum of the votes obtained by the different names and write them down on a separate sheet of paper. The last Scrutineer, as he reads out the individual ballots, pierces each one with a needle through the word *Eligo* and places it on a thread, so that the ballots can be more securely preserved. After the names have been read out, the ends of the thread are tied in a knot, and the ballots thus joined together are placed in a receptacle or on one side of the table.

70. There then follows the third and last phase, also known as the *post-scrutiny*, which comprises: 1) the counting of the votes; 2) the checking of the same; 3) the burning of the ballots.

The Scrutineers add up all the votes that each individual has received, and if no one has obtained two thirds of the votes on that ballot, the Pope has not been elected; if however it turns out that someone has obtained two thirds of the votes, the canonically valid election of the Roman Pontiff has taken place.

In either case, that is, whether the election has occurred or not, the Revisers must proceed to check both the ballots and the notes made by the Scrutineers, in order to make sure that these latter have performed their task exactly and faithfully.

Immediately after the checking has taken place, and before the Cardinal electors leave the Sistine Chapel, all the ballots are to be burnt by the Scrutineers, with the assistance of the Secretary of the Conclave and the Masters of Ceremonies who in the meantime have been summed by the junior Cardinal Deacon. If however a second vote is to take place immediately, the ballots from the first vote will be burned only at the end, together with those from the second vote.

71. In order that secrecy may be better observed, I order each and every Cardinal elector to hand over to the Cardinal Camerlengo or to one of the three Cardinal Assistants any notes which he may have in his possession concerning the results of each ballot. These notes are to be burnt together with the ballots.

I further lay down that at the end of the election the Cardinal Camerlengo of the Holy Roman Church shall draw up a document, to be approved also by the three Cardinal Assistants, declaring the result of the voting at each session. This document is to be given to the Pope and will thereafter be kept in a designated archive, enclosed in a sealed envelope, which may be opened by no one unless the Supreme Pontiff gives explicit permission.

72. Confirming the dispositions of my Predecessors, Saint Pius X, Pius XII and Paul VI, I decree that—except for the afternoon of the entrance into the Conclave—both in the morning and in the afternoon, after a ballot which does not result in an election, the Cardinal electors shall proceed immediately to a second one, in which they are to express their vote anew. In this second ballot all the formalities of the previous one are to be observed, with the difference that the electors are not bound to take a new oath or to choose new Scrutineers, *Infirmarii* and Revisers. Everything done in this regard for the first ballot will be valid for the second one, without the need for any repetition.

73. Everything that has been laid down above concerning the voting procedures must be diligently observed by the Cardinal electors in all the ballots, which are to take place each day, in the morn-

ing and in the afternoon, after the celebration of the sacred rites or prayers laid down in the *Ordo Rituum Conclavis*.

74. In the event that the Cardinal electors find it difficult to agree on the person to be elected, after balloting has been carried out for three days in the form described above (in Nos. 62ff) without result, voting is to be suspended for a maximum of one day in order to allow a pause for prayer, informal discussion among the voters, and a brief spiritual exhortation given by the senior Cardinal in the Order of Deacons. Voting is then resumed in the usual manner, and after seven ballots, if the election has not taken place, there is another pause for prayer, discussion and an exhortation given by the senior Cardinal in the Order of Priests. Another series of seven ballots is then held and, if there has still been no election, this is followed by a further pause for prayer, discussion and an exhortation given by the senior Cardinal in the Order of Bishops. Voting is then resumed in the usual manner and, unless the election occurs, it is to continue for seven ballots.

75. If the balloting does not result in an election, even after the provisions of No. 74 have been fulfilled, the Cardinal electors shall be invited by the Camerlengo to express an opinion about the manner of proceeding. The election will then proceed in accordance with what the absolute majority of the electors decides.

Nevertheless, there can be no waiving of the requirement that a valid election takes place only by an absolute majority of the votes or else by voting only on the two names which in the ballot immediately preceding have received the greatest number of votes; also in this second case only an absolute majority is required.

76. Should the election take place in a way other than that prescribed in the present Constitution, or should the conditions laid down here not be observed, the election is for this very reason null and void, without any need for a declaration on the matter; consequently, it confers no right on the one elected.

77. I decree that the dispositions concerning everything that precedes the election of the Roman Pontiff and the carrying out of the election itself must be observed in full, even if the vacancy of

the Apostolic See should occur as a result of the resignation of the Supreme Pontiff, in accordance with the provisions of Canon 333 § 2 of the Code of Canon Law and Canon 44 § 2 of the Code of Canons of the Eastern Churches.

CHAPTER VI – Matters to be observed or avoided in the election of the Roman Pontiff

78. If—God forbid—in the election of the Roman Pontiff the crime of simony were to be perpetrated, I decree and declare that all those guilty thereof shall incur excommunication *latae sententiae*. At the same time I remove the nullity or invalidity of the same simoniacal provision, in order that—as was already established by my Predecessors—the validity of the election of the Roman Pontiff may not for this reason be challenged.

79. Confirming the prescriptions of my Predecessors, I likewise forbid anyone, even if he is a Cardinal, during the Pope's lifetime and without having consulted him, to make plans concerning the election of his successor, or to promise votes, or to make decisions in this regard in private gatherings.

80. In the same way, I wish to confirm the provisions made by my Predecessors for the purpose of excluding any external interference in the election of the Supreme Pontiff. Therefore, in virtue of holy obedience and under pain of excommunication *latae sententiae*, I again forbid each and every Cardinal elector, present and future, as also the Secretary of the College of Cardinals and all other persons taking part in the preparation and carrying out of everything necessary for the election, to accept under any pretext whatsoever, from any civil authority whatsoever, the task of proposing the *veto* or the so-called *exclusiva*, even under the guise of a simple desire, or to reveal such either to the entire electoral body assembled together or to individual electors, in writing or by word of mouth, either directly and personally or indirectly and through others, both before the election begins and for its duration. I intend this prohibition to include all possible forms of interference, opposition and suggestion whereby secular authorities of whatever order

and degree, or any individual or group, might attempt to exercise influence on the election of the Pope.

81. The Cardinal electors shall further abstain from any form of pact, agreement, promise or other commitment of any kind which could oblige them to give or deny their vote to a person or persons. If this were in fact done, even under oath, I decree that such a commitment shall be null and void and that no one shall be bound to observe it; and I hereby impose the penalty of excommunication *latae sententiae* upon those who violate this prohibition. It is not my intention however to forbid, during the period in which the See is vacant, the exchange of views concerning the election.

82. I likewise forbid the Cardinals before the election to enter into any stipulations, committing themselves of common accord to a certain course of action should one of them be elevated to the Pontificate. These promises too, should any in fact be made, even under oath, I also declare null and void.

83. With the same insistence shown by my Predecessors, I earnestly exhort the Cardinal electors not to allow themselves to be guided, in choosing the Pope, by friendship or aversion, or to be influenced by favor or personal relationships towards anyone, or to be constrained by the interference of persons in authority or by pressure groups, by the suggestions of the mass media, or by force, fear or the pursuit of popularity. Rather, having before their eyes solely the glory of God and the good of the Church, and having prayed for divine assistance, they shall give their vote to the person, even outside the College of Cardinals, who in their judgment is most suited to govern the universal Church in a fruitful and beneficial way.

84. During the vacancy of the Apostolic See, and above all during the time of the election of the Successor of Peter, the Church is united in a very special way with her Pastors and particularly with the Cardinal electors of the Supreme Pontiff, and she asks God to grant her a new Pope as a gift of his goodness and providence. Indeed, following the example of the first Christian

community spoken of in the Acts of the Apostles (cf. 1:14), the universal Church, spiritually united with Mary, the Mother of Jesus, should persevere with one heart in prayer; thus the election of the new Pope will not be something unconnected with the People of God and concerning the College of electors alone, but will be in a certain sense an act of the whole Church. I therefore lay down that in all cities and other places, at least the more important ones, as soon as news is received of the vacancy of the Apostolic See and, in particular, of the death of the Pope and following the celebration of his solemn funeral rites, humble and persevering prayers are to be offered to the Lord (cf. Mt 21:22; Mk 11:24), that he may enlighten the electors and make them so like-minded in their task that a speedy, harmonious and fruitful election may take place, as the salvation of souls and the good of the whole People of God demand.

85. In a most earnest and heartfelt way I recommend this prayer to the venerable Cardinals who, by reason of age, no longer enjoy the right to take part in the election of the Supreme Pontiff. By virtue of the singular bond with the Apostolic See which the Cardinalate represents, let them lead the prayer of the People of God, whether gathered in the Partiarchal Basilicas of the city of Rome or in places of worship in other particular Churches, fervently imploring the assistance of Almighty God and the enlightenment of the Holy Spirit for the Cardinal electors, especially at the time of the election itself. They will thereby participate in an effective and real way in the difficult task of providing a Pastor for the universal Church.

86. I also ask the one who is elected not to refuse, for fear of its weight, the office to which he has been called, but to submit humbly to the design of the divine will. God who imposes the burden will sustain him with his hand, so that he will be able to bear it. In conferring the heavy task upon him, God will also help him to accomplish it and, in giving him the dignity, he will grant him the strength not to be overwhelmed by the weight of his office.

CHAPTER VII – The acceptance and proclamation of the new Pope and the beginning of his ministry

87. When the election has canonically taken place, the junior Cardinal Deacon summons into the hall of election the Secretary of the College of Cardinals and the Master of Papal Liturgical Celebrations. The Cardinal Dean, or the Cardinal who is first in order and seniority, in the name of the whole College of electors, then asks the consent of the one elected in the following words: *Do you accept your canonical election as Supreme Pontiff?* And, as soon as he has received the consent, he asks him: *By what name do you wish to be called?* Then the Master of Papal Liturgical Celebrations, acting as notary and having as witnesses two Masters of Ceremonies, who are to be summoned at that moment, draws up a document certifying acceptance by the new Pope and the name taken by him.

88. After his acceptance, the person elected, if he has already received episcopal ordination, is immediately Bishop of the Church of Rome, true Pope and Head of the College of Bishops. He thus acquires and can exercise full and supreme power over the universal Church.

If the person elected is not already a Bishop, he shall immediately be ordained Bishop.

89. When the other formalities provided for in the *Ordo Rituum Conclavis* have been carried out, the Cardinal electors approach the newly elected Pope in the prescribed manner, in order to make an act of homage and obedience. An act of thanksgiving to God is then made, after which the senior Cardinal Deacon announces to the waiting people that the election has taken place and proclaims the name of the new Pope, who immediately thereafter imparts the Apostolic Blessing *Urbi et Orbi* from the balcony of the Vatican Basilica.

If the person elected is not already a Bishop, homage is paid to him and the announcement of his election is made only after he has been solemnly ordained Bishop.

90. If the person elected resides outside Vatican City, the norms contained in the *Ordo Rituum Conclavis* are to be observed.

If the newly elected Supreme Pontiff is not already a Bishop, his episcopal ordination, referred to in Nos. 88 and 89 of the present Constitution, shall be carried out according to the usage of the Church by the Dean of the College of Cardinals or, in his absence, by the Subdean or, should he too be prevented from doing so, by the senior Cardinal Bishop.

91. The Conclave ends immediately after the new Supreme Pontiff assents to his election, unless he should determine otherwise. From that moment the new Pope can be approached by the Substitute of the Secretariat of State, the Secretary for Relations with States, the Prefect of the Papal Household and by anyone else needing to discuss with him matters of importance at the time.

92. After the solemn ceremony of the inauguration of the Pontificate and within an appropriate time, the Pope will take possession of the Patriarchal Archbasilica of the Lateran, according to the prescribed ritual.

Promulgation

Wherefore, after mature reflection and following the example of my Predecessors, I lay down and prescribe these norms and I order that no one shall presume to contest the present Constitution and anything contained herein for any reason whatsoever. This Constitution is to be completely observed by all, notwithstanding any disposition to the contrary, even if worthy of special mention. It is to be fully and integrally implemented and is to serve as a guide for all to whom it refers.

As determined above, I hereby declare abrogated all Constitutions and Orders issued in this regard by the Roman Pontiffs, and at the same time I declare completely null and void anything done by any person, whatever his authority, knowingly or unknowingly, in any way contrary to this Constitution.

Given in Rome, at Saint Peter's on February 22, the Feast of the Chair of Saint Peter, Apostle, in the year 1996, the eighteenth of my Pontificate.

Acknowledgments

This book was born in a discussion over luncheon with J. Alan Kahn, the President of Barnes & Noble Publishing, and Michael Fragnito, the Vice President and Publisher of Barnes & Noble Publishing's General Trade division. Alan's inspiration and excitement, and Michael's editorial and publishing acumen fueled the composition of *Selecting the Pope* in a way unique to my two decades of experience as an author, editor, and publisher. I thank them for the opportunity to take this journey through history and into the future.

My literary agent, Jacques de Spoelberch, smoothed the path and walked with me, as ever. Meredith Peters proved to be the Supreme Editor that an author (this author, in particular) needs in those crunch times of blown deadlines and last-minute corrections, as well as a more than competent "pontiff" (i.e., "bridge builder") herself. Sharmilla Sinanan saved my bacon many times and in more ways than one. I would also like to thank Midori Nakamura, the designer of this book, Gerald Levine, the production manager, and Monique Peterson, for her careful fact-checking and copyediting.

Prof. Alan Delozier and Dr. Kate Dodds, who provided me with refuge and with access to invaluable resources in the Special Collections Department of the University Library at Seton Hall, remind me why several popes were librarians before they were popes.

Msgr. Robert J. Wister, also of Seton Hall University, not only contributed an introduction to the book, but he also read and critiqued it carefully. Then Msgr. Frank Seymour, the Archivist of the Archdiocese of Newark, New Jersey (among many tasks and talents), gave it yet another much needed once-over, if not a complete absolution. My deepest thanks to both men.

Always, my wife, Maureen, and sons, Patrick and Bryan, are called upon to offer those seemingly little sacrifices of time and patience that seem to add up in ever larger sums as the years—and the books—roll by. I am especially grateful to them for remaining cheerfully available to me even at the worst moments of authorial and paternal grumpiness.

Index

abdication, of pope, 17, 18.
  See also resignation
acceptance, of election,
  83–84
acclamation, election by, 51,
  77
Adversus Heraesus, 13
Africa
  cardinals from, 112
  church in, xi, xiii
  new dioceses in, 34
  pope from, 16, 118
Agagianian, Cardinal
  Gregory Peter XV,
  40–41
Agapitus I, 20
Alberic II, 23
Alexander I, 13, 24
Alexander III, 25
Alexander VI, vii, 30
Alexandria, 5, 14
American Catholic Church
  current state of, 89–92,
  95–100
  identity of, 95–96
  importance of, 91
  new dioceses in, 34
  pluralism and, xxiv
  sexual scandal in, xvii,
  89–92, 95–100
Anicetus, 13–14
Anterus, 17
anti-Catholicism, in media,
  91–92
Antioch, 5, 14
antipopes
  election of, 27
  first, 16
  in sixth and seventh
  centuries, 20, 21
  in tenth century, 23
  in twelfth century, 25
anti-Semitism, 38
Antonelli, Cardinal
  Giacomo, 34
Antoniutti, Cardinal
  Ildebrando, 42
apostasy, of Marcellinus, 18
Apostles' Creed, 7

Apostolic Constitution. *See*
  Universi Dominici Gregis
apostolic constitution,
  definition of, 48
Apostolic Palace, 55
Apostolic Penitentiary, 50,
  56, 57, 61
apostolic succession
  bishops in, 7, 102,
  103–104
  in early church, 16
  primacy and, 6–8
Aquinas, Thomas. *See*
  Thomas Aquinas, Saint
archbishop and metropolitan
  of the Roman
  Province, pope as, 5
archbishop, position of, 7–8
Arian heresy, 18, 19
Arinze, Francis, 116
Asia
  cardinals from, 112
  church in, xi, xiii
  new dioceses in, 34
  pope from, 118
Asia Minor, 9, 12
Athenagoras I, 24
Attila, 18
Austria, veto power of, 35, 66
authority
  in apostolic succession, 7
  of bishops, 15
  in *Dictatus Papae*, 25
  during vacancy, 57
ballot
  burning of, 79–80
  description of, 78
  procedure for, 77–81
basilica of St. John Lateran,
  3, 56
Basle, Council of, 30
Benedict II, 21
Benedict IV, 23
Benedict XV, 36–37, 84
benediction, of new pope,
  84–85
Benelli, Cardinal Giovanni,
  xiii–xv, 43–44, 58

bishop(s)
  in American scandals,
  98–99
  in apostolic succession,
  7, 102, 103–104
  appointment of, 59
  collegiality of, 101–105
  development of office, 15
  election of, 13
  position of, 7
  resignations of, 90
  translation of, 22
bishop of Rome
  establishment of, 13–14
  pope as, 3, 83
Bologna, 36
Bonaventure, 28
Boniface I, 18
Boniface VI, 22
Boniface VIII, 27–28
Book of the Popes (*Liber
  Pontificalis*), 18
Borgia, Cesare, vii
Borgia, Lucretia, vii
Boston, scandal in, 90–91
bribery, 30
Bruno. *See* Leo IX
Byzantine empire,
  detachment from, 21

Cadaver Synod, 23
Callistus I, 16, 17
Callistus III, 40
Calvin, John, 31
camerlengo
  at conclave, 50, 80
  after death of pope, 55–57
  reception of, 84
  secrecy of conclave and,
  74
candidates. *See also papabili*
  exclusion of, 35–36, 51,
  66, 82
  speculation about,
  112–119
canon law, revision of, 36, 37
canonization
  of Joan of Arc, 37
  of Pius X, 36